MW01138431

I TATTI STUDIES IN
ITALIAN RENAISSANCE HISTORY

Published in collaboration with I Tatti
The Harvard University Center for Italian Renaissance Studies
Florence, Italy

GENERAL EDITOR
Nicholas Terpstra

A VEIL OF SILENCE

Women and Sound in Renaissance Italy

JULIA ROMBOUGH

Harvard University Press

Cambridge, Massachusetts

London, England

2024

First printing

Library of Congress Cataloging-in-Publication Data

Names: Rombough, Julia, 1987– author.
Title: A veil of silence : women and sound in Renaissance Italy / Julia
    Rombough.
Other titles: I Tatti studies in Italian Renaissance history.
Description: Cambridge, Massachusetts : Harvard University Press, 2024. |
    Series: I Tatti studies in Italian Renaissance history | Includes
    bibliographical references and index.
Identifiers: LCCN 2023044127 | ISBN 9780674295810 (cloth)
Subjects: LCSH: Women—Italy—Florence—Social conditions—History. |
    Noise—Social aspects—Italy—Florence—History. | Silence—Social
    aspects—Italy—Florence—History. | Domestic space—Italy—Florence—
    History. | City and town life—Italy—Florence—History. | Florence
    (Italy)—History—1421–1737.
Classification: LCC HQ1149.I8 R663 2024 | DDC 305.40945/511—
    dc23/eng/20231019
LC record available at https://lccn.loc.gov/2023044127

For Daniel

CONTENTS

A NOTE ON DATES, CURRENCIES, AND MEASUREMENTS

The Florentine new year began on March 25, the Feast of the Annunciation. All dates in this book have been modernized, so that a Florentine record dated February 15, 1594, is given here as February 15, 1595. Dates in endnote transcriptions that fall between January 1 and March 25 have been left in the Florentine style (*stile fiorentino*) and marked [*sf*] to alert readers.

A variety of currencies and coin types circulated in Renaissance and early modern Florence. Merchants and bankers used a gold currency for international trade. From 1530 onward, this was based on the scudo, which was itself based on the earlier florin. Accountants organized their ledgers according to three noncirculating silver currencies: lire, soldi, and denari; 1 lira = 20 soldi = 240 denari. In the mid-sixteenth century, one scudo was worth around 7 to 7.5 lire. The fees and fines discussed in this book were usually calculated according to scudi and lire. Florentines used a variety of other copper and silver coins for daily purchases. In 1561 a mason might earn a daily wage of roughly 1.625 lire, and a bushel of wheat cost around 2.5 lire.

Florentines measured spaces and materials by the braccio (pl. braccia). A Florentine braccio was around 58.36 centimeters, or roughly two feet long. The braccia measurements in this book have been converted to meters and rounded up when necessary to reflect the intended measurement more accurately. For example, a spatial measurement of 100 braccia has been converted to 60 meters.

A VEIL OF SILENCE

Introduction

*I*N 1620 Sister Perpetua Lapi, abbess of the Sant'Onofrio convent in Florence, described the incessant noise that plagued her midsize community of nuns. In a sternly worded letter to the local archdiocese, the abbess explained that "as governess of this sacred building, I must always block out all scandals that could give growth to evil thoughts" and went on to list the "evil" sounds she and her fellow nuns "experienced all night long," describing "many dishonest words, noises, and extraordinary shouting." The racket, she claimed, came from "those labeled as prostitutes who stay opposite our convent." Women sex workers and their clients labored and socialized late into the night in nearby homes and streets. The shouts, laughter, fighting, and howling associated with sex work drifted over the convent walls, piercing the pious silence Abbess Lapi sought to enforce. The abbess ended her letter with a demanding plea that church and civic authorities take action to maintain quiet around her convent, boldly stating, "I can no long support that my nuns have become defiled by so many wicked words and by the filth that they hear."[1]

Abbess Lapi's noise complaint used categories of quiet and noise to articulate highly gendered concepts of purity and social status. The noisy "filth" she associated with sex workers was directly linked to the bodily, spiritual, social, and sexual defilement she claimed marked these "scandalous" women. Shielding her community of nuns from such "evil" sounds was, in the abbess's estimation, critical to maintaining the purity of her convent and its residents. The noise complaint served to establish a sonic boundary distinguishing pure from impure women. By calling on concepts of noise and silence, Abbess Lapi worked to construct and enforce hierarchies of femininity and class, associating elite and honorable women with quiet and silence and nonelite and dishonorable women with noisy chaos. Lapi's claim that nuns were "defiled" by the sounds of sex work reflected her anxiety that these gender, class, and sonic boundaries could be so easily transgressed.

A rich documentary record reveals the chatter, shouting, clamor, laughter, fighting, singing, music, and urban bustle that animated late Renaissance Florence. Amid Florence's dynamic soundscapes, a heightened emphasis on sonic regulation emerged in the sixteenth and seventeenth centuries. Residents complained about noise pollution with new force; civic and church legislation aimed to monitor soundscapes with greater precision; average Florentines were charged with crimes of making noise (far baccano); and a wealth of prescriptive health and spiritual writings asserted that urban noise was a caustic force that could corrupt the body, the soul, the body social, and the environment. Conversely, quiet, silence, and "good" sounds were upheld as markers of individual, social, and environmental well-being and of gender order. Precise sounds were assigned moral meanings by various urban and religious authorities. Quotidian soundscapes, and reactions to them, were a "semiotic system" that reflected the city's complex social, religious, and political relationships.[2] Concerns about noise pollution were particularly acute in and around communities of women. Urban authorities were uniquely worried about how noise stood to impact the bodies and souls of the thousands of girls and women who lived in the city's many enclosed institutions.

A Veil of Silence reveals the uniquely gendered history of sound and silence in late Renaissance Florence, examining the soundscapes in and around residential institutions for girls and women and considering the sonic regimes and daily acoustics of cloistered life. Institutional soundscapes emerged as flash points for larger debates about gender, class, urban governance, health, and Catholic reform in sixteenth- and seventeenth-century Florence. Women's enclosures were central nodes around which the larger Florentine soundscape was both shaped and contested. Particular sounds took on an outsize significance in these spaces, and new efforts were undertaken to regulate the sounds women and girls both made and heard. This intense sonic focus was propelled by the record-setting pace at which civic and ecclesiastical enclosures expanded, resulting in previously unseen rates of long-term institutionalization focused primarily on the enclosure of girls and women. A vast network of nunneries, charity homes, hospitals, youth homes, reform houses, and asylums housed thousands of girls and women for long periods—and often for life. These institutions expanded significantly in both number and size over the late Renaissance period, collectively housing more girls and women than in any previous time. As a seemingly never-ending stream of girls and women entered various institutions, urban and ecclesiastical authorities were tasked with regulating their sonic experiences with new precision.

Ideally, enclosures were marked by silence and quiet—interjected only by the godly sounds of prayer, sanctioned music, and bells. Idealized soundscapes were directly linked to the idealized femininities institutional authorities sought to foster; quiet and silence were thought to purify the body and soul and to encourage feminine chastity, modesty, and penitence. It was with this in mind that the Malmaritate house, a civic charity home for "badly married" women fleeing spousal abuse or engaged in sex work, stated that as part of its reforming regime women were "to remain withdrawn in silence."[3] The Santa Caterina conservatory, a civic youth home for impoverished girls and young women, likewise devoted a chapter, "On Silence," to its book of statutes and outlined the many ways in which its wards were required to maintain "continual silence."[4] Similarly, Le Murate, a Benedictine monastery and one of Florence's largest sixteenth-century nunneries, expanded on deeply rooted monastic traditions that praised "profound silence" and recorded punishments for specific types of noisemaking, noting, for example, that "whoever makes noise by dropping a knife or something else on the floor [in the refectory] rises to her feet before the abbess and makes a visible sign."[5] Civic laws, for their part, increasingly forbade particular sounds in public spaces adjacent to girls' and women's institutions, attempting to regulate the sounds that enclosed residents heard as well as those they made. A 1642 law was carved in stone and placed on the outer wall of the San'Orsola convent and is a typical example. The law forbade anyone "to make noise or sing during the day or night within 150 braccia [90 meters] of the church and around the convent."[6] All of these regulations associated quiet with institutional regulation, gender order, and spiritual and urban discipline. Women's institutions were a notable presence in virtually every Florentine neighborhood and bordered many of the city's important squares and intersections. Taken together, these enclosures formed a collection of soundscapes that stretched across the city, from the center to its outer periphery. Thus, while cloistered girls and women were physically and visually separated from the larger city behind high walls and gates, they played a crucial role in shaping the Florentine soundscape, and their communities were pivot points around which broader sociosonic regulations turned.

Sonic regimes in and around enclosures parsed and publicized hierarchies of femininity, class, and social position. Noisy scandalous women, silent repentant women, and quiet pious women were all increasingly identifiable by their sonic associations. These sonic identities ran parallel to boundaries of class, social position, and religious status, as well as notions of sexual purity. Institutional growth also coincided with profound political and religious shifts to further produce a unique sonic culture in Florence. Urban officials in the newly established Medici Duchy of Florence and the Grand Duchy of Tuscany used the city's many cloisters as justification for an expanding body of sonic legislation that sought to regulate the activities, movements, and sensory productions of Florentines who lived and lingered near institutions. These groups included women sex workers; vendors who loudly hawked their wares in streets and squares; homosocial gatherings of male youths who gathered to posture, play games, and perform music; and aggressive or violent men who shouted, fought, and often harassed girls and women. Sonic regulations around gendered enclosures were thus a disciplinary mechanism for both cloistered residents and the broader Florentine population. The civic focus on sonic discipline coalesced with a series of broader religious reforms that placed new emphasis on silence and quiet as markers of elite decorum and Catholic piety. In Tuscany, church reformers strove to establish sacred soundscapes as part of their broader mandate of spiritual renewal and Catholic reform. Ecclesiastical authorities framed quiet and silence as potent spiritual aids that could scour the body and soul of sin and promote penitence. Women's institutions, and their soundscapes, were at the center of the intersecting social, political, and religious shifts that defined early modern Florence. Analyzing the shouts, cries, laughter, singing, and daily racket in and around these gendered sites provides new insight into everyday experience in women's communities and the complicated relationships that tied cloistered girls and women to the early modern city.

Despite wide-ranging efforts to enforce quiet and silence, institutions brimmed with vibrant soundscapes. The fortresslike walls that enclosed many communities often failed to block out the sounds of the city—sounds that drifted over walls, through windows, and into listening ears. Neighboring streets, squares, and buildings resonated with sounds made by those who lived and lingered nearby. Moreover, Florentines often purposely gathered outside institutions, shouting and calling out to the cloistered girls and women living inside. Others visited enclosed residents in the institutional parlor—socializing, trading news, discussing family and current affairs, and conducting business. Cloistered communities also prepared foods, medicines, art, and ritual objects, both for their own consumption and for the marketplace.[7] Many institutions produced textiles—mainly silks—in busy workshops within the enclosure complex. All these activities created a sonic register that mixed with the silences, prayers, and musical performances ideally associated with institutional life.

Women and girls had varied reactions to these dynamic soundscapes. Some, like Abbess Lapi, framed any unsanctioned sounds as "noise" and claimed that "evil" sonic incursions "defiled" vulnerable communities of women. Many others found rules of silence oppressive, and they rejected, challenged, or simply ignored sonic regulations as they chatted, sang, shouted, laughed, and cried. Those who found regimes of silence particularly intolerable sometimes left or escaped their institutions, even climbing out windows and over cloister walls. The broader Florentine community, for its part, often paid little heed to rules enforcing quiet—if it was even aware of these rules at all. Sex workers and their clients continued to live and work near nuns; merchants loudly sold their wares outside women's institutions; youths gathered to play games, shout, and socialize in the streets adjacent to girls' and women's enclosures; coaches rattled down streets; and life bustled on in Florence. A voluminous paper trail of noise complaints, sonic legislation, criminal records, institutional documents, and private letters reveals that regulatory sensory efforts often went unachieved and enclosure soundscapes remained mutable and multilayered. Authorities continually struggled to uphold any sonic boundary separating cloistered residents from the larger urban soundscape. Enclosed communities of women were part of an interconnected and dynamic network embedded within Florence's urban fabric. In this context, sounds and silences were used as a means of asserting authority, of social regulation, and also as tools of resistance and of challenge; listening to the sounds of early modern Florence reveals how diverse groups of women navigated their spatial and social experiences via the soundscape.

Sound and the City

Florentine civic authorities in the late medieval and early Renaissance centuries invested unique political, social, and religious significance in the urban soundscape.[8] A collection of fourteenth- and fifteenth-century civic laws aimed to regulate when and where music could be performed throughout the city, and by whom.[9] Moreover, Florence's fifteenth-century republican government carefully ordered the timing and flow of bell ringing throughout the city, crafting an "acoustic regime" that oriented Florentines in time and space and communicated interlocking messages about urban governance, sound, and civic identity.[10] Sonic concerns framed many of Florence's major architectural undertakings in the fifteenth century, prompting what Niall Atkinson has termed a focus on "the acoustic art of city building." Bell towers, stone corridors, city walls, and cobbled streets were all part of the "hearing architecture" of the city and created a built environment that was marked by "the active participation of the building in producing aural communities." Atkinson argues that in this reverberant ambience, "Florentines were extremely intent listeners and acute interpreters of the noises their city made" and the soundscape was "a landscape of sounds that was a crucial component in the construction, maintenance, and orchestration of urban life."[11] By calling on R. Murray Schafer's notion of a "soundscape" to describe an acoustic environment that shaped, and was shaped by, those who inhabited it, this acoustic focus allows us to consider how specific sounds stood to articulate and also challenge social norms, political authorities, religious customs, and spatial meanings.[12] For example, bell ringing brought harmony and order to the city, not only by marking the passage of time and important events but also through the "complex rules, regulations, and customs" that dictated when and how certain bells could be rung and in what relational order to other bells, acoustically shaping the social, religious, and political topography.[13] Sometimes Florentines willfully disrupted this careful orchestration. In 1378 the disenfranchised wool workers at the heart of the Ciompi Revolt disregarded bell-ringing regulations to signal their rebellion against the republican government and to communicate their demands for better working conditions, guild privileges, and political representation. As Atkinson explains, the first moments of the revolt were signaled by the frantic ringing of a parish church bell, which "set off a chain reaction of responses from bell towers around the city. . . . From tower to tower, from bell to bell (*di campana in campana*), all of Florence was engulfed in the sound" of insurrection. Pealing bells signaled an acoustic rejection of the political regime as the "Ciompi found access to a corporate voice and countered the official sounds of the city."[14] The Ciompi Revolt was ultimately short-lived, and republican authorities reasserted dominance over the city's politics and acoustics, punishing leaders of the revolt for illicitly ringing bells. Yet in the ensuing centuries the rebellion persisted in Florentine political and social memory as a potent reminder of the power of sound as a tool of regulation and of resistance.

Efforts to regulate soundscapes, to limit noise, and to discipline noisemakers became more pervasive and widespread in the sixteenth and seventeenth centuries. These efforts were primarily focused on the sounds of sociability—loud gatherings in public spaces, general urban racket, and the sounds associated with particular trades and industries. This heightened emphasis on sonic regulation can be linked to several factors, some specific to Florence and some shared throughout the Italian Peninsula and larger Christian world. First was the ascendence of the Medicean principate in Florence and Tuscany (1532–1737), which ushered in a new ducal—and later the grand-ducal—regime in the wake of the collapse of the republic. The transitional duchy and Grand Duchy of the mid-sixteenth to early seventeenth century marks a critical period in the city's history and stands as an important example of an early modern political regime with absolutist tendencies.[15] A series of Medici rulers, beginning with Cosimo I de' Medici (r. 1537–1574), enacted sweeping reforms during these decades that aimed to centralize governance, consolidate dynastic Medici rule, and bureaucratize the emerging state. Previously independent magistracies, religious organizations, and institutions saw their finances and management increasingly controlled by the Medici and their government agents.[16] Simultaneously, new legislation pursued social discipline with greater force through the successive production and reproduction of regulations limiting, among other things, "racket," "tumult," and "noise."[17] Sonic regulation played a notable role in the emerging political and social character of ducal and grand-ducal Florence, and Medici rulers pursued sensory discipline as a means to consolidate urban and social influence and in the name of good governance.

A second factor was shifting urban demographics. Many cities expanded significantly over the course of the sixteenth, seventeenth, and early eighteenth centuries, and most urbanites lived in cramped spaces with varying levels of infrastructure. These "cheek by jowl" conditions produced new anxieties about class, health, and urban planning.[18] Spatial and social tensions were expressed via sensory issues: complaints about the sounds of certain groups, concerns about the stench of urban industries, and disdain for the sight of dilapidated homes, lean-tos, and crowded streets.[19] Recent studies have also revealed the highly mobile nature of early modern populations. Throughout the Italian Peninsula, people were on the move. Merchants, refugees, migrant workers, soldiers, sex workers, artists, enslaved peoples, and a host of others flowed in and out of Italian hubs for a variety of reasons.[20] Some stayed only temporarily, while others settled for the long term. The net result of this dynamism was that many cities were growing, undergoing large-scale public works, and populated by diverse groups, most of whom lived in close quarters. Urban sounds, and efforts to contain them, highlighted the complex social and sensory geographies that defined early modern cities. In this context, moralizing urbanites complained about the sounds, smells, sights, and filth they associated with sex workers, the working poor, street criers, traveling merchants, migrant laborers, enslaved people, beggars, and other precarious or marginalized individuals. It was this attitude that prompted the Genoese physicist and health writer Giovanni Battista Baliano to bleakly claim that "the poor . . . live in filthier homes and rooms; they keep their clothes and bodies fouler."[21] A similar disdain led Senofonte Bindassi, a Venetian poet, to disparage the "screams and screeches of so many who live in the cities of the world."[22] More often than not, descriptions of the urban soundscape were deeply imbedded with issues of class, gender, ethnicity, and privilege, and these were driving factors in the efforts to identify and limit noise pollution.

Florence's growth over the course of the sixteenth and seventeenth centuries was not as dramatic as other European centers like London or Paris, but the city nonetheless expanded modestly while also suffering episodic population crashes from successive waves of plague, pandemic, war, and famine. Despite these catastrophes, new walls were constructed in 1557 to encompass the growing city, and by 1642 the population had reached 74,682.[23] As Florence and the surrounding Tuscan territories expanded and underwent important political shifts, concerns and complaints about noise pollution became more prevalent. Most significant for this study was the dramatic growth in number and size of residential institutions for girls and women. These enclosures, which can to a certain extent be conceptualized as communes within the commune, expanded at an unprecedented pace, prompting crowded living conditions and sensory tensions that echoed those of larger urban settings. Issues of class, social status, infrastructure, and gender were thus particularly acute in and near urban cloistered communities and were expressed through an escalating series of noise complaints and sonic legislation.

Catholic reform and the religious upheavals of the Reformation contributed yet further emphasis to sonic regulation in Florence specifically and the Christian world more broadly. Soundscapes, and efforts to regulate them, reflected the religious tensions that gripped Christian communities during the early modern centuries. In protestant contexts like Lutheran Germany, preachers enacted an "acoustic semantic change" that sought to silence the sounds associated with Catholicism. These preachers advocated for reforms to bell ringing, stripping away the "pomp" they associated with "vain and ostentatious" bells favored by "papists."[24] In Italy, reformers similarly worked to craft soundscapes that reflected reinvigorated church mandates. The emphasis on spiritual renewal, liturgical and priestly reform, and devotional standardization at the heart of much Catholic reform brought a new focus to the senses in both practice and thought. For example, many church reformers pursued a visual "aesthetic" marked by simplicity, instructiveness, and "decorum" in altarpieces and other devotional artworks, and they critiqued the sensuous, allegorical, and highly realist works that some Renaissance artists produced.[25] Many of these same reformers advocated for a sonic aesthetic marked by uniformity, simplicity, and quiet. Strictures against "worldly" melodies and compositions abound in the repetitive exhortations of bishops and archbishops who admonished clerics "that neither by day or night may they play lutes nor other instruments, nor sing *versi, canzone, sonetti* and other amorous and worldly things."[26] These types of edicts expanded on the "vague prescriptions" of the Council of Trent (1545–1563), which had outlined limits around sacred music and art.[27] Similarly, church authorities discussed the importance of "active listening" in churches and encouraged parishioners to sit silently and attentively during services.[28] The decrees of the Council of Trent, only marginally concerned with lay practices, also proclaimed that "they shall also banish from churches . . . vain, and therefore profane conversations; all walking about, noise, and clamor."[29] The edict was an attempt to halt common practices whereby priests and parishioners used church services as a time to conduct business, socialize, or squabble, and they aimed instead to foster new modes of oral and aural decorum that would reflect a reinvigorated church. Spiritual and pastoral manuals likewise praised the value of silence and framed it as an active force that cleansed both body and soul. Sonic discipline thus developed as an important element of Catholic reform and was directly linked to the entwined concepts of bodily and spiritual discipline championed by many reformers. Yet, as scholars of music, art, and ritual have shown, the application of these sensory reforms was uneven and patchy at best. Local communities often ignored or were unaware of efforts to rein in the sensuous, and "popes, cardinals, and bishops . . . [had a] great diversity of attitudes about what was appropriate, what was not."[30] At all levels, Catholic devotion and sensory practice remained multidimensional, flexible, and richly steeped in pre-Tridentine traditions throughout the sixteenth and seventeenth centuries. Nonetheless, the political, demographic, spatial, and religious shifts that characterized early modern Florence brought a new focus to the senses and soundscapes. This was particularly the case in and around the city's many gendered enclosures where thousands of girls and women lived.

Senses, Bodies, and Gender

Early modern Europeans made important links between the senses, bodies, and gender. Prescriptive writings discussed the crucial role of the senses in shaping femininities. In Giovanni Domenici's popular fifteenth-century conduct manual and household guide, *Rule for the Management of Family Care* (1401), which was dedicated to the influential noblewoman Bartolomea degli Alberti, the Florentine preacher had warned of women's natural tendencies toward sensory indulgence, which, he purported, led them into sin, much like when "Eve took a great risk to have another look at the apple." He outlined the various ways that women needed to carefully regulate their sensory intake and avoid sinful indulgence—advising, for example, that "when in the city . . . keep the eyes downcast and fixed to the earth." Similarly, Domenici warned against smelling things "for superfluous pleasure" and recommended that women eat simple foods and avoid elaborately flavored dishes without the express permission of their husbands. Hearing and speaking required particularly careful attention. Domenici advised Bartolomea to "stretch open the ears to hear the divine commands, celestial advise, divine praise, the holy doctrine, the misery of the afflicted ones, and the melodies of the birds making sweet verses to their Lord." He claimed that it was through these positive sounds that "the sustenance of the soul enters." Domenici was, however, also quick to advise Bartolomea "not to hold the ears open to fairy tales and songs" and warned her that "if you hear the hissing serpentine tongue of slanderers, flee or shut up the ears." He also advised women to give the "sacrifice of your lips" by remaining silent and warned them not to "gossip, or talk of other things except briefly and truthfully . . . do not say an idle word."[31] For preachers like Domenici, sensory regulation, and sonic discipline in particular, was crucial to the production and regulation of normative femininity.

Gendered sensory discourses were directly linked to early modern theories of the body and sex. In particular, the senses were understood to act on the physical body as powerful shaping forces. At the core of this belief was humoral theory and the traditions of Hippocratic, Aristotelian, and Galenic thought. Humoral theory claimed the body was governed by four humors: blood, black bile, yellow bile, and phlegm. While individual bodies varied in their humoral makeup, or complexion, well-balanced humors were unanimously understood as the key to health while imbalanced humors prompted illness and disorder. The humors were primarily influenced by "nonnaturals," factors that acted on, entered into, and altered the human body and its humors.[32] Nonnaturals were generally agreed to be air, motion and rest, sleep and waking, things taken in, things excreted, and passions and emotions.[33] The senses occupied a unique position in the realm of the nonnaturals, operating in multiple spheres of influence. Sound was understood to be air itself, a force physically taken in by the body, and an agent that prompted passions and strong emotions.[34] The other senses were similarly complex: smells entered into the body via the nose, lodged themselves within the internal body, produced strong emotions and passions, and were also excreted from the body and dispersed through space.[35] Images were similarly thought to physically pierce the body with beam-like rays.[36] Most importantly, the senses blurred the boundary between an individual and the larger environment; sounds, smells, sights, textures, and tastes penetrated the body and flowed in and out of the body's sensory receptors, prompting consequential internal and external changes.

Sound in particular acted on the body and the environment with distinct implications and was framed as a material agent that had material effects on the physical body, the community, and the environment at large. For example, medical and scientific treatises from the period discussed how sounds stood to directly influence air quality, either thickening or thinning the air and thus polluting or purifying it. Curative sounds like bell ringing and cracking artillery were said to break up and disperse polluting haze that was described as "thick and like the water of swamps."[37] Health writers similarly discussed how positive and healthy sounds could fortify both body and soul. Silence, quiet, music, birdsong, and other sounds that were deemed "positive" purportedly had the power to treat a variety of ailments ranging from snakebites to plague. Medical writers circulated stories about how individuals "nearly beyond hope of health, have been healed by the delights of music."[38] Conversely, sonic "filth" and unhealthy sounds that were labeled noise were understood to corrupt, rattling through individual bodies and the body social and causing illness and malaise as they disrupted the humors, the internal organs, and other key bodily processes. Noise was similarly thought to harm the soul, leading the sixteenth-century priest Onofrio Zarrabini to claim that "just as our body has five senses, there are five windows through which death enters into us."[39] Medical manuals therefore recommended a variety of ear treatments to cleanse the body of sonic discord, "to remove noise" from the ears, and to rebalance the humors.[40] Italian "agents of health" published a flurry of manuals and treatises over the course of the early modern centuries, many of which discussed the effects of sound on the body; health and spiritual writings alike encouraged a unique focus on soundscapes and sonic regulation.[41] Many of the ideas circulated in these medical, scientific, and spiritual discourses drew on the classical writings of antiquity and were published with new rapidity as part of the rise of "healthy living" literature and a new "culture of prevention" that emerged during this period.[42] In this context, health writers repeatedly advised their readers to carefully monitor surrounding soundscapes, to guard their ears from unhealthy sounds, to purge their bodies of noise, and to attend to their sonic health.

The crucial role of the senses in health, humoral, and bodily theory had important implications for the entwined constructions of sex and gender. According to dominant early modern theories, sex and gender were paradoxically both fixed and malleable states. Female bodies were thought to be identifiable by a series of natural characteristics distinguishing them from opposing male bodies. Female bodies were wet, cold, soft, weak, and porous; they were also considered particularly sensuous and were framed as unstable entities from which sounds, smells, and fluids often seeped in and out with little regulation.[43] The porous and seeping nature of the female body also meant that senses physically penetrated the body more easily, making girls and women more susceptible to the effects of loud noises, sumptuous flavors, illicit sights, and fragrant odors. Male bodies, by contrast, were framed as dry, hot, hard, strong, and less permeable.[44] These binary characteristics were understood to play a key role in the development of sex characteristics, including the shaping of reproductive organs, body hair, and other physical features. They were also purported to have important social implications, accounting for women's supposed intellectual incontinency and their inclination toward sensory indulgence. Yet bodies and their associated categories of sex and gender could also shift and change, disrupting this binary in complex ways. Male bodies were sometimes thought to leak, lactate, or menstruate and female bodies could become hot, hard, and dry.[45] Moreover, early

modern investigations of trans individuals and intersexed bodies, or
bodies labeled as intersexed, complicated binary discourses and ultimately
reveal the historicity and subjectivity of both sex and gender.[46] Thus, while
normative discourses upheld a strict sex and gender binary, early modern
Europeans also continually recognized the mutable nature of both the
body and the social constructs of gender. Bodies, sex, and gender could
change and were all thought to be deeply affected by surrounding sensory stimuli.

Faced with this instability, conduct manuals, health writings, and religious sermons outlined sensory regimes that aimed to stabilize the
body and its associated concepts of sex, gender, and sexuality.[47] It was this
type of thinking that prompted fiery preachers like Bernardino of Siena
(1380–1444) to rail against unmonitored sensory indulgence and to suggest, for example, that "taste is the first sensual portal that leads youth
to a life of seemingly sodomitical debauchery."[48] In a 1424 Lenten sermon
in Florence, Bernardino had chastised "druggists, who sell pine nut pas-
tries, zuccata [candied fruit], marzipan, and sweet cakes" to male youths
and claimed that these sweet flavors prompted dangerous sensory
arousals, passions, and emotions that filled young men with "sodomitic
lust."[49] Similarly, sound was thought to mold women's bodies, minds, and
souls, with profound consequences. The early modern physician Scipione
Mercurio claimed that loud shouts and noise could alter one's humoral
balance and "pale the face and tremble the heart" even of "courageous
men" and were thus uniquely dangerous for women, whom he claimed
were physically, spiritually, and intellectually weaker. Mercurio warned
women how noise "cools the blood, disturbs the spirits, pales the face, induces fevers, causes passions, produces defect" and stressed how important it was for women to avoid loud crowded public gatherings and to
shelter themselves in quiet and private environments.[50] These types of
medically situated discourses drew on the same set of assumptions that
prompted writers like Giovanni Domenici to advise women to keep their
eyes downcast, their taste palates bland, and to "shut up the ears" and
"sacrifice of your lips" by remaining silent. A wide swath of early modern
writings appealed to the broadly held notion that women were at once
uniquely vulnerable to sensory agitation and also more sensuous and
prone to unregulated sensory "indulgences." It was this same logic that
led the medieval French writer, André le Chapelain, to claim in his popular

twelfth-century text, *The Art of Courtly Love,* that women are "loud-mouthe" and "keep up a clamor all day like a barking dog." As Constance Classen has noted in her analysis of this rhetoric, "women's compulsive orality was considered another product of their feminine fluidity: they gushed with speech as they gushed with body fluids. This connection was not merely symbolic[,] for feminine volubility was held by some to result from uterine vapors irritating the brain."[51] Body, sense, sex, and gender were intimately enmeshed concepts and had profound consequences for gendered theory and practice in early modern Europe.

In late Renaissance Florence, sensory discourses, medical thought, and spiritual theories of sound and its effects all coalesced with the rising rates of gendered institutionalization to produce unprecedented efforts to carefully regulate urban and institutional soundscapes. Regulating the sounds that enclosed girls and women made and heard was crucially important because sound was considered central to the regulation of normative femininity, bodily health, and spiritual purity. Institutional, ecclesiastical, and civic authorities understood the city's many enclosed communities to be sites of precarious femininity, packed full of thousands of girls and women who each required careful sonic regulations to discipline and care for their bodies and souls. It was this very notion that led Abbess Lapi to describe the sounds of sex work that penetrated her cloister as "evil," molesting, and defiling.

Institutions for Girls and Women

Florence's institutional landscape transformed over the course of the sixteenth and early seventeenth centuries to accommodate record high numbers of girls and women who lived in a diverse range of residential enclosures including nunneries, youth homes, reform houses, and charity homes. Individuals entered distinct enclosures under varying circumstances and experienced institutionalization differently depending on the intersections of class, religion, race, ethnicity, vocation, and personal circumstance. Institutional expansion occurred simultaneously along two key axes: ecclesiastical and civic. A rich field a scholarship has examined how convent populations soared in sixteenth- and seventeenth-century Florence and on the Italian Peninsula more broadly.[52] Catholic reform, a competitive marriage economy, and local political and religious shifts resulted in astoundingly high rates of monachization. By the seventeenth century, close to half of Florence's noblewomen lived within a convent or monastery.[53] Histories of hospitals, poorhouses, and prisons have likewise shown how emerging models of care and discipline changed the nature of nonecclesiastical institutionalization during this period. New types of civic institutions were rapidly founded and attended to specific social groups through sustained enclosure.[54] In Florence the growth of ecclesiastical and civic homes for girls and women far outnumbered those for boys and men because systemic inequalities meant that girls and women were more vulnerable to poverty and precarity and because patriarchal norms asserted that they required nearly constant guardianship.

Institutions varied greatly in terms of demographics, size, and mandate. Some nunneries were extremely prestigious and housed patrician girls and women who contributed large dowries and wielded impressive social, religious, and political capital. Other convents were humbler and housed more women from nonelite families—families who, like their elite counterparts, relied on nunneries to safeguard female relatives, to elevate family honor, and to offload girls and women who were deemed disabled, "troubled," or unmarriageable. Nunneries were intensely stratified communities. The rank of choir nun was all but exclusively reserved for elite women, and only choir nuns could hold administrative positions. Lower-class girls and women were usually relegated to the status of servant nun and tasked with carrying out the manual and domestic labors key to daily operations.[55] During this period, rural women streamed into Florentine nunneries in growing numbers, while some patrician Florentine women undertook new patterns of migration out of the city and into rural nunneries. In rural settings, *contadine* nuns struggled to match the considerable resources urban-born women often brought with them, making it easier for urban families to take command of the rural nunneries they patronized.[56] Enslaved and servant girls and women occupied the lowest social strata in the convent microcosm, mirroring the larger society of early modern Europe. Though not uncommon, enslaved girls and women were not a consistent presence in Florentine nunneries. They did not take formal vows and instead labored to fulfill the needs and desires of wealthy choir nuns, as in when a number of seventeenth-century Medici women were gifted enslaved black women when entering their respective convents.[57] Other institutions explicitly barred enslaved women in their enclosures. The Orbatello, a civic charity for impoverished widows, banned enslaved women from the institution and claimed, as justification, that whenever they were admitted the other women were "disturbed and perturbed."[58] The experiences of enslaved residents are difficult to recapture in great detail, in large part because their histories are silenced by most archival records. The sparse references that survive, while illuminating, are often frustratingly vague, reflective of the profound marginalization these individuals experienced.

Civic institutions likewise varied significantly in demographics. Some were general poorhouses with open-door policies, though increasingly institutions aimed to carefully discriminate regarding whom they accepted. These homes focused on niche groups of the "worthy poor" and moved away from general hospitals that characterized fourteenth- and fifteenth-century Europe, where the sick, poor, and pilgrims were often housed together for shorter stays.[59] When the Malmaritate home opened in 1580, for example, it made clear that it was a charity only for married sex workers and women fleeing "bad marriages" and not a general charity house. The book of governance outlined in detail how "the old are not for this home.... The sick should not be accepted ... pregnant women are not accepted."[60] The upper classes usually avoided entry into civic charities because family networks provided a socioeconomic safety net that charity and reform houses aimed to mimic. Yet Florentine elites remained intimately involved in the operation and management of civic homes as confraternity members, patrons, and business partners.[61] Residential profiles in civic enclosures were thus less stratified than nunneries, but institutional demographics remained fundamentally linked to dynamics of class.

Despite the important differences that distinguished Florence's many enclosures, a number of shared characteristics link the diverse communities this book examines. First, they were all Catholic. Nunneries constituted a key element of the church structure and were important sites of local religiosity that bound together individuals, families, communities, and the church. Civic institutions fell beyond the direct administrative purview of the church, but their daily operations remained deeply tied to Catholic notions of piety and civic religion. Attending to the souls of institutional wards was equally important as attending to their basic needs of food and shelter. While the vast majority of residents were Catholic, non-Catholics or neophytes occasionally lived in the city's institutions. A 1448–1552 list of women in the Le Murate nunnery recorded "Lucretia the Jew" among their numbers.[62] Residential records for the Orbatello widows' home reported that in 1668 "Maria, the former Jew," joined the community. Similarly, in 1677 "Maria Verginia, the baptized Muslim" entered the Orbatello and was joined in 1679 by "Maria Maddalena, the baptized Muslim."[63] Some institutional authorities and residents were eager to participate in narratives of Christian triumphalism and appear to have sought out Jews, Muslims, and recent converts to bring into their communities; as Tamar Herzig notes, "converting the Jews remained an important expression of Italian nuns' religiosity throughout the age of Catholic Reform."[64] In 1636 Florence also established a House of the Catechumens to further "encourage" potential Jewish and Muslim converts and to educate neophytes in Catholic doctrine. Houses of Catechumens opened throughout the Italian Peninsula, spurred by the missionizing zeal of the Reformation, and residents were subjected to intense pressure to convert to Catholicism "of their own free will" in these homes.[65]

A second characteristic linking Florence's diverse network of female institutions was the rampant practice of forced enclosure. Some women willingly and eagerly sought entry into ecclesiastical and civic enclosures, but many residents, if not most, were institutionalized either directly against their own will or as the result of limited choice. The relationship between Catholic reform and forced enclosure was paradoxical. Edicts from the Tridentine period sought, at least in theory, to curb the rampant practice of forced enclosure in nunneries. The Council of Trent stipulated that girls could not take the habit until the age of sixteen, that their profession must be "pious and free," and that no girl or woman could be forced "to enter a monastery against her will, or to assume the habit of any religious order, or to declare her profession."[66] In reality, however, these rules were easily ignored or maneuvered around, and officials often did little to limit the practice. In fact, profession rates soared to previously unseen highs in many Italian cities during this period, including Florence. Similar dynamics prevailed in many civic institutions. While Florence's impoverished and vulnerable often actively petitioned for entry into one of the city's charity houses, many girls and women hoped to avoid these same institutions. Charity homes sometimes doubled as prisons and

workhouses and often adopted punitive practices in their efforts to rehabilitate residents. In particular, women sex workers, or those deemed at
risk of falling into sex work, were regularly forced into charity homes or
convents after being apprehended by city officials for various offenses.[67]
Civic institutions may have strived to discriminate carefully regarding
whom they accepted, but they also kept residents under duress to fulfill
mandates focused on the preservation of feminine honor through long-
term enclosure. For many, charity and reform homes were bleak places
and best avoided.

Rising rates of forced enclosure dovetailed with a renewed focus on
strict cloistering that was championed by many Catholic reformers.
Unprecedented numbers of girls and women were institutionalized during
this period, and they lived under increasingly strict cloister rules that
sought to carefully regulate their movements and activities.[68] Ideally, the
cloister was designed to act as a seal, sealing in vulnerable, problematic,
and pious girls and women and sealing out the broader world along with
its corrupting influences. Tridentine decrees reaffirmed and strengthened
Periculoso, a papal decree first issued in 1298 that had ordered female monastics to live in perpetual enclosure in order to "safeguard their hearts
and bodies in complete chastity" and to protect them from "the public
and worldly gaze and occasions for lasciviousness."[69] Tridentine rules
sought to expand *Periculoso* and to enforce cloistering more universally.
Edicts from the council ordered "that the enclosure of nuns be carefully
restored, wheresoever it has been violated, and that it be preserved, wheresoever it has not been violated." The decree also stated that "for no nun,
after her profession, shall it be lawful to go out of her convent, even for a
brief period, under any pretext whatsoever, except for some lawful cause,
to be approved of by the bishop."[70] Tridentine decrees spurred a series of
local apostolic visits to nunneries throughout the Italian Peninsula that
sought to root out lax cloisters. Convent visitors dispatched to Tuscan
nunneries described the insufficiently high cloister walls and poorly policed gates that weakened cloisters, and they complained about nuns who
lived "without fear of anyone" and largely did as they pleased, acting with
a level of autonomy that some church authorities deemed unacceptable.[71]
Indeed, behind the protective barrier of the cloister many communities
were effectively self-governed on a day-to-day basis. Nuns could, and did,
capitalize on this to enjoy varying degrees of agency and influence.

Tridentine efforts to strengthen cloisters thus aimed to also enforce greater external oversight on nunneries, often putting new pressures on institutionalized women. For those who were enclosed against their will this could be unsufferable. Arcangela Tarrabotti, a prolific writer and unwilling nun in seventeenth-century Venice, described how the twin realities of forced enclosure and strict claustration were akin to being "trapped in a treacherous net, robbed of precious liberty," and she critiqued parents who insisted on "burying [girls] alive in the cloister for the rest of their lives."[72]

The push for strict claustration also had profound effects in unvowed institutions, including tertiary homes and the many civic enclosures this book considers. In 1566 Pope Pius V, under pressure from reformers like Charles Borromeo, issued the papal bull *Circa pastoralis* ordering strict cloistering as a requirement for all communities of women.[73] The bull was particularly concerned with tertiary houses, where pious women did not take formal religious vows and traditionally had more flexible and varied rules of enclosure. Many tertiary communities resisted the bull, but in the following decades visitations and papal decrees continued to push for their strict enclosure with varying degrees of success. Over time, a general trend emerged where many unvowed communities succumbed to ecclesiastical pressure and adopted formal vows and permanent cloistering.[74] Elite Florentines who operated civic institutions likewise embraced strict enclosure as an institutional ideal. Over the course of the sixteenth and seventeenth centuries many charities shifted to housing girls and women for longer periods of time, often for life, and under stricter cloisters. For example, when Florence's Santa Caterina home for abandoned children opened in 1590 near the outer edge of the city under the direction of a group of pious noblemen, the house operators only intended the charity to remain open for three years as a temporary measure in response to famine-induced precarity. The charity aimed to safeguard girls in need and to prepare them to live with relatives, enter into a domestic service contract, get married, or join a nunnery. By the end of the third year, however, many girls were still living in the institution and the city moved to establish a permanent home that would bring in more girls and house them for longer.[75] The grand duke gave permission for the charity to move to a larger location in Via San Gallo on the north side of the Arno River, closer to the city center. Santa Caterina's records described this as "a worthy place to build a home that was capable of housing many girls, and all for the honor and glory of God and to keep many girls from the hands of the devil."[76] Many Santa Caterina wards went on to stay in the institution for the rest of their lives. Other charity homes became more enclosed by transitioning into convents. The Pietà home, another youth conservatory, was also established as a temporary shelter but by 1634 had transitioned to a fully cloistered third-order convent.[77]

Institutionalization could become a lifelong reality in yet other ways. Many wards were funneled through an institutional pipeline, shuffled from one enclosed institution to the next. For example, infant wards in Florence's expansive Innocenti foundling home often remained in the complex well into adulthood, only to then transition directly to another charity home or nunnery where they lived for the remainder of their lives. Lists of institutional residents sometimes allow us to track these dynamics across numerous institutions. In 1636 a young woman named Maddalena di Giovanni entered the Orbatello charity home, where the record books carefully noted that she was "a Pietà girl."[78] It is unclear what circumstances prompted Maddalena to leave the youth conservatory, which had transitioned to a fully cloistered nunnery just two years earlier, or when she had left the Pietà. Perhaps with no other opportunities immediately available to her, Maddalena opted to enter another charity home, continuing the cycle of institutionalization. At the Orbatello, Maddalena joined women such as Albiera Della Ginerva Delli Innocenti, Anastasia Delli Innocenti, and Caterina Delli Innocenti, just a few of the women who had been raised in the Innocenti and taken the foundling home as their surname before moving to the Orbatello.[79]

Of course, lifelong institutionalization was not the case for all residents. Some nuns successfully petitioned to have their vows dissolved and left the cloister. Some girls and women took advantage of dowry programs offered in select charity homes and used these funds to arrange marriages. Others left to move in with family members, friends, or enter a domestic service contract. Some women fled or escaped, and others simply moved out of their own accord. A dynamic network of institutions opened and operated in sixteenth- and seventeenth-century Florence, housing thousands of girls and women from across the socioeconomic spectrum. These institutions varied in important respects, and individuals experienced enclosure in complicated and personal ways. Collectively, however,

Florentine enclosures were linked by a series of interconnected dynamics. They expanded in number and size, and housed residents for longer periods of time, often under stricter cloisters. Within this context, sonic regulation and rules of silence were framed as crucial to the maintenance of the cloister, to communal order, and to the discipline and care of female bodies and souls. The daily sounds and silences that resonated in and around these sites provide new insight into the complicated history of gendered enclosure in Florence.

Sources and Chapters

How can we recover historical sounds that, by their very nature, are fleeting and leave no lasting trace? My research has involved searching out both direct and indirect references to sound in letters, legislation, criminal records, institutional documents, and prescriptive health and spiritual writings. There is a certain irony in using written records in an attempt to move beyond the textual and the visual. Nonetheless, these sources contain valuable information about the early modern soundscape. More simply, they are often all that remains of an otherwise ephemeral past. At times the search for sound turned up archival silences. Often my research involved inferring sounds from descriptions of urban activities and interactions in which they are not explicitly referenced. Other sources contain rich and detailed descriptions of the clatter, racket, din, shouting, laughter, bell ringing, birdsong, and everyday vocalizations that filled early modern Florence.

But how much do these written descriptions of sound reveal about what Florence actually sounded like, and what do they tell us about the experiences of girls and women? Important echoes of the urban sensate are recorded in these documents and leave traces of the sounds and silences that resonated throughout Florence. Yet textual descriptions of sound are also highly discursive and ultimately reflect the complex manner in which the senses are "value-coded," "emotionally charged," and "interiorized by the members of society in a deeply personal way."[80] Moreover, written sources are a mediated "staging of sound" and "textualization of sound" that is fundamentally linked to positionality.[81] To examine the premodern soundscape, my analysis takes as a starting point David Howes's assertion that the senses are "heavy with social significance" and "the human sensorium . . . never exists in a natural state. Humans are social beings, and just as human nature itself is a product of culture, so is the human sensorium."[82] What institutional authorities like Abbess Lapi framed as "dishonest words, noises, and extraordinary shouting" were almost certainly interpreted differently by those who made these sounds and by other groups who heard them. For many these vocalizations would not have been considered "evil" at all, and instead were the routine articulations of urban life. Descriptions of sound thus depend entirely on how certain groups understand their social position and their claim to urban spaces and soundscapes. It was with this notion in mind that Peter Bailey described noise primarily as a cultural construction and labeled it "sound out of place," building on Mary Douglas's study of dirt as "matter out of place"; both distinctions ask us to recognize how the articulation of material and immaterial boundaries align with the articulation of sociocultural boundaries.[83] In their concern for regulating sounds out of place and identifying "unwanted sounds" in and around women's enclosures, Florentine authorities and some institutionalized women were, in fact, focused on identifying unwanted individuals and out-of-place activities.[84] Locating noise meant locating noisemakers and labeling transgressive identities, activities, and sounds on both sides of the cloister wall. Distinctions between good and bad sounds and between silence and noise were expressed alongside parallel boundaries that aimed to distinguish the pious from the impious, the wealthy from the impoverished, the honorable from the dishonorable, and the clean from the polluted.

The soundscapes examined in this book are fundamentally entangled with issues of social position, authority, discipline, challenge, and resistance and ultimately reveal how the senses were key building blocks for social boundaries.[85] A gendered analysis of the early modern sound scape lays bare these connections. Mark Smith has noted how many nineteenth- and early twentieth-century sensory histories, while innovative in their focus, tended to assume "a uniformity of sensory experience among all classes and genders," treating "everyone in the past as one, undifferentiated sensory clump." As Smith points out, this approach "elides and flattens a complex cultural and social topography" that shaped past societies—one in which the sensate had shifting and deeply personal implications that were fundamentally shaped by the intersections of gender, class, race, ability, and a host of other factors.[86] By focusing on gender, embodiment, class, and social experience, this book considers how dominance over a soundscape meant dominance over a particular space and those who inhabited it; in Florence the quest for quiet served to enshrine a unique set of social, gender, and religious hierarchies and to identify different types of women in a series of social asymmetries.[87] Efforts at sonic regulation were often unsuccessful, however, and noisemakers like the sex workers who lived and worked near the Sant'Onofrio nunnery usually resisted, ignored, or were entirely unaware of efforts to limit their sounds as they continued to live loudly. In doing so they pushed back against claims that they, and their sounds, were out of place or unwanted in the city.

Florentines had a variety of words to describe noise. The most common were *baccano*, *rumore*, *tumulto*, *strepito*, and *bruttura*. Often they described particular features of the soundscape they interpreted as noisy, including *gridi* (shouts and screams), *voci* (voices), and *suoni* (sounds). When Italians used these words, they offered socially and culturally specific interpretations of what they heard and imagined. These descriptors tell us less about decibel level (the intensity or loudness of a given sound) and more about the "social temperament, class background, and cultural desire" of those doing the describing.[88] As such, this book is less interested in what early modern Florence *actually* sounded like and much more interested in what sonic descriptions reveal about social relationships, spatial experiences, and bodily practices. My approach to interpreting silence is similar. As Mark Smith explains, "sound itself cannot properly be understood unless we think of it as constituted, at least in part, by silence(s)."[89] When Italians discussed silence and quiet, *silenzio/silentio* and *quiete*, they understood these resonances not simply as the absence of sound but as active agents within a soundscape and social space. Institutional, church, and civic authorities worked to craft and maintain enclosure soundscapes resplendent with silence as a means of communicating specific notions of gender, sociability, and spirituality. Throughout the book, *silence* and *noise* are treated primarily as social concepts that provide insight into the unique auditory cultures of Renaissance Florence.

The chapters in *A Veil of Silence* examine urban and institutional soundscapes from a variety of perspectives, considering the sounds that enclosed girls and women both made and heard alongside broader cultural, medical, and religious discourses on sound and hearing. Chapter 1 considers the institutional shifts that marked the early modern centuries, outlining key features of Florence's diverse network of enclosures for girls and women and introducing the communities at the heart of the book. In the sixteenth and seventeenth centuries a series of religious, civic, and social factors converged to prompt the rapid growth of civic and ecclesiastical institutions. As a result, thousands of girls and women from varying circumstances lived in strictly enclosed spaces for protracted periods of time, and often for life. This chapter traces the broad contours of girls' and women's experiences in civic and ecclesiastical homes by analyzing the factors that pushed individuals into enclosures and the daily regimes they encountered. Florentine institutions worked to provide guardianship and care while also disciplining, classifying, and regulating the female population. Sonic regimes that prioritized silence, quiet, and sacred sounds were crucial to all of these programs of care, charity, and discipline.

Chapter 2 considers the sounds that enclosed girls and women heard, examining the soundscapes that surrounded Florence's expansive network of girls' and women's institutions. What did daily life in Florence sound like, and how did Florentines variously respond to the noise, chatter, and clatter that reverberated through the streets? Cloistered women complained about urban noise pollution with new regularity and force in the sixteenth and seventeenth centuries, and urban and church officials expressed heightened concerns about shouts, songs, and racket near these communities. Three distinct sociosonic groups were identified as particularly noisy: women sex workers, rowdy male youths, and aggressive and violent men. Examining archival records related to each group reveals how noise complaints were directly linked to issues of class, gender, social status, and physical space. Girls' and women's communities were at the center of many of the sonic tensions that animated Florence, and diverse groups of women used noise complaints as a means to claim space and to assert their presence in the noisy city.

Chapter 3 examines medical, environmental, and spiritual theories of sound and hearing, investigating how early modern Italians understood sound to act on the physical body, the environment, and the soul. Drawing on a wide range of health and spiritual writings, I show how early modern Italians understood sonic health as a basic requirement for bodily and spiritual well-being. Health manuals outlined positive and negative

sounds in detail and discussed their impact on the body and the environment, continually reminding their readers of the importance of aural
health. Spiritual writers likewise understood sound to be a powerful agent
that directly influenced both body and soul, and Catholic reform advocated for new modes of oral and aural comportment focused on quiet,
silence, and attentive listening. Bodily health, spiritual health, and sonic
health went hand in hand, and prescriptive literature repeatedly discussed
the active power of sound and the importance of carefully regulated
soundscapes. These broader discourses on sound and the body allow us
to more fully consider why sonic regulation mattered so much to civic,
religious, and institutional authorities in Florence and its uniquely gendered implications.

Chapter 4 analyzes the pursuit of quiet in and around institutions
for girls and women, considering the sounds that enclosed women made
and heard. Institutional, ecclesiastical, and civic authorities all worked to
regulate cloistered soundscapes with new precision in the sixteenth and
seventeenth centuries. Authorities framed silence as crucial to the care
and discipline of cloistered communities and made direct links between silence, feminine purity, and reform. Despite these efforts, cloistered girls and women often ignored sonic regulations and lived loudly,
and institutional and church authorities continually struggled to rein in
the vibrant sounds of everyday life. During this same period, civic officials
published an increasing number of secular laws that sought to regulate
the sounds Florentines made near women's institutions. This emerging
sonic legislation was linked to Florence's shifting political character, and
civic authorities identified girls' and women's institutions as important
sonic sites that required particular civic attention. Here, too, despite best
efforts, enclosure soundscapes remained dynamic and multilayered, and
Florentines usually ignored or were unaware of the civic pursuit of quiet.
Cloistered communities continually resonated with the sounds of urban
sociability. Examining these dynamic soundscapes, in both their idealized and everyday forms, reveals gendered histories of sound, silence, and
noise in the Renaissance city.

CHAPTER ONE

Space: Communities of Girls and Women

*I*N 1618 the Medici grand duchess, Maria Maddalena d'Austria, named herself governess of the Orbatello home for impoverished widows, adding the charity to a growing portfolio of civic and religious institutions she patronized. As part of her role, the grand duchess wanted to know "the state of the house of the Orbatello, [including] how many rooms there are and in what condition."[1] Civic magistrates noted that they would visit the institution to determine its state of affairs. Several decades earlier, in 1585, when a Florentine magistrate had crafted a similar report, the news had not been good. A letter had described "the many disorders we have found" and spoke of the women "of suspected dishonor and of the poorest example" living in the complex, and of the men who passed in and out of the enclosure largely unaccounted for.[2] To add to the troubles, the complex had fallen into disrepair. Several of the ground floor apartments were uninhabitable because they were "too damp," and the building was in need of substantial renovations.[3] Lodgings were crowded, as multigenerational families crammed themselves into the small apartments. Despite rules stating that boys over the age of twelve could not reside in the institution for fear of scandal, mothers regularly kept their sons living with them for much longer.[4]

The Orbatello was one of the Florence's older charitable homes for women, founded in 1371 as a communal living complex for poor women and widows by the wealthy banker Niccolò degli Alberti in an act of civic piety.[5] By the time the grand duchess requested a report on the institution in the seventeenth century, the Orbatello had undergone significant changes. In 1401 the powerful captains of the Guelf Party took over the Orbatello's finances and management. The community was located in a walled complex on Via della Pergola, north of the imposing Cathedral of Santa Maria del Fiore. Institutional records described the complex as "a completely enclosed building. . . . One enters and exits through a single door . . . and there are 27 houses along three sides with a ground floor and balcony, which are given to poor people to live in for the love of God and no rent is collected."[6] Perhaps most significantly, by the seventeenth century the demographics of the institution had shifted. Impoverished widows still lived in the complex, but nonwidowed women were increasingly moving in.

Beginning in the 1580s, with the consent of Grand Duke Francesco I de' Medici, the Orbatello began to accept an increasing number of women from the nearby Innocenti foundling home.[7] The Innocenti was facing mounting debts and overcrowding, as many abandoned infants remained in the institution well into adulthood. This was particularly the case for girls and women who did not have the same apprenticeship opportunities or freedoms as male youths. The Innocenti, seeking to alleviate costs associated with long-term care, relied on the Orbatello to take in wards who had reached adulthood. These Innocenti women were not widows, but they had lived all but their entire lives in an institution. With nowhere else to go and no immediate marriage prospects, Innocenti women made the short move down the street to the Orbatello—from the foundling home directly to the widow's asylum, from one institution to another. There Innocenti women paid their way by joining the Orbatello community in producing silks and other textiles, a trade Innocenti wards were taught in childhood. Yet the Orbatello struggled to accommodate these new residents and to make sure they complied with house rules. In 1585, frustrated institutional authorities declared that "the Innocenti women, under penalty of the loss of their room, are obliged to obey the priest just like all the other women, and they or any others are not allowed to go outside of the institution without a license of permission."[8] Many Innocenti women, for their part, seemed unwilling to follow these rules. Perhaps eager to generate income on their own terms and to exercise new freedoms after years of watchful guardianship in the foundling home, the Innocenti wards quickly gained a reputation for ignoring the Orbatello's rule of enclosure and coming and going from the complex as they pleased. Some went further and appear to have used the institution as a base for sex work.[9] These women and the men they invited into their apartments were almost certainly the individuals of "suspected dishonor" referenced in official letters.

According to urban authorities, a particularly problematic effect of the "many disorders" at the Orbatello was the noise and disturbance it created. Young men and youths loitered in the street outside the enclosure, shouting for the girls and women living inside, playing instruments and noisy ball games, and otherwise "croaking" and "cooing."[10] The relative laxity of the cloister, with its largely unmonitored gate and crumbling walls, opened the complex up to the sounds and activities of surrounding shops on Via della Pergola and Via degli Angioli. Men who sneaked into the institution to solicit sex, visit with residents, or conduct business created their own scandalous sounds. By 1606 some of the Innocenti women had established a school in the complex to teach young Orbatello residents to read; the shouts, screams, and delights of children as they learned and played was identified as a particularly noisy problem.[11] Frustrated magistrates forwarded a list of suggestions to the grand-ducal offices in an attempt to remedy the situation. First they advised the renewal of an old ban that strictly outlawed men from entering the institution and prohibited silk merchants and shopkeepers who came to conduct business from approaching any closer than the outer door.[12] Next they recommended the Orbatello shift its living arrangements, confining younger women to the inner courtyard apartments, while older widows occupied apartments backing onto the public street and outer door. They hoped this protective ring of "old and more venerable" widows would deter the noisy youths who loitered in the street, and if nothing else they hoped the older women would "remedy or at least report the disorders."[13] A number of edicts and bans were further produced in the following years as part of a continual attempt to limit "disorders" at the complex.[14] In

1606, authorities proclaimed that Innocenti women could continue to teach Orbatello children in the school but that "there should not be such noise that it disturbs the other women who live in said convent or in the apartments were the teachers teach; in short, these activities will only be tolerated when there is every sort of modesty and quiet."[15]

Concerns about "disorders" and noise at the Orbatello reflect a broader preoccupation for the disciplined enclosure of girls and women in early modern Florence. That the Orbatello's daily affairs occupied authorities up the ranks to the grand duchess is indicative of several defining features of Florence's many institutions for girls and women. First was the interconnected nature of the city's expansive institutional network. Civic and ecclesiastical enclosures, while distinct, remained linked—both in shared governance strategies and, as in the case of the Innocenti and the Orbatello, demographically as some residents moved from one institution to another. Second, reports of "disorders" at the Orbatello reveal the daily realities of institutional life and the diverse reactions girls and women had to the regimes they encountered in these homes. Essentially all institutions promoted ambitious mandates that aimed to foster specific understandings of gendered purity and honor. As in the case of the Orbatello, enforcing "modesty and quiet" was at the core of these mandates. But these efforts were complicated by a reality whereby many institutions were cash strapped, overcrowded, and filled with independently minded entrants. Like the willful Innocenti women, many residents ignored or resisted house rules—particularly those that sought to limit their movements and vocalizations. Despite these challenges, authorities persisted in their efforts to bring the city's thousands of enclosed girls and women to heel. Indeed, the grand duchess's inquest into the Orbatello's daily affairs reveals how Medici rulers understood institutional management, and the enclosure of girls and women in particular, as an important element of civic and grand-ducal governance.

This chapter provides an overview of the communities at the center of this book. I begin by tracing the remarkable growth, in both number and size, of civic and ecclesiastical enclosures roughly between 1550 and 1650. Next I examine the social, familial, religious, and political factors that prompted urban authorities and elite citizens to open and operate an unprecedented number of institutions. Equally important are the realities that drove nonelite, working-class, and impoverished girls and women into residential institutions, sometimes of their own volition but often by force or because of profoundly limited options. To explore these dynamics, I focus on records from the Orbatello widow's complex, the Convertite convent for penitent sex workers, and the Malmaritate charity home for "badly married" women (see Figure 1.1). Taken together, these three institutions provide a view into a wide cross-section of Florence's female population, including young and old; single, married, and widowed; vowed and unvowed; and those deemed honorable and dishonorable. Both the Convertite and the Malmaritate focused primarily on reforming sex workers and women deemed "scandalous." An analysis of Florence's shifting policies toward sex work reveals how many girls and women ended up in these residential enclosures and the programs of sexual reform, enforced modesty, and paternalistic supervision they encountered. The experiences of marginalized women are contrasted with those of elite women who gathered in the city's many nunneries. By briefly analyzing how noblewomen crafted influential networks within the cloister and contributed to the broader political and religious landscape of Florence, I further explore how class dynamics patterned institutional profiles. To analyze these histories, I draw on a rich body of scholarship that has examined Italian Tridentine and Catholic Reformation convent cultures. Finally, this chapter considers how an emphasis on silence, quiet, and carefully monitored soundscapes prevailed in all Florentine institutions for girls and women. Regulating sonic experience was a central component in all institutional regimes.

Institutional Expansion in Late Renaissance Florence

A visitor to late Renaissance Florence would have been struck by the sheer number of residential institutions in the city: nunneries, monasteries, hospitals, asylums, conservatories and poorhouses. Some were humble homes and barely distinguishable from neighboring buildings. Others, like the Orbatello, were noticeable because of their imposing gates and the signs and symbols decorating the exterior, albeit sometimes crumbling, walls. Others were grand architectural complexes like the Innocenti foundling home, designed by Filippo Brunelleschi and lauded as a site of great civic pride. The city's many nunneries were usually notable for their high cloister walls enclosing both small and large complexes with

Figure 1.1. Locations of (1) Sant'Elisabetta delle Convertite, (2) the Orbatello, and (3) Casa delle Malmaritate. Stefano Buonsignori, map of Florence, 1584 (copy from 1695), Harvard College Map Library.

Courtesy of the Digitally Encoded Census Information Mapping Archive (DECIMA).

gardens, dormitories, refectories, and churches. Together these institutions were a near constant presence on the city's topography, cropping up in almost every neighborhood and spread throughout all four urban quarters. In 1550 Leandro Alberti devoted a section of his popular survey of Italian cities, *Descriptions of All of Italy*, to Florence's "excellent buildings" and noted "memorable charitable buildings and hospitals, like the hospital of S. Maria Nuova . . . superior to all the hospitals of Italy, [and] the hospital for the poor infants [the Innocenti], along with other similar charitable buildings of which they say there are thirty-seven. And likewise, one finds . . . seventy-six religious monasteries for men and women."[16] Descriptions of early modern Florence reflected an unmistakable feeling that the city was filled with the institutionalized, whose presence, while largely hidden from public view, composed a defining feature of the city's character.

Florence witnessed stunning growth in both the number and size of its residential institutions in the sixteenth century. New enclosures were opened at a rapid pace, and older complexes saw their populations grow. The vast majority focused on enclosing girls and women. A few charities for boys and men did open during this time, such as the Ospedale dei Poveri Fanciulli Abbandonati, an orphanage for abandoned boys that opened its doors in 1542. Monasteries for male religious also saw modest increases. In their foundational study of the 1427 Catasto [tax assessment], David Herlihy and Christiane Klapisch-Zuber counted 554 to 566 monks in Florence.[17] By 1551 the city had twenty-two monasteries and 656 male religious; by 1632 six new monasteries had been added, altogether housing 966 vowed men.[18] The relatively modest increases in male institutionalization were far outstripped by the exponential growth of civic and religious institutions for girls and women. In the 1550s alone three civic institutions were founded for vulnerable girls without guardianship: the Ospedale di Fanciulle Abbandonate di Santa Maria Vergine (1552), the Casa della Pietà (1554), and San Niccolò (1556). By the end of the decade, these homes collectively housed around 260 girls at a time.[19] In the late sixteenth century, the city further expanded its institutional network, opening the Malmaritate in 1580 as a refuge for married sex workers and women fleeing spousal abuse. In 1588 the Ospedale della Carità opened as group home for destitute young women. The city simultaneously continued operations at established charities like the Innocenti and the Orbatello, taking in an increasing number of wards.[20] In 1590 the Santa Caterina house opened, primarily as a refuge for abandoned girls considered at risk of entering the sex trade. Institutional growth continued in the seventeenth century—notably, with the founding of the Ospedale dei Mendicanti, a large poorhouse opened in response to the begging and poverty crisis of 1619–1622.[21] The Mendicanti accommodated both sexes, in separate quarters, housing 497 women and 160 men in 1632, but it quickly transitioned to almost exclusively house women and their children.[22]

Perhaps even more dramatic than civic institutional growth was the pace at which nunneries expanded and profession rates soared. A 1384 survey of Florence's convents had reported only three hundred nuns.[23] A 1422 convent visitation reported a mere 229 professed nuns in the city.[24] The 1427 Catasto, though incomplete in reporting convent populations, noted a modest increase of roughly five hundred to 520 nuns in urban convents.[25] Over the next century and a half, nunneries expanded at a dizzying rate. By 1552, forty-four religious houses were listed within the city walls, collectively housing 2,658 professed nuns, roughly 11 percent of the total female population.[26] By 1632 the number of nuns had jumped even higher, to 3,887.[27] The ratio of women religious to the total urban population also increased exponentially over these centuries. In 1384 roughly one in every 141 residents was a nun. By 1427 this had narrowed to one nun for every seventy-two inhabitants. By 1552 the ratio was even smaller, with one nun for every twenty residents.[28] By 1632 the ratio had shrunk yet again, with roughly one nun for every seventeen residents (see Figure 1.2).

Census records allow us to estimate the total number of girls and women living in Florence's many civic and ecclesiastical enclosures. In 1561 Duke Cosimo I commissioned the comprehensive Decima census. Scribes and notaries were dispatched to systematically walk through the city, carefully tallying how many men, women, and children lived in the roughly nine thousand residences they visited, their occupations, and the taxable values of each residence.[29] While institutions were exempt from this taxation, population figures for most of the city's enclosures were nonetheless recorded. According to the 1561 census, roughly 14 percent of the city's girls and women lived in an institution: 4,175 out of 29,782 girls and women and of a total population of 59,216. By

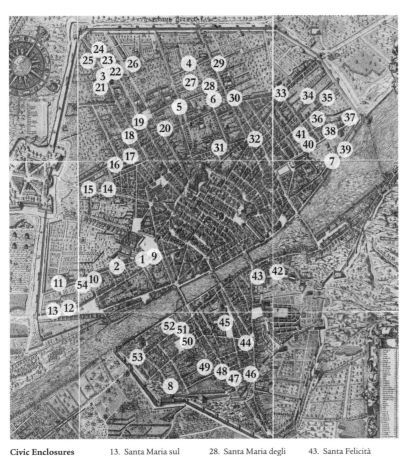

Civic Enclosures

1. Ospedale della Carità
2. Malmaritate
3. Santa Caterina
4. Pietà
5. Innocenti
6. Orbatello
7. San Niccolò di Ceppo and Santa Maria Vergine
8. Mendicanti

Convents

9. San Pagolo
10. San Martino
11. San Jacopo di Ripoli
12. Sant' Anna
13. Santa Maria sul Prato
14. Foligno
15. San Giuliano
16. Santa Bernaba
17. Sant' Orsola
18. Sant' Apollonia
19. Santa Caterina da Siena
20. San Niccolò
21. San Luca
22. Santa Lucia
23. Sant' Agata
24. San Clemente
25. Chiarito
26. San Domenico
27. Crocetta
28. Santa Maria degli Angeli
29. Santo Silvestro
30. Santa Maria di Candeli
31. Santa Maria Nuova
32. San Pier Maggiore
33. Sant' Ambrogio
34. Santa Verdiana
35. Le Murate
36. San Jacopo
37. Montedomini
38. Monticelli
39. Le Poverine
40. Capitolo
41. San Francesco
42. San Giorgio
43. Santa Felicità
44. San Pier Martire
45. Santo Spirito
46. Annalena
47. Santa Chiara
48. Convertite
49. La Nunziatina
50. Santa Monaca
51. San Frediano
52. Santa Maria degli Angioli in Borgo S. Frediano
53. Agnolo Raffaello
54. San Martino

Figure 1.2. Enclosures for girls and women, ca. 1632. Note that the locations, names, and affiliations of many institutions changed over the course of the sixteenth and seventeenth centuries. Stefano Buonsignori, map of Florence, 1584 (copy from 1695), Harvard College Map Library.

Courtesy of the Digitally Encoded Census Information Mapping Archive (DECIMA).

1632, when a new census was conducted, just under 19 percent of the female population lived in an enclosed institution, 5,929 out of 31,494 girls
and women and of 65,331 total residents.[30] These are conservative estimates that often do not account for boarders, servants, enslaved girls
and women, and those who moved in and out of institutions or were
otherwise unaccounted for.[31] It is likely, therefore, that by the early to
mid-seventeenth century around 20 percent of the city's girls and women
resided within an institution at any one time. Moreover, girls and women
who weren't enclosed almost certainly knew somebody who was: a sister,
daughter, relative, friend, business associate, or loved one. These relationships pulled even more Florentines into the orbit of institutionalization.
Whether due to those living in an institution, the visiting of residents,
the provision of services to enclosed communities, or the patronizing of
a charity home or nunnery, enclosures for girls and women permeated
the social fabric of Florence at multiple levels. The figures above reflect a
fundamental demographic shift over the course of the centuries of the
late Renaissance. Taken together, nunneries, reform houses, conservatories, and shelters expanded to house thousands of girls and women at
any one time, cutting across the lines of class, age, economics, and social
status. Examining these institutions collectively allows us to fully consider the pervasiveness of enclosure: residential communities were not
only a regular feature on the city's topography but housed a significant
portion of the female population, more than in any earlier period in
Florentine history.

The Push to Enclosure

What accounts for the remarkable rise in female institutionalization in
early modern Florence? A series of shifts and events, some general to the
Italian Peninsula and some specific to Florence, coalesced to encourage
both civic and religious authorities to open and operate an unprecedented
number of enclosures. First, were the social realities that plague, famine,
war, and poverty wrought on Italian cities. Florence suffered a series of
compounding financial crises and famines over the sixteenth and early
seventeenth centuries, leaving many destitute. Twin epidemics of plague
and famine hit the city in 1522–1523 and again in 1526–1528. Famine
continued to roll through Florence in the ensuing decades, notably in

1539–1540.[32] A devastating famine engulfed the city once again in 1551, and the population fell to 59,000 when just three decades earlier it had topped out at 80,000.[33] Several decades later, in 1620–1621, Florence suffered another epidemic that claimed approximately three thousand lives over the course of eight months.[34] In 1630–1631, Florence suffered from yet another brutal plague and ensuing famine that gripped much of northern Italy and devastated urban populations throughout the region over the course of several years. In the late sixteenth and seventeenth centuries Florence also contended with a series of economic depressions that impacted the city's centrally important textile industry.[35] Poverty and precarity were ubiquitous in early modern cities like Florence; charitable institutions aimed to meet the practical needs of an urban population that regularly experienced hunger, illness, and violence, as well as the needs of the many girls and women who became impoverished.

New charities also addressed what scholars have identified as pervading anxiety about the large numbers of unmonitored girls and women in Italian urban centers.[36] Patriarchal norms meant that girls and women were often economically reliant on male family members and were also thought to require near constant guardianship. Despite this systemic inequality, women were a driving force in Italian economies—making and marketing a plethora of goods, managing familial and personal finances, and enacting economic and personal agency in diverse ways.[37] Yet it is also undeniable that girls' and women's opportunities were profoundly constrained compared to those of their male counterparts. Of course, there was no universal experience, and class, social status, race, ethnicity, ability, and a host of other factors shaped individual experience. For example, patrician widows could enjoy significant autonomy and financial freedom, whereas working-class women were often plunged into poverty when a spouse died. Locally born women often had well-established networks that allowed them to survive lean years by calling on reciprocated forms of peer support, whereas foreign-born or migrant women could experience isolation and xenophobia, further exacerbating their social and financial precarity.[38] Whatever the circumstances, all women had to navigate the bounds of patriarchy carefully. This meant that epidemics of illness and plague, war, migration, economic depression, and shifting personal circumstances left many vulnerable and, most concerning to paternalistic civic authorities, beyond direct male supervision.[39] Charity homes aimed to provide much needed social services while also establishing programs of institutional care rooted in patriarchal guardianship.

The Florentine confraternities and the wealthy individuals who were involved in opening and operating civic charities also established these enclosures as an expression of piety. This quickened the pace of institutionalization, as urban elites eagerly sought vulnerable populations to house in their new charity homes. Emerging models of Catholic care increasingly advocated for strategic and disciplined *caritas*: organized charitable giving that aimed to offer assistance to the needy and advocated for a sustained disciplinary approach to social reform. *Caritas* moved away from the more sporadic, spontaneous, and personal modes of charity and *misericordia* that typified the medieval centuries when needy community members often received help by right.[40] The push toward disciplined care spurred the foundation and reorganization of charitable institutions—most notably for girls and women—where reform and charity found routinized expression through long-term enclosure. Financial ambition worked alongside these changing charity practices. Many wealthy individuals and families participated in operations of charity in order to raise capital. Most often this took the form of silk work—a Florentine industry that relied primarily on the low-paid labor of girls and women. By 1663, women performed 84 percent of the silk work in Florence, and girls and women undertook textile work in most of the city's charity homes and nunneries, often working on contracts that were brokered by the wealthy families involved in running or patronizing these enclosures.[41] For example, once precarious young girls entered the Santa Caterina conservatory they were quickly put to work producing silks and embroideries, skills they were taught by masters of the trade who were hired by the house.[42] Santa Caterina's financial records confirm the steady pace at which the youths labored; records from 1611 listed silk production, gold embroidery, and weaving as key sources of income for the house. The institution brought in income from "silk work," which may have involved weaving simple cloths, ribbons, and taffetas or the more intensive labor of reeling, twisting, and spinning silk filaments; "goldwork," fine embroidery with gold thread; and "weaving work," likely in silks and linens and perhaps some wools (see Figure 1.3).[43] The names of many of Florence's premier families, including the Capponi, Medici, and

Figure 1.3. Karel van Mallery, after Jan van der Straet (aka Johannes Stradanus or Giovanni Stradano), "The Reeling of Silk," plate 6 from *The Introduction of the Silkworm [Vermis Sericus],* ca. 1595, engraving, Metropolitan Museum of Art, New York.

Strozzi, are listed in Santa Caterina's financial records as both patrons and business partners.[44] The profits from this labor not only supported the institution's daily operations but also offered the wealthy Florentines affiliated with the charity direct access to a cheap labor force and the valuable goods it produced; these goods were then sold in local and foreign markets. For impoverished girls and women, textile work was presented as a means to economic stability, a path to honorable labor, and a project in communal and self-discipline. For elite Florentines, these de facto workhouses provided an opportunity to bolster one's upper class status as a charitable Catholic citizen, all while ensuring financial returns and access to a profitable labor force.

Nunneries likewise saw their numbers rise dramatically during this period as the result of complex dynamics. Many scholars have analyzed how elite Italian families faced a highly competitive marriage market and rising dowry prices. They often opted to place a daughter or several daughters within prestigious convents or monasteries, which required lower dowries than those needed for premier marriage arrangements, allowing families to consolidate funds for strategic marriages that bolstered familial status.[45] Sharon Strocchia has shown how Florentines were among the earliest Italians to engage in this type of strategizing, a key factor that partially explains the rising number of convents and monasteries in Florence from the fifteenth century onward.[46] Behind nunnery walls, sisters, nieces, aunts, and cousins continued to work for the benefit of the family—sometimes rising to positions of authority within the institution, advancing family patronages, and building extensive religious and social networks.[47] Marriages and nunneries thus emerged as two hubs of patrician familial strategizing. As newer and larger nunneries were founded in the late fifteenth and sixteenth centuries, middle-class and working-class families also increasingly looked to these institutions to offset marriage costs, raise familial status, and shelter family members.[48] This strategizing compounded with local political and religious shifts such as foreign invasions, the Savonarolan movement, and regime changes and collectively encouraged thousands of girls and women to take the habit.[49] Of course, families and individual women also acted out their genuine religiosity by taking religious vows. Nunneries were important sites for renewed piety, ecclesiastical reform, and the emphasis on pastoral care at the root of Catholic reform.[50] As in the case of civic charities, piety and practical needs mixed together to produce a high frequency of institutionalization.

Local political shifts were a final crucial factor in rising rates of institutionalization, particularly in Florence's many civic enclosures. The grand duchess's interest in the Orbatello's affairs in the early seventeenth century was far from purely charitable. Or, to put it differently, charity and institutionalization were deeply entwined with the emerging self-interests of the Medici government. For much of the Orbatello's history, the resident widows had effectively self-governed their community. Despite the official authority of the Guelf Party, which distributed resources and paid salaries, Orbatello residents had a long tradition of deciding who entered the complex and often claimed autonomy over daily life in the charity home.[51] The grand duchess's inquest into Orbatello affairs in the early seventeenth century marked a shift in the institution's governance and reflects a broader trend whereby the Medici supervised girls' and women's institutions with new precision as part of their increasingly centralized and bureaucratized style of governance.

Ducal and grand-ducal oversight of the city's enclosures began with
vigor in the mid-sixteenth century. When Cosimo I de' Medici ascended
to power in 1537, cash poor and eager to assert control, he found a wealth
of resources, both economic and political, in the city's expanding institutions and charitable endeavors. Medici rulers quickly framed themselves
as fathers and mothers of the city's needy and capitalized on paternalistic
models of care to assert authority over Florence's vast institutional
network. Of key interest to the Medici was oversight not only of the
thousands of residents who were packed into enclosures but also of the
upper-class women and men who oversaw these enclosures. Institutional
affiliation allowed Medici rulers an unparalleled view into virtually all social and political classes in the city: secular and religious, rich and poor,
young and old.[52] In 1542 Cosimo I therefore placed all Tuscan *ospedali*
under the control of his newly founded magistracy, the Provedditori sopra
li Derelicti e Poveri Mendicanti; the policy was continued by subsequent
Medici rulers Francesco I (r. 1574–1587) and Ferdinando I (r. 1587–
1609).[53] Through a series of policies and magistracies, these three Medici
dukes crafted a supervisory apparatus to effectively channel funds and resources from previously independent Tuscan institutions directly to the
centralizing Medici government. Large charitable homes like the Innocenti offered important financial resources from which the Medici then
borrowed credit, invested funds, and extracted labor.[54] Philip Gavitt sum-
marizes this practice succinctly, explaining that "by bringing charity into
their personal orbit, the Medici could both tighten their control over
the state and gain access to credit without imposing excessive taxes."[55]
Medici dukes and duchesses thus relied on expanding civic institutions
to establish a highly centralized system of governance, a strategy that
partially explains their eagerness to patronize institutions and to support the creation of new enclosures. The proliferation of charity homes
and the rampant institutionalization of girls and women was intimately
linked with the emerging political character of the Medici Duchy and
Grand Duchy.

Medici oversight also extended to the city's many nunneries, though
here issues of jurisdiction could prompt blistering tensions with ecclesiastical authorities who had official command of these communities. In a
clear effort to bring the city's nunneries under more direct ducal supervision while actively blocking competing ecclesiastical power, Duke Cosimo

I ordered a comprehensive convent census in 1548–1552 immediately after his political rival Antonio Altoviti was appointed archbishop of Florence in 1548 in an act of spite by Pope Paul III of the Farnese family. In 1548 Cosimo I blocked Altoviti from entering Florence to assume the position and continued to do so until 1564. That same year he began officially probing convent affairs with a census.[56] The census carefully recorded the patronymic of each nun, highlighting the extent to which Florentines ensured the survival of family ties within the convent. Cosimo's inventory of convents and nuns provided him with valuable information about the identities of the city's thousands of nuns, their familial affiliations, and their possible political leanings, laying bare connections between nunneries and the influential families he sought to keep in check. With a comprehensive list of the connections between nunneries and the Florentine elite, Cosimo I and his appointed magistrates had a template on which they could judge future requests made by particular institutions and their possible political implications. The census reflects the extent to which women religious were integral to the larger institutional, political, religious, and social fabric of Florence. It is notable, for instance, that Cosimo ordered no comparable census of the city's male religious houses.

Nonelite Women in Institutions

Petitions on behalf of women seeking entry into the Orbatello widows' asylum reveal the pressures many nonelite women faced and the realities that pushed working-class and impoverished girls and women into the city's expanding institutional network. A series of 1554 supplication letters on behalf of Luchretia, "the widow of Buonfiglio the sword maker," described her precarious state. Luchretia petitioned "to have a room in the Orbatello, first because she is pregnant and is a person for whom this is scandalous [i.e., a single mother], and because she [already] has four girls and one boy that every passing day will give more concern to the magistrates because they are needy."[57] Luchretia's mother, also a widow, had lived in the Orbatello for the past twenty-four years and was working hard to petition for her daughter and grandchildren's entry to the complex, where they would join her.[58] Ultimately Luchretia's application was successful and she moved into the institution, likely returning to the same apartment where she had been raised as a child. The cycle of widowhood, poverty, and institutionalization stretched across three generations of Luchretia's family; the Orbatello provided a lifeline that helped this multi-generational family survive and stay together.

But Luchretia was just one woman in need among many. By 1562, 178 residents were living inside the Orbatello's twenty-seven apartments.[59] A great many more women petitioned for entry to the asylum than were accepted. Between 1588 and 1620 an average of only 5.15 new residents a year were accepted, not including entrants' children.[60] A 1631 letter to the Medici grand duchess reveals just how many women were turned away; it explained that six vacant apartments in the institution had become available and listed twenty-two supplicants and their dependents deemed worthy of consideration. Of this already curated short list, the grand duchess accepted seven.[61]

While many civic charities touted the value of an open-door policy, this was tempered by a reality where strategically worded petitions, patronage networks, and family affiliations were often key to gaining institutional entry. The fact that Luchretia could count on her mother to petition on her behalf from within the Orbatello was no doubt crucial in the decision to admit her. The new Catholic emphasis on *caritas* also prompted efforts to only admit the "worthy poor" to charitable homes. For women, this meant highlighting their sexual and social modesty to appeal to the archetype of penitent femininity that charities sought to foster. One such supplication from the Orbatello, dated 1553 and written on behalf of the young, recently widowed Francesca, described her as a "most poor and honest person"; without aid, said the petition, she could not feed her three young children, leaving the family on the brink of starvation.[62] Supplicants also gathered letters of reference from notable citizens who vouched for their honor. When Lessandra degl'Innocenti requested entry to the Orbatello in 1618, a letter addressed to the grand duchess explained how Lessandra had left the Innocenti to work as a servant in the house of Francesco Miniati but that chronic headaches and other illnesses rendered her unable to carry out her duties. Officers of the Guelf Party reported that Lessandra was seeking shelter in the Orbatello to "have guardianship for the preservation of her virginity."[63] Lessandra's application also included a character reference from Benedetto Nacchianti, a confessor at the esteemed Basilica di Santa Croce. Nacchianti noted that Lessandra had indeed worked as a servant for Francesco Miniati and that he had "known Lessandra for many years" and could confirm that she was "a good girl who confesses and receives communion often and frequents the church."[64] In a similar vein, the Pietà home for vulnerable girls abandoned its open-door policy by 1570 in favor of a mandate whereby new entrants were "nominated" by leading citizens. Self-interest was never far off in this kind of decision-making. Pietà nominees were often the illegitimate children of courtiers.[65] Many of the noblemen involved in opening the youth home were likely looking for spaces to house illegitimate children they had fathered, with minimal cost to themselves, all while increasing their community standing as charitable citizens. These factors, in combination with resource shortages and overcrowding, meant that, even when girls and women wanted to, gaining entry to a civic institution could be difficult. Simultaneously, it meant that many others—in particular, the illegitimate children of the elite—were placed in institutions with little to no consideration for their own wishes.

Sex Work and Institutionalization

What happened to girls and women who were turned away from charity homes like the Orbatello? Perhaps they sought shelter in one of the city's other charity houses. Others may have scrambled to make ends meet by scraping together small jobs, benefiting from the help of neighbors, or begging. Some children may have been sent into conservatories like the Ospedale dei Poveri Abbandonati for boys and Santa Caterina or the Pietà for girls, where basic necessities would be provided. Some women in these circumstances engaged in sex work to support themselves and their families. Had Luchretia been turned away from the Orbatello, she may have found sex work one possible avenue through which to generate income. Nor would it have been unheard of for Luchretia's eldest daughter, the sixteen-year-old Domenica, to enter the sex trade.[66]

Perhaps more than poverty, sex work troubled moralistic Florentines and drove the development of institutions designed to divert girls and women from sex work and to "reform" sex workers. Conservatories like the Casa della Pietà, San Niccolò, and Santa Caterina were opened precisely to divert youths like Domenica from this trajectory. The 1613 Santa Caterina book of statutes explained that "during the reign of Don Ferdinando de Medici, Grand Duke of Tuscany [r. 1587–1609], there was the greatest famine throughout all of Italy, and thus many poor girls gave themselves to prostitution because of hunger. . . . Many God-fearing noblemen, with the favor of the Most Serene Grand Duchess, complained of the many poor girls that went to the streets."[67] Established institutions like the Convertite convent similarly worked alongside newly founded civic homes like the Malmaritate to "reform" adult women sex workers. By the early seventeenth century, Florence was operating a host of residential institutions designed specifically for women sex workers and "at-risk" youths. All of these enclosures mixed charity, sexual discipline, labor, and penitence.

This institutional strategy marked a shift away from the city's earlier approach to managing the sex trade, which, when it wasn't turning a blind eye, sought to expel women sex workers beyond the city walls. A late thirteenth-century law had stated that *meretrici* (sex workers) were to remain at least 1,000 braccia—more than a half kilometer—outside the city walls. A 1325 law stipulated that sex workers could enter the city on Mondays but were otherwise to remain outside the city walls, where their perceived moral and sexual dishonor would not damage civic purity.[68] In 1403 the Ufficiali dell'Onestà (Office of Decency) was founded to legislate and police sex work, operating under a rotating board of appointed officials.[69] In 1547, as part of Duke Cosimo I's reforms, the Onestà abandoned efforts to expel sex workers from the city. Instead it identified eighteen street sections where sex workers could legally live and work, policed those workers (and, to a lesser extent, their pimps and clients), and required women to officially register as *meretrici* and pay a registration fee every four months to the Onestà.[70] Many women avoided registration, preferring to work illegally as fees cut into their profits and often worked to further entrap them in poverty; many women were also reluctant to have the pejorative label *meretrice* attached to their names in civic records.

Civic and religious authorities upheld the title of *meretrice* as a totalizing spiritual, social, and labor identity, but the realities of sex work were much more complex. Some women practiced sex work intermittently, while others engaged the occupation more regularly and for many years. Many women worked multiple jobs, engaging in various forms of sex work, textile work, and other trades to differing degrees. Most importantly, it is difficult to know how girls and women with proximity to the sex trade self-identified. Archival records essentially never present these women on their own terms and rarely record their direct speech. Instead their experiences are filtered through the lens of authorities who sought to marginalize and criminalize women whom they labeled as "immodest" and sexually deviant. Many who had the specter of *meretrice* or *mala vita* (wicked life) attached to their name likely did not self-identify as such. All of these factors make it difficult to accurately assess the prevalence of sex work and self-identified sex workers in sixteenth- or seventeenth-century Florence. Nonetheless, Onestà registry books provide some valuable insights. For example, in 1614 the city registered ninety-seven women as *meretrici* in civic record books.[71] The vast majority were entered into the registry on a single day, November 7. This was the result of civic efforts to quickly gather money for the perpetually underfunded Sant'Elisabetta delle Convertite convent, the city's Augustinian convent for repentant sex workers.[72] Implored by Convertite governors who described the desperate poverty of the convent, civic officials were tasked with immediately raising funds for the impoverished nunnery. The Onestà opted to offer active sex workers a onetime incentive: register with the Onestà and pay a single tax, and then an exemption from some future taxation would be issued and a portion of the collected funds would be dispensed to the needy Convertite nuns. The hurried script that recorded dozens of names that day suggests that many sex workers found this an attractive incentive or, perhaps more likely, were forced to register by pressured magistrates. In the following years, Onestà registration rates fell back to predictably lower numbers of a few dozen. In 1617, for example, only thirty women were registered with the office.[73] The sudden spike in 1614 is a testament to the large numbers of girls and women who avoided civic efforts to police and profit from their labor and hints at the pervasiveness of the unofficial sex trade.

By the mid-sixteenth century, fines and fees from sex work lined the pockets of Onestà magistrates and provided revenue for the Medici government, but civic authorities, religious officials, and many citizens continued to bemoan the scandal they believed sex workers wrought on the city.[74] To address these concerns Florentine authorities relied on institutionalization—in particular, through the Convertite convent for repentant sex workers located in Via Chiara in the working-class Santo Spirito quarter on the southwestern edges of the city. The Augustinian convent had been founded in 1329 by the lay confraternity Santa Maria delle Laudi to serve as a house where "converted" women made the transition from sex workers to penitent nuns.[75] Florence's Convertite was one of the many *convertite* convents that spread throughout the Italian Peninsula over the course of the fourteenth and fifteenth centuries.[76] When it first opened, the house had been located "near the old walls of the city of Florence," and by 1333, stones from the city walls themselves were being used to continue the construction of this "most pious work."[77] By the mid-sixteenth century, the Convertite convent and its population had expanded several times. Only twenty-five women lived in the convent in 1368, but this had almost quadrupled to ninety-two in the 1548–1552 census. By 1620 the population had again more than doubled, with 206 recorded residents.[78] The convent complex also expanded to include, among other things, a scriptorium; separated *parlatori* (parlors or meeting rooms) for men, women, and nuns; two granaries; a chicken coop; a prison; three floors of dormitories; a church; and a large refectory.[79] The institution was no longer backed against the city's crumbling walls, as new walls had been built in 1557 to refortify and encompass the expanding city. It is also notable that Via Chiara was also one of the streets legislated for legal sex work in the 1547 laws. Active sex workers and converted women lived in close proximity on the city's working-class periphery.

In its day-to-day governance, the Convertite was similar to the city's many other nunneries. Women took monastic vows; the institution was strictly cloistered; daily life was structured around the sacred rhythms of prayer, sacral obligations, and the divine office; and the convent was part of the city's sacred topography. But life in the Convertite was also marked by themes of gendered shame, sexual reform, and incarceration. The convent had claimed penance as key from its inception, recording that residents were "to pass time as a penitent of God's mercy . . . and remain in perpetual reclusion."[80] But the Convertite also had a reputation for laxity. Despite strict cloister rules, the institution often housed women for short periods when they were sent to the convent for temporary confinement for petty crimes or when deemed in need of immediate aid. As a result, the convent had a more flexible cloister than many other nunneries while also advocating for strict regimes of gendered shame and penitence.[81] Moreover, without the valuable dowries that middle- and upper-class entrants brought to elite nunneries, the Convertite was chronically underfunded and relied on charitable donations and civic support for survival. In the 1548–1552 convent census, the nuns capitalized on the attention of civic magistrates to stress their poverty, also noting that their numbers had recently dropped as the result of a devastating plague. The convent requested a subsidy every three to four months and emphasized that it could not accept any new women unless they were sex workers who desperately needed to convert.[82] Because of its financial circumstances and unique institutional mandate, the Convertite was more reliant on civic support than other Florentine nunneries and also subject to greater civic involvement in its affairs. Thus, while the convent officially fell under ecclesiastical jurisdiction, it was uniquely imbedded within the web of Florentine civic governance and charity, bridging civic and ecclesiastical models of institutionalization.

A prime example of civic involvement in Convertite affairs was legislation that aimed to raise funds for the convent. City laws used active sex workers' incomes to support Convertite operations. A 1533 law dictated that *meretrici* who died without children or legitimate heirs would have a quarter of their estate handed over to the Convertite.[83] In 1577, in keeping with this law, Maddalena di Piero della Torre left the convent "a quarter of her estate according to the custom of prostitutes and the law made in 1533."[84] Maddalena may have had little choice in the matter, but it is also possible that she had planned to bequeath funds to the convent in a final act of piety and goodwill toward her peers. Often, however, the law reflected an intention and was an unachieved policy as women found creative ways to allocate any assets they had on their own terms. Similarly, a 1560 law stipulated that sex workers who did not voluntarily report themselves to the Onestà were to be fined a lifetime tax of six scudi per year, paid in quarterly installments, a portion of which was distributed to the Convertite.[85] Here again, many women no doubt sought to avoid fiscal and civic intrusion into their affairs.

In 1580 Florence opened the Malmaritate home for "badly married" women, yet another institution focused on reforming sex workers that was operated by the confraternity of Compagnia di Santa Maria Maddalena sopra le Malmaritate. According to the Malmaritate's 1582 book of statutes, the institution aimed to reach "the great multitudes of women of *mala vita* in the city of Florence, many of whom would return to penitence if they had a place in which to retreat."[86] The Malmaritate sometimes sheltered women fleeing spousal abuse and violence, but most of the asylum's residents were married sex workers. Of course, these two realities were far from mutually exclusive and they regularly overlapped. Married women were not exempt from the same social and financial pressures that affected vast numbers of unmarried and widowed women. Nor was it uncommon for married women to engage in sex work, looking for the same financial gains as unmarried women. Often this work was encouraged and sometimes even forced on them by their husbands, who acted as their pimps. In 1596, for example, Christofano di Giovanni Tedesco was sentenced by the Onestà to "one year of exile in Livorno . . . for having driven his own wife away from him to live licentiously."[87] Church laws and social norms meant that married women could not simply divorce their husbands, nor could they take monastic vows in the Convertite. The Malmaritate therefore sought to temporarily cloister "badly married" women, enclosing and reforming a segment of the female population otherwise overlooked by Florentine institutions. The Malmaritate was much smaller than both the Convertite and the Orbatello and could only house around thirty women at a time. Comprehensive residential records have not survived for the institution, but anecdotal sources suggest it maintained a relatively full house in its earlier decades.[88] By the time of the 1632 census, however, the home was all but empty, housing only four wards and one servant. It is unclear what accounted for this low number, as the Malmaritate's day-to-day records have not survived.[89]

The Malmaritate organized itself much like a convent and daily life was structured according to a monastic model. Residents were to live, work, sleep, and eat communally, wear the same simple robes, and remain strictly cloistered during their tenure in the home. The building included "five rooms by the street, including the kitchen, the small *parlatorio* and entrance room, at the back of which one passes into a backyard enclosed by high walls. Going up a set of stairs one finds a little choir correspondent to the church, and continuing up these stairs one reaches the first floor consisting of three rooms over the garden . . . five rooms facing the street, two of which are very small, and following the same stairs one reaches the second floor and finds seven rooms."[90] Unlike a convent, the ultimate goal was to rehabilitate these "badly married" women and return them to their husbands and families to live new pious lives. To this end, the Malmaritate sought to provide economic

alternatives to the sex trade, primarily silk work contracts brokered by
confraternity members involved in the Malmaritate's governance.[91]

Like the Convertite, the Malmaritate was located on the outskirts of
the city—in this case, on Via della Scala in the Santa Maria Novella quarter,
north of the Arno River and west of the important Basilica di Santa Maria
Novella. The surrounding area was largely made up of the working class
and home to much of the city's wool and silk production. The 1632 census
listed twenty-six weaving and eight spinning households on Via della Scala
alongside a mix of tanners, woodcutters, tailors, widows, and sex workers.[92]
Several sanctioned sex work zones also surrounded the Malmaritate: Via
Palazzuolo, one street to the south, and Via Codarimessa directly to the
north; in fact, the neighborhood accounted for the highest concentration
of registered sex workers in Florence beyond the central brothel.[93] The
Convertite, Malmaritate, and Orbatello were all located in the city's
working-class outskirts and were surrounded by active sex work zones.
These shared social geographies are significant: Convertite and Malmaritate residents lived not only at the geographical edges of the city but also
on its social periphery. On the one hand, both institutions strove to rein-
tegrate "scandalous" women into respectable Florentine society. On the
other, the very location of these institutions near the edges of the city and
surrounded by active sex work zones served to highlight and reinforce
their marginal social, economic, and spatial realities.

Resisting Enclosure

Some women no doubt sought entry into the Convertite or the Malmaritate willingly, perhaps seeking respite from dangers associated with sex
work or marriage. Indeed, sex workers lived at high risk of violence and
assault. In 1596 alone at least thirteen men were fined by the Onestà for
assaulting women sex workers.[94] While the Onestà promised registered
meretrici an avenue to pursue legal action against their assailants in exchange for registration fees, the systemic realities of misogynistic violence
far outweighed the magistracy's case-by-case, and often lackluster, attempts to seek justice for women victims. For example, one of the men
fined by the Onestà in 1597, Batistino di Jacopo "the pimp," repeatedly
attacked sex workers. Batistino appears in Onestà records in 1597, 1602,
and 1605 for having "given punches in the face to Portia del Piragin," "for

having badly beaten Giulia di Michele his prostitute," and "for having badly beaten Margherita Carissi."[95] For each of his recorded crimes, Batistino was required to pay a small fine to the Onestà. Only after his third fine in 1605 was he prohibited from setting foot on Via Giardino, a sanctioned sex work street, for a period of two months.[96] These fines and prohibitions would have done little to protect women from Batistino's violent attacks. Moreover, recorded instances of assault reflect only a fraction of the violence that women sex workers actually experienced. Above all, the historical record is clear that male perpetrators, whether clients or pimps, were punished in disproportionately small numbers and with mild sentences. Entry into institutions like the Convertite or the Malmaritate stood to offer some refuge from this reality.

Yet while the record is clear that sex workers often faced real dangers in Florence's streets, private homes, and brothels, it is equally clear that many—if not most—loathed life in institutions like the Convertite and the Malmaritate. More often than not, women were forced into these institutions as punishment for perceived sexual crimes—namely, adultery and sex work—or as victims of sexual and physical assault. For example, when Camilla di Silvestro was charged in 1598 for having sex with Vincenzo, a man who was not her husband, she was given the choice between ten months in the Stinche (civic prison) or a stint in the Malmaritate.[97] Similarly, sex workers who failed to pay fines to the Onestà, or were otherwise apprehended, were often sent to the Convertite for incarceration. In 1524 the city had ordered a woman named Barbara to the "convent of Convertite of Florence, [which] she cannot leave for a month under the penalty of 21 Florins."[98] Reform and refuge homes often doubled as prisons, and authorities consistently blurred the boundary of culpability between victim and assailant, disciplining women within these institutions regardless of the circumstances that brought them there.[99]

Faced with the prospect of living the remainder of their lives as strictly cloistered nuns, some Convertite residents opted to leave. In 1594 Antonia d' Ostro Bolognese was sentenced to whipping and a pecuniary fine of fifty scudi for "having left the convent of the Convertite where she had taken the nun's habit and having returned to the dishonest life."[100] Several years earlier in 1577, Lessandro di Ludovico had been imprisoned for five years for bringing a rope ladder to the Convertite walls to aid two nuns in their escape from the convent.[101] Many women in the Malmaritate similarly found enclosure intolerable and fled. Onestà records from 1586 note that Caterina da Carniguano, "the prostitute, [who] had entered into the Malmaritate, and then left, . . . is again leading a dishonest life."[102] The Malmaritate's book of governance admitted that the institution could not officially, or in good conscience, keep all women against their will. It noted that "to hold by force all those that would want to go from here would cause too much confusion in the house, and often women would need to come to penitence violently."[103] Nonetheless, house governors tried to keep their wards enclosed, stating that "in order to prevent the scandal that arises if women flee here, and with the fear of penalty let alone they should think of fleeing, we want those who flee . . . to give to this pious house twenty scudi."[104] This would have been a relatively small sum to wealthy Florentines, but was designed to pressure working-class and impoverished women into staying put. The Malmaritate also adopted more concrete strategies to enclose residents, noting that "the garden area is protected by spikes on top of the garden wall, so that no one is able to enter inside without breaking them, and whenever this occurs, it will be immediately discovered and our sisters will see who they are."[105] House governors claimed these protections served to keep intruders out, but they no doubt also functioned to keep women in. It is unclear how successful these strategies were, but records of women fleeing in the night, escaping from windows, or being abducted—as when Zanobi Spini was arrested in 1604 by the Otto di Guardia, the city's policing magistracy, for abducting three women from the Malmaritate to bring them back into the sex trade—all suggest that the house often failed to keep women in the home or to collect their fines.[106] Enclosure records are full instances that attest to the widespread reality of forced enclosure and the dramatic measures some women took to escape this fate.[107]

Ultimately, Florentines expressed a deep ambivalence toward women sex workers. Religious and civic authorities claimed that *meretrici* lived a "wicked life" but also claimed they were a necessary evil, providing men sexual outlets that, while sinful, were considered preferable to same-sex intimacies or adulterous relationships with married women.[108] The city therefore established bureaucratic mechanisms to police and profit from sex work. Moreover, the Convertite aimed to lift women out of sex work but relied directly on income from the active sex trade to fund these efforts. The net result of this ambivalence was a rise in institutionalization. New charity homes like the Malmaritate and well-established institutions like the Convertite stood to assuage moral anxieties about sex work without requiring civic and religious authorities to address systemic issues of misogyny, gender inequity, and class inequality that pushed many women into vulnerable circumstances to begin with. Instead the onus of reform was placed on individual girls and women, and institutions served as disciplinary centers that facilitated personal repentance. Inside these enclosures, authorities worked to reform girls' and women's bodies and souls regardless of the circumstances that brought them to the institution.

Elite Women: Nunneries, Patronage, and Piety

Middle- and upper-class women experienced a different reality, free from the grinding financial and social precarity so many of the city's nonelite women experienced. Despite profound economic and class differences, elite girls and women also found their lives increasingly institutionalized over the sixteenth and seventeenth centuries, almost always in nunneries. This phenomenon stretched throughout Italian cities but was unmatched in other European regions.[109] Once inside a nunnery, the experiences of elite Florentines differed significantly from those of the marginalized girls and women in charity homes or underfunded nunneries like the Convertite.

Not all patrician nuns lived in premier convents, though in general their social status sheltered them from the hard labor and punitive forms of discipline experienced in many of the city's charity and reform homes. For example, institutional residents across the spectrum, in civic and ecclesiastical enclosures alike, engaged in textile work to support themselves and their institutions, but not all textile work was the same. Those in charity homes like the Malmaritate and the Orbatello often worked to mass-produce silks and some linens and wools, work they were required to undertake in order to pay their way and to reform their bodies and souls through "honorable" labor. This was hard work that could involve a range of tasks, including boiling silk cocoons; separating filaments; winding rough threads onto spindles; and twisting, reeling, and spinning textiles to prepare them for further production. This kept the girls and women bent over boiling, odiferous vats, hunched over spindles and looms as they passed the shuttle back and forth, lifting and draping . soaking wet fabrics, and, at times, working their fingers raw. By contrast, wealthier nunneries and elite nuns were actively involved in the silk trade but often subcontracted out the intensive labor of boiling silk cocoons, twisting and winding filaments, and preparing the material for spinning. This allowed elite institutions to focus their labors on the most profitable and final stages of silk production. Even then, many patrician nuns would have actively overseen this work but rarely engaged in protracted heavy labor themselves.[110]

Within Florence's nunneries, patrician women contended with their own class dynamics as they jostled for influence and institutional command. The stakes were nowhere near as high as those faced by the impoverished girls and women who confronted very real possibilities of starvation, homelessness, or abandonment. Nonetheless, patrician social dynamics played an important role in patterning institutional profiles. Rising to a position of authority in one of the city's prestigious nunneries was no small feat. Florentine families laid claim to particular cloisters through cherished patronage networks they had cultivated over generations. Families also stacked preferred institutions with multiple family members, building a network of alliances and support within nunneries that helped certain relatives rise to positions of authority. For example, according to the 1548–1552 convent census, thirty-seven nuns lived in San Pier Martire, an austere Dominican convent on the southern outskirts of Florence. The abbess, Brigida di Piero Dazzi, could count on the support of two other nuns from the wealthy mercantile Dazzi family, Clementia di Antonio Dazzi and Oretta di Jacopo Dazzi. Likewise, four other pairs of sisters from different families lived in the institution alongside numerous cousins and aunts, not to mention matrilineal relatives who were perhaps part of the community but less discernable in the census's patrilineal focus.[111] Similarly, the wealthy San Domenico nel Maglio convent in the city's north end had long been a patrician stronghold where women from elite families clustered. As Sharon Strocchia has shown, the nunnery relied heavily on private family wealth, and patrician nuns oversaw vast income and property profiles from within the cloister, continuing to work for the benefit of their families.[112] Among the thirty-four nuns living in the convent between 1448 and 1552, four came from the powerful Albizzi family: Cherubina di Benedetto degli Albizzi, Clementia di Niccolò degli Albizzi, Fiammetta di Antonio degli Albizzi, and Margherita di Lucantonio degli Albizzi. The community also housed two women from the eminent Bardi family, three women from the Gherardini family, and two women from the wealthy mercantile Rucellai family.[113] These clusters of patrician relatives not only provided networks of companionship and support but also helped certain nuns and their families rise to positions of authority and influence within their nunneries and, sometimes, to lay claim to the neighborhood enclaves where convents were located.

Faced with this competitive reality, women with less prestigious patrician names or from less established networks often stood little chance of rising to positions of authority. Records from the Convertite convent provide valuable insight into how some elite women and their families navigated these dynamics. The vast majority of Convertite nuns came from nonelite families and many, if not most, had some association with sex work. But patrician women did occasionally take vows in the Convertite. In 1620 the Convertite nuns composed a list "of all noble nuns and gentlewomen who found themselves in our venerable convent . . . from the year 1455 until this present year of 1620."[114] Over the course of 165 years, a total of forty-three noblewomen from the city's lesser patrician families took vows to the convent. Of this carefully preserved list, ten occupied the position of abbess, in nearly consecutive order.[115] Convent scribes diligently preserved these elite names and entry dates, marking the patrician nuns as distinct from the larger Convertite population. The list served to proudly highlight the nunnery's ability to attract aristocratic women.

But the list also raises questions: Why would elite women enter this perpetually underfunded convent rife with associations to sex work? What would compel noble families, fixated as they were on preserving the value of their family name, to encourage kinswomen to live among socially maligned sex workers in an impoverished convent? It is possible that patrician entrants understood their decision, or their family's decision, as an act of piety and a firm rejection of the comforts that typified some wealthy nunneries and often drew the ire of reformists. Taking vows in the Convertite echoed stories of Christ living among sex workers, lepers, and sinners. Some elite women and their families may have been compelled to imitate these rich spiritual narratives. But the decision was also likely driven by more "worldly" social and political factors. While perhaps unlikely to break through the ranks in elite and prestigious convents, noblewomen from less well-connected families or patrician women deemed "problematic" were all but guaranteed to rise to the top of the Convertite community.[116] As the successive chain of patrician abbesses reveals, non-elite Convertite nuns could not match the influence that aristocratic entrants brought to the institution. The list of patrician nuns in the Convertite attests to yet another way that class dynamics prevailed in Florence's enclosures for girls and women.

Whether elite or humble, the capillary reach of Florentine nunneries rendered these institutions foundational building blocks of the city's character. In the Florentine context, this was part of a larger phenomenon of female institutionalization, one that saw thousands of diverse girls and women entering or being forced into a wide range of civic and ecclesiastical communities. Convents, though distinct, were part of the broader institutional fabric of Florence. It is only by examining nunneries and civic institutions together that we can fully consider the scope and diversity of enclosure during this period.

Rules of Silence and Pious Soundscapes

All Florentine institutions upheld silence and quiet as crucial to their daily programs of care and discipline. For nuns, silence stood as a marker of spiritual privilege and was key to the preservation of gendered piety and reformed spirituality. For women of the *mala vita* living in the Convertite and the Malmaritate, silence was a form of penance and a debt owed for their sinful pasts. For youths in conservatories and "honorable" impoverished women in the Orbatello, silence was framed as crucial to the development and performance of respectable femininity and to the care of vulnerable female bodies and souls.

The earliest major religious rules contained sparse references to silence. The Augustinian rule noted only the importance of listening "without disturbance or strife" and to chanting "only what is prescribed."[117] The Benedictine rule went further, ordering monastics to "close your mouth on evil and perverse talk, do not get in the habit of long-winded conversations, do not engage in empty babbling or joking, don't indulge in prolonged or explosive laughter."[118] As these rules were handed down to monasteries and convents of various orders throughout the medieval and early modern centuries, they formed sonic foundations on which institutional regulations often expanded. Rules of silence found new expression as part of the Observant Movement in the fourteenth century when contemplative and mendicant orders alike emphasized silence as part of their "fervor for renewal." Observant houses advocated for "a widespread form of penitential spirituality that privileged poverty, asceticism, and contemplative silence."[119] In the mid-sixteenth century, rules of silence once again took on new significance as a crucial aspect of Catholic reform and the strict cloistering that Tridentine authorities sought to establish. Nunneries like Florence's Le Murate expanded on early monastic rules to make specific regulations, such as "on Wednesdays and Fridays everyone remains silent, saying ten times the psalm *Misere Mei Deus,* and those who break the silence without reason recite the psalm five more times in penitence." Individual nuns were celebrated for their silence, as when Valentina Buonsignori, a Le Murate nun, died in 1558 and was memorialized for having lived "with rigorous observance in every monastic discipline, especially the holy virtue of silence, for about fifty-three years."[120] Seventeenth-century recommendations for new convent entrants likewise stipulated that all professed nuns needed to maintain a "sacred silence" that gave them "little time to speak and waste precious time on useless and idle conversations."[121] The Catholic Reformation's focus on the "sensuous" and exhortations on the importance of sonic decorum coalesced with the focus on cloister reform that preoccupied many Tridentine era authorities; as a result, enclosures for girls and women emerged as important sensory sites where issues of sound, gender, space, and spirituality blended together. Over the fifteenth, sixteenth, and seventeenth centuries an escalating series of rules repeatedly proclaimed that silence and quiet were crucial markers of Catholic spirituality and of pious femininity.

    In diverse institutions the monastic emphasis on silence mixed with specific institutional mandates of gendered reform, care, and charity. For example, Convertite convents highlighted silence as critical to both sexual and spiritual repentance. Florence's Convertite noted the importance of "perpetual reclusion" just as the nearby Convertite house in Pistoia ordered that "in choir and in church, not only during the blessed mass but also at any other time, the due silence must be observed . . . [and] similarly when eating in the refectory . . . and especially when reading and in the dormitories."[122] The Convertite convent of Cortona, an enclosed tertiary Franciscan community, likewise recorded in its undated post-Tridentine book of order that "silence will be observed in all places" in order to achieve repentance and spiritual purification.[123] A monastic emphasis on silence likewise trickled down to unvowed institutions like the Malmaritate, which stated that as part of its reforming program, resident women were to "remain withdrawn in silence."[124] The institution claimed that a clean break from the sounds of the city and noise signaled social, moral, spiritual, and bodily transitions in progress. Silence was presented as a debt owed for past sexual sins and a symbol of repentance. The Malmaritate's book of statutes made direct links between silence, sexual reform, and gendered reform, noting that "while they are under our care the residents will remain quiet, scandalous and *convertite* only in name." The institution claimed that "we must reduce only to memory all that these women have been . . . therefore no one should give an ear when they should speak . . . knowing it is their nature to never be satisfied and to sow discord."[125] This sonic program was rooted in a number of assumptions. First, "scandalous" women were inherently noisy and sought to "sow discord" with their vocalizations. Second, enforcing silence facilitated the transition from a dishonorable to a penitential woman. And third, Malmaritate regulations warned that "experience demonstrates that every time resident women talk with others, they are more restless."[126] Of course, a refusal to listen to residents or allow them to speak to outsiders also meant that house authorities could ignore the complaints of women being held against their will, an approach that no doubt contributed to the harsh conditions leading many women to leave the institution.

Youth conservatories like the Santa Caterina home also echoed monastic rules by including a chapter titled "On Silence" in its book of statutes. The institution proclaimed that silence was required, "in the morning one hour before saying the Most Holy Rosary, also during the day one hour before saying the third part of the Rosary. In the church there is continual silence. In the dormitory when the bell rings that signals sleep and even in the morning when [the girls are] called to work [there is silence]. In the refectory while eating there is silence, also in the morning during general communion and especially when in mass. And those who transgress these rules go for discipline to the Prioress."[127] Santa Caterina regulations also aimed to limit wards' verbal exchanges with outsiders and

stipulated that children who wanted to speak with relatives or visitors at
the institutional gate needed the explicit permission of the prioress and
were warned that they must "speak loud enough to be heard by the *ascoltatrice* [an appointed listener], who will always be present."[128] Those who
disobeyed were barred from speaking with anybody at the gate for six
months, and relatives who turned up at the institution hoping to con-
verse with a child more than once a week were to be turned away. Santa
Caterina regulations further outlined that a subprioress, "a discrete and
prudent girl," would be appointed to help the prioress keep order in the
home. Key among her duties was the responsibility of "vigilantly" ensuring
that other wards "observed the rule of silence."[129] Any breaches of silence
were to be immediately reported to the prioress, and noisemakers were to
be sent for discipline. In 1570, new statutes for the Pietà charity home
for precarious girls had likewise sought to instill stricter sonic regulations
and explicitly outlawed popular songs within the institution. House governors expressed fears that these secular melodies would drift out of the
institution and be heard by passersby, casting doubt on the piety and solemnity at work within the house. The Pietà rules particularly forbade
love songs and suggestive lyrics and ruled that girls caught singing salacious tunes could be whipped or ordered to kiss the feet of all other girls
in the home.[130] Much like how regimes of silence aimed to transform
scandalous women into penitential women, sonic regulations in youth
homes worked to strip precarious youths of any sounds associated with
the "wicked" or secular life and to craft new monastic-like sonic behaviors that gestured toward feminine purity and discipline as understood
by civic and ecclesiastical authorities. It was along these same lines that
the Santa Caterina house also taught its young wards pious sonic
performances to accompany an institutional baseline of silence—namely,
prayer and song. The book of statutes recorded how those who "who do
not know what to do will ask the priest. [They must be] taught to sing
the notes or words of the sermon songs while in line for matins."[131]

In civic and ecclesiastical homes alike, silence was ideally interrupted
only by the carefully regulated sounds of bells, the divine office, sacral
obligations, and sacred music. Prayerful utterances were a central component of the convent soundscape, and their efficacy was thought to be
augmented by a baseline of silence that otherwise prevailed. Daily life was
also marked by the predictable sound of bell ringing. The institutional

bell called girls and women to prayer, signaled meals, and marked death within the institution, functioning as "a primordial auditory site" and central piece of sonic architecture around which communities organized their identities and daily rhythms.[132] Music also pierced the institutional silence. Many convents hired instructors to teach song and music within the cloister and paid accomplished musicians to perform during their ceremonies. Nunneries were known to actively recruit girls and women with voice and musical training into their communities, knowing they could attract crowds to the convent church to hear a particularly talented virtuosa and hear new compositions performed by prestigious choir nuns concealed behind the church grille.[133] Some Catholic authorities expressed deep anxieties about nuns' musical performances, and worried about music's ability to arouse and excite audiences and performers alike.[134] This prompted intermittent attempts to ban polyphony and enforce plainchant in Italian nunneries. Tridentine convent visitations oscillated between allowing polyphonic singing under limited circumstances and banning it altogether to preserve nuns' "purity of heart."[135] Reformers like Carlo Borromeo, Francesco Bossi, Gabriele Paleotti, and Antonio Seneca worried about how layered melodies stood to overly excite nuns' vulnerable bodies and spirits and warned that "playing vain instruments such as viols and violins shall no longer be tolerated, nor do we approve of novices during the probationary year—a time of mortification—attending to polyphonic songs which relax the spirit and true observance of their vows."[136] Nonetheless, Italians flocked to hear cloistered women perform music, and polyphonic compositions remained an important component of many institutional soundscapes; as Colleen Reardon notes, "musical performance by holy women in early modern Italy was not always characterized by conflict and subject to repression," despite the reformist zeal and rhetoric of some church authorities.[137]

Florence's expansive network of girls' and women's institutions aimed to craft carefully curated soundscapes throughout the life cycle: beginning in childhood, in youth conservatories like Santa Caterina, where girls were taught silence, prayer, and sacred song; in reform houses like the Malmaritate and Convertite, where silence was central to sexual and spiritual repentance; and prevailing in the city's many nunneries, where silence, prayer, and sacred music injected the urban soundscape with the sounds of piety and purity. From the Innocenti to the Orbatello, the Convertite to the Malmaritate, and from conservatories to convents, Florentine institutions housed girls and women from virtually every set of circumstances and all stages of life. The astounding rise in both the number and size of these enclosures reveals the careful attention civic and ecclesiastical authorities devoted to caring for, disciplining, and classifying diverse groups of girls and women. When the Malmaritate demanded that "scandalous" women "remain quiet," when officers of the Orbatello warned institutional wards that they must live in "modesty and quiet," and when monastic rules repeatedly prioritized contemplative silence, each institution reiterated the importance of sensory regulation as a central component in the larger project of gendered care.

The record high numbers of girls and women who lived in diverse enclosures in early modern Florence were part of a larger urban project that sought to organize the female population into a comprehensive system of distinct moral, social, and spiritual categories: the vulnerable poor, dishonorable sex workers, repentant *convertite*, and honorable nuns. Furthermore, distinct institutions served to separate one group from the other—confining the vulnerable poor to institutions like the Orbatello and Santa Caterina, repentant women of the "wicked life" to reform houses like the Convertite and the Malmaritate, registered sex workers to specific urban zones legislated by the Onestà, and to keep any possible scandal far away from the city's many brides of Christ. Sonic regulation was a crucial element of this classificatory process, and while rules of silence and quiet prevailed in all institutions, the unique significance attributed to silence varied depending on institutional type. For those who carried the stain of the *mala vita*, silence was a mark of shame and repentance; for "at-risk" youths, silence was a symbol of gendered piety and spiritual education; and for women religious, silence was a spiritual privilege and a marker of religious obedience. In all of these instances, quiet and silence were directly associated with gendered discipline and care. Despite these lofty aims, however, daily life in and around Florentine enclosures was often marked by a far noisier reality.

CHAPTER TWO

Noise: Urban Soundscapes and Gender

*N*EARLY EVERY EVENING, the Augustinian nuns of Santa Maria di Candeli found themselves besieged by the sounds of shouting, laughter, sex, and socializing. By the 1560s nuns of the mid-size convent in the northeastern Santa Croce quarter had come to expect a nightly barrage of lewd words, shouts, screeches, fighting, and racket—sounds that drifted into their cloister from the street outside. The sounds came primarily from a group of women sex workers who lived and labored in the nearby homes and streets, and from the men and youths who visited the area to socialize and solicit sex.

According to civic laws, however, sex workers were well within their rights to occupy the area. The Candeli convent was located on Via Pilastri, just one block east of the Orbatello widow's complex (see Figure 2.1). Civic laws from 1547 had designated a nearby section of Via Pilastri as one of several sanctioned sex work zones spread throughout the city. Magistrates of the Onestà actively relegated sex workers to this area in an effort to limit perceived immorality to precise "vice" zones. Via Pilastri cut along the north end of the Santa Croce quarter and eventually intersected with the important Sant'Ambrogio parish church and adjacent Benedictine

Figure 2.1. Via di Pilastri and locations of (1) the Santa Maria di Candeli convent and (2) the Orbatello complex. Stefano Buonsignori, map of Florence, 1584 (copy from 1695), Harvard College Map Library.

Courtesy of the Digitally Encoded Census Information Mapping Archive (DECIMA).

convent near the eastern edge of the city. The surrounding neighborhood was traditionally home to the working class and to much of the city's wool-working industry. The nearby Piazza Sant'Ambrogio was a popular meeting place for games, gambling, and a host of community and religious rituals, and sex workers had long used the square to attract clientele.[1] In 1461 the city had enacted laws that forbade sex workers from loitering near the Sant'Ambrogio church and square, an edict that was continually renewed throughout the sixteenth and seventeenth centuries with little success.[2] By the mid-sixteenth century, city officials opted for a different approach and demanded that sex workers and their clients instead move up the street and confine their salacious activities to the newly prescribed stretch of Via Pilastri.

This brought sex workers and their clients to the doorstep of the Santa Maria di Candeli convent. To separate these pious brides of Christ from women of the *mala vita* (wicked life), civic officials banned registered sex workers from living or working in the buildings immediately surrounding the Candeli convent.[3] Yet narrow streets, high-density buildings, and the realities of day-to-day life meant that many ignored or were unaware of the rule. Moreover, these laws did little to stop the sounds associated with sex work from spilling over the prescribed boundaries and penetrating the convent.[4] The issue came to a head in the mid-sixteenth century when sex workers moved into the area in growing numbers, in part encouraged by new civic legislation. In 1560 Giulia Napoletana, a sex worker, was "imprisoned for living [too] near the convent of the Candeli."[5]

In 1563 "many youths" were fined for "having gone in the night to the house of Tonina [a sex worker] in Via Pilastri and making noise and brawling."[6] In 1563 Francesca da Pistoia, "a prostitute in Via Pilastri," was fined for roaming the streets at night without permission.[7]

The Candeli nuns were unwilling to accept the scandalous noises they associated with sex workers, sounds they claimed threatened their honor and disrupted their devotions. In 1568 they addressed a letter to the ecclesiastical office that oversaw Tuscan nunneries. The letter described how, because of "the shouting, noise, and other dishonest words that the nuns experience all night long from their church and dormitory, caused by the prostitutes who live in Via Pilastri and near the convent, they are greatly disturbed and molested; not only when they find themselves reciting prayers in church, but also in their individual cells."[8] The nuns explained that "the noises, actions, and words spoken give scandal not only to these servants of God but also to many honorable people." The letter concluded by stating "we demand the prostitutes remove themselves."[9] Officials responded with a standard notation of "sta bene" (it is fine), acknowledging their intent to pursue the nuns' demands. It is unlikely, however, that the Candeli nuns, civic officials, or church authorities had much success in cleansing the area of these sounds. Archival records show that sex workers and their clients continued to frequent Via Pilastri long after the nuns had written their noise complaint. In 1589 the Otto di Guardia sentenced the servant Pasquino da Ruota for "having made noise" in Via Pilastri, where he had likely gone in search of sex, and for having fought and insulted a man named Giuliano Chiareschi.[10] On June 15, 1594, the Onestà fined the "prostitute Margherita Brunelleschi who stays in Via Pilastri . . . two gold scudi for having been found dressed as a man during the day without a license or note."[11] Loud socializing, sex work, and continual traffic in and out of the area continued to mark Via Pilastri and the Candeli convent soundscape years after the nuns wrote their complaint.

The thousands of strictly cloistered girls and women living in Florentine enclosures may have been physically separated from the rest of the city behind enclosure walls and gates, but they remained intimately enmeshed in the larger urban soundscape. Sounds from surrounding streets, squares, homes, and shops regularly seeped into their institutions. For those who were enclosed against their will, these sounds may have been a welcome interruption to the monotony and isolation of cloistered life and a cherished connection to the communities that bustled just beyond their walls. For others, like the Candeli nuns who complained about noise, these sounds were perceived as a violation of the sacred rituals nuns enacted and an affront to the privileged status some cloistered women enjoyed. Institutional authorities, for their part, interpreted the unsanctioned sounds that drifted into enclosures as scandalous intrusions that threatened the integrity of the cloister and violated the vulnerable bodies and souls these communities housed.

This chapter examines the everyday sounds that enclosed girls and women heard and analyzes key elements of Florence's social soundscape. In the sixteenth and seventeenth centuries, institutional authorities and some enclosed women complained about noise pollution with new regularity. As enclosures for girls and women expanded, separating these communities from the broader urban soundscape became particularly challenging. Limited space within the city walls meant that cloisters often neighbored sex work areas rife with bawdy sounds, squares where people gathered for work and play, shops and marketplaces where salespeople hawked their wares, and private homes where residents worked, lived, and socialized. While urban institutions had always contended with multilayered soundscapes, the sheer number of enclosures with large populations that spread throughout the city in the sixteenth and seventeenth centuries meant that severing sonic ties to the larger city was all but impossible, something that increasingly vexed institutional authorities and some enclosed women. At the same time, Catholic Reform and shifting early modern charity practices placed new emphasis on strict cloistering and long-term enclosure. In this context, sonic intrusions were framed not only as disruptive, but also as a threat to the very integrity of enclosure and the highly gendered programs of care and discipline diverse institutions pursued.

While a rich body of scholarship has analyzed the "permeable" nature of Italian cloisters despite Tridentine efforts to enforce *clausura* (enclosure), few studies have considered how urban sounds of sociability and daily sonic exchanges were a key element of this permeability.[12] Officials in institutions like the Convertite, the Malmaritate, the Orbatello, and the city's many nunneries continually struggled to regulate sonic production around their institutions and often contended with noisy realities. In particular, three distinct but connected groups repeatedly appear in

Florentine noise complaints: women sex workers, rowdy male youths, and aggressive men. Examining the sonic concerns related to each group reveals how noise complaints served as a proxy for persistent anxieties about feminine purity, the working classes, and dangerous or disruptive homosocial gatherings. These anxieties were particularly acute in and around women's institutions and the private homes of Florentine women.

The Noisy City

In October 1581, one year after the Malmaritate house opened, a man named Pier Francesco da Diaceto was arrested for "making noise in front of the monastery [of the Malmaritate] and throwing stones at the windows."[13] Pier Francesco had been the pimp to one of the Malmaritate's recently admitted women and had come to talk with her. Turned away, he flew into a rage, shouting in the street, hurling stones at the windows, making noise, and refusing to leave. The Malmaritate cloister was designed precisely to sever communications between men like Pier Francesco and women residents, whom the house governors hoped would "return to penitence if they had a place in which to retreat."[14] Achieving any complete separation or "retreat" was difficult, however. Upon entering enclosed institutions, the city's thousands of institutionalized girls and women did not abandon the sonic or social ties that bound them to the city. In fact, women's enclosures were often the explicit targets of shouting, stone throwing, music playing, or illicit conversations as outsiders attempted to communicate with enclosed relatives, friends, lovers, and business partners. These sonic interactions ranged from hurried whispers near the institutional gate or cracks in the enclosure walls, to sanctioned visits in the *parlatorio* (parlor) under the alert ears of *ascoltatrici* (appointed "listeners" whose job it was to monitor these interactions), to aggressively loud sonic assaults from the street designed to shock and shame enclosed women.

When Pier Francesco hurled stones and shouted outside the Malmaritate, he was participating in a long tradition whereby Italians shamed, mocked, and sought revenge through noisy stoning. Stoning was explicitly antiauthoritarian and often directed at urban officials, prominent statues, and civic buildings.[15] Women's institutions stood as symbols of carefully guarded femininity and of civic and religious order and were thus prime targets for this type of aggressive scorning. In 1603 and 1604 the cardinal legate in Perugia complained about the noisy hail of stones continually lobbed at the city's convents and monasteries, "disturbing their quiet . . . and those Reverend Mothers were coming [to complain of being] disturbed in their orations."[16] Similarly, in 1625, the Florentine nuns of Santa Maria di Montedomini, a Franciscan convent in the Santa Croce quarter, wrote to the archdiocese lamenting the chaos they experienced from the "stones and balls that are often thrown at their windows."[17] Pier Francesco's noisy assault outside the Malmaritate is one of many instances whereby Florentines willfully transgressed the sonic boundaries designed to isolate enclosed women.

By the turn of the seventeenth century, essentially all of Florence's institutions for girls and women had made official, and often repeated, complaints about noise around their cloisters. For example, a 1549 law by the Guelf Party pertaining to the Orbatello proclaimed that "in the future no person regardless of status or position can go in the street of the Orbatello or nearby places, especially during the night, to serenade . . . nor play instruments of any sort, nor sing, or stop to listen to any of the above mentioned activities under the penalty of our arbitration."[18] In the summer of 1561, the Convertite similarly reported "that around their convent and church there is so much racket of instrument playing, singing and other disturbances and gatherings, and it has prevented them the consolation of the divine offices."[19] In response, the Otto di Guardia legislated that those living or passing within 200 braccia (roughly 120 meters) of the Convertite were forbidden "to make racket of any sort, to play instruments, to sing, or to make other resounding noises, to play with balls or any other kind of game under penalty of the arbitration of the Magistracy."[20] In November 1581, directly after Pier Francesco had hurled stones, shouted, and made noise outside the Malmaritate, the city enacted a law that banned anyone "from going toward or entering inside the door of the new monastery . . . in Via della Scala, where the Malmaritate converts are congregated . . . to bother or pester any of these *convertite* . . . or to speak to any of them in any way."[21]

Alongside these complaints was a steady stream of petitions by the city's nunneries. In January 1552 the Florentine nuns of San Pier Martire, a Dominican convent on the southern outskirts of the city, complained to the Otto di Guardia about the incessant noise surrounding their convent. In response, the Otto legislated that "in the future no one can go within 120 meters of this convent to sing, throw stones, gather or make other noises under penalty of 20 scudi."[22] But the law did little to deter groups from gathering near the convent to socialize. A year later the nuns claimed they were still harassed by these sounds, and in 1552 the Otto enacted sonic legislation again, prohibiting "anyone [from] playing games anywhere near that convent . . . nor making or saying any kind of filth or dishonest words . . . under the penalty of 20 scudi."[23] In 1557 the convent was torn down to allow for refortifications of the city walls, and the San Pier Martire nuns moved to a new complex near Palazzo Pitti, the new residence of the Medici duke and duchess.[24] If the nuns had hoped their new location would offer more regulated soundscapes, they were quickly disappointed. Here, again, they were plagued by noises that drifted over their cloister walls. This time the sounds came from women sex workers and their clients who solicited business in the surrounding area. Several decades later, in 1607, the Onestà proclaimed in a somewhat exasperated tone its hope that "in the future these nuns will not have any more disturbances from prostitutes who live near their convent and particularly closest to where they have their dormitory."[25] Florence's archives are filled with similar reports and reflect a daily reality in which institutions were inundated with the sounds of the city. Over the course of the mid-sixteenth to the early seventeenth centuries, civic and church officials processed noise complaints from women's institutions essentially every year, often recording numerous complaints per year, each describing the "shouting," "racket," and "tumult" that cloistered women were said to experience.[26]

Noise complaints were replete with a series of intersecting gender, class, and religious dynamics. These are particularly clear in the case of the San Pier Maggiore nuns and their quest to enforce quiet around their nunnery. In 1561 the eminent Benedictine monastery lobbied the Otto di Guardia with a noise complaint. The elite nuns disparaged "the great racket made in this square all day by [those] playing ball games so that it is a great impediment to the divine offices."[27] The nuns demanded the city control the "disorder" caused by noisy street games and the gatherings they attracted in the square outside the institution. Civic officials responded by affixing a paper to the church door that forbade *giucare a cocomeri* (ball games) by *ortolani* (greengrocers who sold produce in the square), *artigiani* (artisans), *plebes* (the nonnobility), or any others and outlined a series of fines and punishments: offenders would be charged 10 scudi and receive public lashings, while nobility could avoid physical punishment by paying an extra five scudi.[28]

San Pier Maggiore was one of the city's wealthiest religious houses and home to women from Florence's powerful nobility. The monastery was located in the prestigious San Giovanni district in a neighborhood nestled just east of the imposing Cathedral of Santa Maria del Fiore. The elite nuns crafted their noise complaint in the midst of a protracted struggle to retain their religious and civic influence in Florence, and it is possible that the noise complaint was linked to the nuns' broader frustrations at their waning presence in public ritual and religious affairs. Throughout the medieval and Renaissance centuries, the nuns had enjoyed an important role in Florence's political, religious, and social culture—in large part because of the impressive lineage of patrician women who took vows in the nunnery and strategically patronized the institution.[29] The nunnery's status was most poignantly reflected in a fictive marriage rite enacted between incoming bishops and the San Pier Maggiore abbesses between 1286 and 1583. The ritual bound the bishop to his see and included a ring exchange, a feast, and a wedding bed ritual that echoed marital rites but maintained monastic chastity. During the rite, the abbess personified the diocese and, as such, represented the Florentine Catholic community at large.[30] In the sixteenth century, however, the San Pier Maggiore nuns began to experience a shrinking role in civic ritual that threatened their traditional ceremonial and civic importance. Florentine bishops increasingly shifted religious influence away from the San Pier Maggiore monastery, concentrating authority within masculine centers of power instead—a process that ultimately led to the abandonment of the fictive marriage ritual in the late sixteenth century and the diminishing role of the nuns in civic religion.

But the San Pier Maggiore women were unwilling to give in to this "progressive erosion of nuns' prerogatives in public ritual" without a fight.[31] Throughout the sixteenth century, the nuns asserted their civic and religious importance by throwing lavish parish feasts and celebrations while continuing to emphasize their essential role in inaugurating new bishops, all of which would have drawn loud and exuberant ritual crowds to the very same square they complained about in their 1561 noise complaint.[32] The nuns' distain for noisy greengrocers, artisans, and nonnobility was thus less concerned with whether people could loudly occupy the square and much more concerned with *which types of people* could occupy the square, under what circumstances, and, ultimately, who had authority to shape the surrounding soundscape and thereby lay claim to the space. The sounds of working-class Florentines at play were framed as an affront to the aristocratic and spiritually privileged status of the San Pier Maggiore nuns. Moreover, the noise complaint reflected the nuns' eagerness to retain control of the square's soundscape and to assert their elite status in the face of a movement to shift religious and civic influence away from the community. Like the Candeli nuns, the San Pier Maggiore nuns used noise complaints to enact their piety and to construct and defend their elite status against the backdrop of noisy working-class Florentines. In this case, sonic descriptions made and marked boundaries distinguishing the religiously, socially, economically, and politically elite nuns from non-elite Florentines who gathered outside their institution. Noise complaints were carefully constructed documents, and the San Pier Maggiore nuns' quest for quiet was rooted in a desire to assert their entwined gender, class, and spiritual privilege in contrast to noisy "others" and to demand civic recognition.[33] For strictly enclosed communities, noise complaints offered a persuasive script that allowed enclosed women to lay claim to the urban spaces surrounding their communities, spaces they could not physically occupy but were eager to assert influence over. Cloistered women may have been unable to leave their institutions, but they demanded public recognition by listening carefully to the highly localized soundscapes that surrounded them.

Noisy Sex Workers

As women's institutions complained about noise with increasing regularity, urban and institutional authorities identified specific social groups as particularly problematic noisemakers. The most common among these were *meretrici* (women sex workers), *giovani* (male youths), and aggressive men. A wealth of archival sources repeatedly discusses each group and their stated sonic infractions. Often, complaints directed at one group overlapped with those aimed at another. Concerns about noisy sex work, for example, took issue with women of the *mala vita*, the sometimes-aggressive men who contracted their services, and the rowdy

groups of youths who gathered in spaces of sex work to socialize and perform normative masculinities in formation. The sonic concerns associated with each group further reveal how the Florentine soundscape was
invested with issues of gender, class, and social status and how noise complaints served as disciplinary mechanisms at these various intersections.

The sounds associated with sex workers ranged from the bell atop her
hat (which Florentine sumptuary laws first mandated in 1384 to signal a
sex worker's presence, with its distinctive ringing as she moved through
the city's streets) to the racket and din created as a by-product of the sex
trade and filling the streets where, from 1547 onward, these women were
mandated to live and work.[34] Sex workers and their clients were continually apprehended and fined for the crime of *far baccano* (making noise).
In February 1565, for example, a Florentine man was charged for having
visited a brothel, only to "later return to make a racket directed at these
women."[35] That same month "Giulia the prostitute in Via Pentolini" was
charged "for having gone in the night with several companions to make
noise outside the house of Lucrezia di Jacopo the grain broker."[36] That
same year the sex worker Lena Bolognese was apprehended for having
shouted, mocked, and publicly fought with another woman.[37] Alongside
the totalizing spiritual, sexual, and legal identities that urban authorities
attributed to sex workers, these women were also assigned a totalizing
sonic identity and were framed as inherently noisy and surrounded by
noise. As such, Florentines often expressed their moralistic distain for the
sex trade via noise complaints.

Sonic records related to sex work fill the magistracy archives of the
Otto di Guardia and the Onestà and reveal that policing the sex trade was
often synonymous with policing noise. From 1547 on, the year sex workers
were legislated to live and work on specific street sections, the Otto di
Guardia and Onestà arrested dozens of *meretrici* and their clients each year
for specific crimes of noise.[38] In May 1560 three male youths who appren-
ticed as weavers were fined for "for having gone in the night to Borgo la
Noce to the house of Bita the prostitute . . . and made noise."[39] In July 1560
"several young noblemen" were fined for socializing in one of the city's
legislated sex work areas and then "having made noise and fought in Via
della Scala near the house of Camilla."[40] In 1575 "four women [sex
workers] living in Via Mozza" were fined for "having made noise at Mariangiola Spagnuola."[41] In 1576 "several prostitutes from Via del Giardino"

were similarly fined for harassing another sex worker named Geronima
Spagnuola and "for having made noise during the night" and lewdly
shouting at Geronima that she should leave Florence and return to Spain
to look for male clients there. Some Tuscan-born sex workers appear to
have resented competing for clients with women they deemed "foreign"
and lashed out at them in noisy outbursts. Noise complaints involving
these "foreign" sex workers also hint at the complex way that histories of
migration, gender, and ethnicity could coalesce in noise complaints and
criminal records. Steady streams of migration shaped early modern urban
demographics, and sex workers in particular often traveled between
urban hubs, settling in various locales for both the short and long term.
We can glimpse some of these migratory histories in sex workers' sur-
names and the identifying data included in Florentine noise complaints.
References to "noisy" sex workers like Antonia d'Ostro "the Bolognese"
and Francesca "of Pistoia" may reference regional movements, while Onestà records about women like Giulia "the Neapolitan," Mariangiola "the
Spaniard," Alessandra "the Albanian," Anna "the Frenchwoman," Barbara
"of Corsica," and Caterina "the German" gesture toward broader penin-
sular and Mediterranean migrations.[42] It is possible, and indeed likely,
that noise complaints directed at non-Florentine sex workers labeled them
as disruptive not only because of their marginal sexual status but also
because of their status as "foreigners." Descriptions of noise could serve as
a foil for compounding social prejudices and provide a window into the
various ways that Florentines sought to identify and discipline those they
deemed "other."

  Cloistered women in particular complained about the sounds of sex
work near their institutions. In a 1562 letter addressed to Duke Cosimo
I de' Medici, the nuns of San Martino, who lived on Via della Scala near
the Malmaritate house, requested that Bruna da Prato "a dishonest
woman of ill fame, not be able to return to a house that she bought near
the convent." The nuns described how Bruna's noisy comings and goings
gave "scandal to the nuns and the other good people who live there."[43]
Similarly, when the Santa Maria di Candeli nuns complained about
noisy sex workers near their institution, they referenced a 1561 law that
banned sex workers from living within 100 braccia (60 meters) of a nunnery and further noted how the law "more or less gives authority for convent deputies to command prostitutes [living even farther than 100

braccia from a nunnery] to leave within fifteen days if they are found to give scandal to nuns."[44] This 1561 law repeated legislation first articulated in 1547 under Duke Cosimo I that had attempted to confine the sounds and sights of sex work far away from women's institutions by decreeing that "prostitutes and dishonest women, single or married, citizens or foreigners cannot live within 100 braccia of any convent of cloistered nuns within the city of Florence, under penalty of 200 lire."[45] This sonic boundary aimed to contain the shouts, screams, laughter, clatter, and lewd words associated with sex work. Yet reports about the "shouting, noise, and other dishonest words" that penetrated the Santa Maria di Candeli convent and the noisy "scandal" the San Martino nuns associated with Bruna reveal how this sonic boundary often failed to contain the sounds associated with the sex trade. The sounds that accompanied sex work regularly infiltrated institutions, even when sex workers lived farther than 100 braccia from institutions.

The sound of rattling coaches also became closely associated with sex work and vice, particularly in and around the city's sanctioned sex work zones, where wealthy clients arrived in clattering vehicles, announcing their intentions as they came and went.[46] Even more troubling to many Florentines were the courtesans and other sex workers who rode about the city in private coaches, often sent by wealthy clients to ferry women to and from private homes. Laws prohibiting sex workers from using coaches were first drafted in 1550 and directly coincided with the sudden rise of coach travel as an elite urban practice.[47] Civic officials continued to publish these laws throughout the sixteenth and seventeenth centuries. For example, a 1577 law prohibited *meretrici* from traveling "around Florence during the day in coaches, carriages, or the like" and stipulated that "prostitutes wanting to take a carriage outside the city must mount and dismount at the city gate and can [only] travel during the night."[48] However, these prohibitions did little to stop the practice. In 1577, criminal records against Monica di Antonio Carbacci described how "although she had lifted herself out of sin, she had relapsed [into sex work] and was living dishonestly in Borgo Santa Croce with the consent of her husband."[49] Monica was accused of "passing through the street [Via Romana] in a coach, [where] she made racket, injurious noise, and impropriety."[50]

The emergence of the coach as a popular means of elite transportation changed intra-urban travel and posed new issues for civic officials

who were tasked with managing streetscapes and noisy traffic. The famed
Venetian architect Vincenzo Scamozzi addressed this challenge in his sem-
inal 1615 text *The Idea of a Universal Architecture,* dedicated to "the most
serene Prince Cosimo de' Medici II Grand Duke of Tuscany." Scamozzi
described the importance of properly paving streets in order to lessen the
noise associated with coaches, and praised "the streets of Rome, Naples,
Genoa, Milan, and some other cities in Italy, not to mention of Germany
and France, which are partially paved by hard stone . . . and in this way
horses and the wheels of coaches make less noise."[51] In Florence, a series
of late sixteenth- and seventeenth-century laws attempted to regulate
coach travel and the frenetic chaos it could create. Laws issued in 1619
by "the most serene Grand Duke of Tuscany . . . and the most dignified
officers of the Otto di Balia" sought to "hinder the disorders and scandals" that often accompanied coach travel and prohibited "insolences"
from "making the coaches race, one coach taking the place of coaches
ahead, crossing in front of others, passing, or reversing in a manner that
gives rise to disorders."[52] However, while the rattling and jostling sound
of private coaches was often perceived as a nuisance, elite Italians also relied on these very same sounds and activities to enact gendered displays
of prestige and power. Upper-class men used private coaches to perform
elite masculinities. The coach became "a mobile extension of individual,
family, and even state honor" and urban streets became "a battleground
over disputes of precedence, rooted in masculine honor" as coach riders
paraded in elaborately decorated vehicles and squabbled over who had the
right-of-way.[53] Conversely, upper-class women used private coaches to
move through the city while remaining largely hidden from public gaze,
thus performing their feminine honor by remaining withdrawn while mobile. The distinctive sound of coach wheels trundling down stone streets
was thus designed to herald elite gendered performances. When "dishonorable" sex workers traveled by coach, they disrupted these entwined
performances of class and gender and shifted the sonic significance associated with the coach. The persistent sound of wheels rolling over stone
and of jostling coaches moving in and out of sex work areas tarnished the
honorable elitism associated with coach travel and loudly publicized
the ease with which class and gender boundaries could be transgressed,
contributing another register to the soundscapes many Florentines associated with immorality, vice, and sexual sin (see Figure 2.2).

Figure 2.2. Grand Ducal law, 1639, prohibiting women sex workers from riding in coaches. Courtesy of the Ministerio della Cultura della Repubblica Italiana / Archivio di Stato di Firenze. The text reads, in part, "*Bando* [announcement] regarding the prohibition against *meretrice* [sex workers] and women of the wicked life who are not allowed to ride in carriages, coaches, horse-drawn litters and the like."

The sounds associated with sex work assume a different significance when examined from the perspective of sex workers themselves. While urban officials, institutional authorities, and some enclosed women used the category of "noise" to construct their superiority in contrast to women they deemed sinful and noisy, these same sounds reflect how sex workers asserted their presence and resisted spatial, social, and sonic marginalization. Most often this resistance was practically driven and likely unconscious. Women like Monica, who loudly passed up and down Via Romana by coach, probably did not consciously interpret the rattling sound of their coaches as an act of resistance against sumptuary laws or urban efforts to marginalize sex workers spatially and sonically. It is far more likely that they were simply doing their jobs. Sex work, like all labor, required sensory productions. Women needed to advertise their services, move about the city, protect themselves, and negotiate with clients. All of this meant that calling, shouting, and "racket" were part of the trade. Consciously or not, however, when sex workers like Monica made these sounds, they asserted their presence in urban spaces and soundscapes. Enclosed women like the Santa Maria di Candeli and San Pier Maggiore nuns attempted to lay claim to their surrounding soundscapes and neighborhoods by complaining about noisy sex workers, but they received pushback from sex workers who ignored or were unaware of attempts to silence them; in doing so these women defied claims that they did not belong in public spaces.

Yet, many sex workers likely also found the sounds associated with their trade tiring and abrasive, much like the other Florentines who complained about the shouting, fighting, and raucous laughter that so often marked spaces of sex work. Registered *meretrici* were forced to live in some of the city's loudest areas and had to contend with the same shouts, screams, and clatter that institutionalized women complained about. Moreover, sex workers were often the direct targets of this aggressive noisemaking, as when three youths in 1560 were fined for having gone "to the house of Bita the prostitute . . . and made noise" or when a man in 1565 was charged for "having visited a brothel" only to "later return to make a racket directed at these women."[54] The direct voices of sex workers are largely absent in magisterial records, making it difficult to discern how they interpreted the sounds that surrounded them. Yet, as I examine in more detail below, some sex workers purposefully brought noise complaints forward to protest the aggressive, violent, and tiresome behaviors of youths and men who loudly harassed them.

Noisy Youths

Early modern Florence was a youthful city. By 1632 a quarter of the city's population was under the age of fifteen, accounting for 8,315 girls and 9,112 boys.[55] Figures for the sixteenth century, though unreported in the 1561 census, were likely much higher: some estimates suggest that closer to one-half the population was under the age of fifteen and around one-third were under the age of eight.[56] The term *giovani* had a broad application in early modern Florence, sometimes referring to boys under the age of fifteen and sometimes to older youths in their late teens and twenties. Civic records assigned the general marker of youth to a wide range of adolescents, teens, and young men.[57] Like sex workers, the city's many *giovani* were considered particularly noisy and were at the center of many noise complaints. Archival sources consistently reference the racket, clamor, and disorder created by youths who roamed neighborhoods

and banded together in gangs, and homosocial gatherings of *giovani* who
loudly socialized in the city's squares and streets.

In 1540 a gang of "twelve youths" were arrested for "having made
noise outside the house of the prostitute Marietta Sportaina, having
thrown stones at the window, [and] looking for a way to batter down her
door."[58] In September of 1539 "certain youths" were processed by the Otto
di Guardia for "having made noise at Moretta the concubine at the Porta
Romana [city gate]."[59] In 1558 "some youths" were prosecuted by the Otto
di Guardia for having gone with weapons and "made noise at the house
of Caterina Seragostini."[60] That same year the Otto di Guardia recorded
how "many male youths" were charged for having gone to "the house of
Piero di Tommaso in Via dell'Agnolo in the night, where there was a gathering and a comedy being performed. . . . The youths opened the locked
door by force with kicks, whistles, stones, and [were] making noise.
And on entering inside, where there were many women and others, they
caused chaos and made violence and tumult, pulling on the suspended
lamp with many pieces of chair to extinguish it, and tearing up a cloth
tapestry."[61] These types of noisy and violent infractions continually drew
the ire of civic officials and reflected broader urban anxieties about
scores of unmonitored and undisciplined youths.

Successive waves of plague, famine, and war meant that many of Florence's *giovani* were orphaned or abandoned and often relied on peer
groups and gangs for survival.[62] Florence opened some charity homes for
abandoned boys during this period, like the Ospedale dei Poveri Abbandonati, and many boys were placed in the Innocenti as infants.[63] But most
youth homes focused on housing young girls. Of the city's 9,112 male
youths under the age of fifteen in the 1632 census, only 248 were officially
registered as institutional wards. Comparatively, more than three times
as many girls under fifteen lived in institutions for impoverished, abandoned, or orphaned children and youths.[64] Compared to young women,
male youths were freer to seek out apprenticeships, make their own way
in the city, and move about without direct supervision. But this also
brought unique challenges, as many were left to their own devices and the
city contended with large numbers of largely unsupervised *giovani*. For
those making their way in the city, banding together into groups of
friends, coworkers, confraternity brothers, and roommates offered both
security and companionship. For example, according to the 1632 census,

186 boys under the age of fifteen lived on Borgo Ognissanti, a main thoroughfare lined with artisan workshops in the western working-class
quarter of Santa Maria Novella, not far from the Malmaritate house. Many
of the youths in Borgo Ognissanti lived together in crowded spaces: an
ironsmith named Giovanni housed six boys under the age of fifteen in his
workshop, Ottavio the goldsmith likewise housed six boys under fifteen,
and Vincentio the goldsmith housed four boys under fifteen.[65] Smithing
relied heavily on apprentice labor, and youths from diverse circumstances
found themselves living on Borgo Ognissanti because of the combined
work, housing, and companionship opportunities these workshops offered; once there, youths built homosocial networks that shaped their
urban experiences.

For both elite and working-class *giovani,* the development and display
of normative masculinities required performances that were by nature
loud: showmanship, fighting, posturing, homosocial gatherings, music,
song, and laughter. Public spaces staged these performances and were the-
aters for the formation of male youth identities, rendering streets and
squares a "thirdspace," an in-between space for those of an in-between
age.[66] Florentines expressed concern about noisy groups who acted as
gangs, roaming neighborhoods, causing disruption, engaging in street
brawls and celebrations, breaking and entering, playing ball games,
throwing stones, frequenting sex work zones, and often violently harassing
girls and women. Over the course of the sixteenth and seventeenth centuries Florentines repeatedly framed concerns about groups of unmonitored
male youths as an issue of noise.[67]

Noisy youths were a particular problem around the city's many enclosures for girls and women. Orbatello records offer a glimpse into these
dynamics. In 1554 an Orbatello governor wrote to the magistrates of the
Guelf Party, listing "the male youths who [illicitly] go into the Orbatello."[68]
The letter described "two servants from the Alto Pascio monastery, who
carry weapons and more often than not come with other youths that I
do not know . . . Matteo, a linen weaver, who stays in Via Nuova with other
youths whose names I do not know . . . many others whose names I do not
know, and Piero the baker in Via dei Servi."[69] These *giovani* were report-
edly making regular trips to the Orbatello, breaking into the widows' complex, and entering the rooms of Marietta di Mona Ermellina, Masa di
Mona Luchretia, Luchretia di Mona Maddalena, Camilla di Mona Pippa,

and Piera de' Monzino.[70] The women may have been using the institution as a base for sex work, and some had perhaps moved into the Orbatello as transfer wards from the nearby Innocenti foundling home. It was precisely these kinds of incidents that would later prompt officials to express dismay over the many "disorders" that plagued the Orbatello.[71] These break-ins were not only scandalous physical violations of the cloister but also sonic violations. Nor were they particularly unique. Only one year earlier, in 1553, the Orbatello had complained about a youth named Piero who repeatedly loitered outside the institution's walls "croaking" and "cooing" for a young woman living inside and continually disturbing the institution with his noisy shouts and songs.[72] While institutions worked to shield girls and women from the broader city and to enforce silence, Florence's noisy *giovani* posed a continual challenge to this project. Loud and often violent incidents only continued over the course of the sixteenth century and into the early seventeenth. In 1572 the Onestà fined a sex worker, Sandra, who was "found opposite from the convent of San Barnaba with two male youths, howling and saying dishonest words without respect to the space."[73] In 1629 the Otto di Guardia arrested four male youths for having gone "near to the convent of San Giuliano in Florence, where they were playing the guitar and singing at the house of a prostitute."[74] Framing disorderly youths as noisemakers allowed civic officials to group a broad set of social concerns about the city's many *giovani* into one category. Loitering, stone throwing, fighting, stealing, gang violence, gender violence, and breaking and entering were all described as issues of noise.

Game playing and gambling also attracted youths and men of all ages into squares and streets and was framed as another persistent sonic problem. Here again, enclosed women were key plaintiffs and provided detailed descriptions of the sounds Florentines made while at play. In 1553 the nuns of Santa Maria degli Angioli and of San Friano both complained about the "ball games and other games played around their convents."[75] Officers of the Otto di Guardia proclaimed that "because of the noise . . . no one is to go within 200 braccia of the convents to play ball games or other sorts of games under penalty of ten scudi and two pulls on the strap."[76] Games like *palla a maglio* (pall-mall) were widely popular across early modern Europe and usually took place in alleys and open squares where players attempted to hit a small ball through a suspended metal hoop with a mallet.[77] The constant whacking of hard balls and mallets against institutional walls, gates, and windows was a continual source of annoyance for many enclosed women, and despite repeated attempts to ban these activities they remained a regular feature of the institutional soundscape well into the seventeenth century. In 1625 the exasperated Santa Maria di Montedomini nuns described the "great racket made day and night in the [adjacent] Piazza della Zeccha with ball games and other gatherings of men."[78]

While gaming and street play was by no means confined to the lower classes, there were class-based concerns embedded in complaints about noisy gameplay. Recent scholarship has revealed the extent to which the early modern social lives of the working classes were experienced on the streets.[79] In Florence, festive brigades known as *potenze* divided the city's working-class districts into self-identifying "kingdoms" and organized games that took over streets and squares.[80] These types of gatherings, while usually tolerated by watchful civic officials, also prompted concerns that they might devolve into violence, brawls, or—worse—civil unrest. The Otto di Guardia, which prosecuted many of the sonic infractions related to gameplay, had been founded in 1378 precisely as a mechanism of public and political surveillance after the Ciompi Revolt briefly overthrew the republican government. In the Otto's early days, officers were tasked with keeping tabs on potential political dissidents, including labor and trade associations, and rooting out conspirators against the republic; this involved keeping a careful watch over boisterous public gatherings, such as gaming tournaments, where political organizing and agitation could take place. By the sixteenth and seventeenth centuries the mandate of the Otto had shifted from political surveillance to a full-fledged criminal office loyal to Medici princely rule, but officers of the Otto were still focused on monitoring public gatherings. Medici dukes and grand dukes were also keenly interested in monitoring street culture and public gatherings. Each morning the secretary of the Otto was mandated to meet with the duke and to report on the previous night's surveillance.[81] This would have involved reporting on the noisy ball games and sonic transgressions described in many of the criminal records mentioned above. Concerns about gameplay, raucous gatherings, and noise all responded to legitimate complaints made by Florentines, but the identification of players as a problematic sonic group also reflected elite governmental concerns about potentially unruly gatherings of working-class men and youths. These concerns were particularly acute near girls' and women's institutions, where precariously cloistered girls and women shared soundscapes with rowdy youths and men.

Noisy Men

On Christmas Morning 1609, Maria Maddalena di Jacopo Domestici, a young Florentine woman, went to the church at the Convertite complex. When she approached the priest to receive communion, a man named Rolando Turco began loudly shouting insults and accusing her of prostitution. Faced with this act of public shaming, Maria Maddalena protested vigorously, asserting that she was an honest woman.[82] Alarmed by the noisy outburst and scandalous claims made on the convent and church premises, archdiocesan authorities undertook an investigation. Ultimately, the archdiocese ruled against Rolando and he was imprisoned in the Stinche civic prison.[83] From prison, Rolando admitted, "I said impertinent words of great scandal in this church."[84] Five months later, he was still incarcerated and petitioning for his release in a letter describing the desperate poverty his wife and six children suffered without his ability to provide income. Rolando's lengthy prison sentence underscores how seriously Italians took public slights of honor and the power of injurious words.[85] Perhaps worse, however, was that he had brought scandal to the Convertite complex by making disruptive and sexualized noise. Rolando's shouting was an affront not only to Maria Maddalena but also to the many repentant women enclosed behind the Convertite cloister, women who were meant to be separated and protected from the scandalous shouts and screams so often associated with sex work and vice. It was Rolando's sonic transgression that prompted the archdiocese to inquire so thoroughly into the incident. Indeed, the case file carefully recorded first-person testimonies describing how Rolando shouted with "a loud and clear voice," "inconsiderately gave scandal to humble people," and "caused great disorder and murmuring."[86]

Florentines, and Florentine women in particular, regularly contended with noisy harassment, and the city's streets could be "mean streets" where men threatened, shouted, and physically and verbally attacked girls and women.[87] These aggressive assaults regularly pierced the protective barrier of homes, institutions, and churches. Of course, women also made noise directed at men and other women in public outbursts. But while civic and religious authorities expressed some concern about these incidents, they were far more concerned with sonic assaults perpetrated by men against women—a type of harassment that occurred more frequently and had profound consequences for women's safety and perceived honor. Decrees from the 1619 Florentine Synod thus sought to curb incidents precisely like the one involving Rolando Turco and Maria Maddalena, decreeing that men were forbidden to "speak dishonorably to women who are going into or leaving churches, and those who do will be punished."[88] Despite these legislative efforts, girls and women regularly experienced noisy assaults by aggressive men. Alongside the wealth of records that describe men who shouted, threw stones, and made noise outside women's institutions, other records provide yet further opportunities to examine the aggressive sounds made by some men and their contribution to Florence's gendered soundscapes. In particular, many noise complaints detail sonic assaults perpetrated by the wealthy and elite, revealing yet other ways in which gender and class shaped the urban soundscape. Noise complaints against elite men show how sonic disputes could provide women a useful legal vocabulary to pursue cases of street harassment and sexual assault.

Patrician men who belonged to military orders like Santo Stefano and San Giovanni emerge as a particularly noisy group in the city's criminal records. The Tuscan order of Santo Stefano was founded by Cosimo I de' Medici in 1561 as a military order that swore perpetual fealty to Medici rule and worked to extend the duchy's influence across the Italian Peninsula, the Mediterranean, and North Africa.[89] Within Florence the order supported charitable works, institutional projects, and civic works. Pledges to the prestigious order were required to prove nobility and carried the names and lineages of many of Tuscany's most cherished families.[90] The international order of the Knights of San Giovanni in Malta were of similarly noble stock; in Florence the Santo Stefano order, and to a lesser extent the San Giovanni order, functioned as an extension of the Medici court.

Noble and celebrated men from military orders were at the center of many violent, disruptive, and noisy incidents as they moved throughout the city, drank in taverns and private homes, frequented sex work areas, socialized, and celebrated. In October 1567 three such noblemen were apprehended for having gone in the night to the house of Caterina de Arno, "the Spanish prostitute," and for having "made noise and breaking her windows with stones."[91] In November of 1569 a Florentine chancellor, Fiorino Fiorini, filed a criminal case claiming that "around two weeks previously, Guidetto Guidetti, a knight of San Giovanni, along with other armed men had approached the house many times where his daughter Giulia, wife of Niccolo Baroncelli, stayed and the knights made noise at them."[92] In his case against the knight Guidetto, Fiorino took care to outline how his daughter was a respectable woman: honorably married, withdrawn in a house, and the daughter of a chancellor. The noisy assault by Guidetto and his fellow armed men was framed as a sexualized sonic assault. Giulia's honor and safety were at risk, not only because of the physical threat suggested by the men's presence outside her home but also simply by the noises they made. The public nature of their heckling and shouting cast doubt on Giulia's respectability: Did she know these men? Had she engaged in an illicit relationship with one of them? Cajoling, hollering, throwing stones, and attempting to force open doors and windows were exactly the kinds of noisy behaviors aggressive men and youths typically undertook outside the homes of sex workers. Much like scandalized nuns who complained about these noises, Fiorino was anxious to ensure that his daughter, and by extension the family's reputation, were not marred by such sonic associations. The incident involving Giulia and Guidetto is similar to what Elizabeth Cohen has termed "house scornings," where Italians enacted revenge by publicly throwing stones, liquids, and ink at the homes of their enemies. House scornings were also sonic scornings, and for women victims, sonic scorning was a common feature of gendered violence.[93] When men shouted, banged on doors, threw stones, and loudly hurled insults at women, Florentines interpreted these as troubling sounds that threatened feminine honor and disrupted civic peace.

The connections between sonic assault, noise, and gendered-based violence are particularly evident in a 1578 case involving several Santo Stefano knights: Carlo Bonsi of Florence, Leandro Flori of Arezzo, and Pasquino of Oliveto. According to Onestà records, the knights had "gone in the night and made noise at the house of Ortensia the prostitute."[94] The men then "entered into the house together by force, and with other knights of Santo Stefano made violence, and with the pummels of their swords and punching they beat Ortensia and threatened her against speaking of it." Unlike Giulia, who was the daughter of a city chancellor, Ortensia did not have a respected family member to carry her case forward or vouch for her honor in the face of this violent sonic and physical assault. Instead she petitioned the Onestà to pursue her aggressors. One year earlier, in 1577, the Onestà had published new laws that claimed to protect registered sex workers in precisely these kinds of cases. In exchange for registration fees paid to the Onestà, the office promised legal recourse for assaults *meretrici* suffered at the hands of clients or pimps. The magistracy outlined a sliding scale of fines and incarceration periods in the Stinche prison for "anyone who molests any [registered] prostitute in any manner of annoyance or injury."[95] The laws were clear that sonic assault was a recognized form of injury that the office pursued. Onestà records explained that "the magistracy considers offenses of molestation *or noise* that have been made."[96] Ortensia's case against the patrician knights therefore carefully highlighted both the physical and sonic assault she had suffered and explicitly recorded how the violent knights had "made noise." The notion that sonic assault constituted a form of personal injury was echoed in other legal records from the period. In Antonio Maria Cospi's 1643 legal text *Criminal Justice,* the Tuscan grand-ducal secretary included "sound, noise, or voice" and "crimes born from the voice, such as blasphemies and injurious words, and other similar [sounds]" in his discussion of corporeal crimes. Cospi explained that sonic assault ought to be considered a corporeal crime because "things that the senses of touch, taste, and sometimes sight, smell, and hearing are subjected to are considered corporeal . . . and we can say the same of sound, noise, or voice . . . because the instrument causing the sound or voice will be material and corporeal."[97] According to Cospi, because sonic assault usually took the form of shouting, screeching, and violent words that were produced by the perpetrator, and because these sounds in turn assaulted and impacted the body of the victim, sonic assault was akin to physical assault and the voice could thus be considered a weapon and grouped alongside other physical and corporeal crimes.

Archival records do not note what, if any, penalty the Santo Stefano knights received for the physical and sonic assault they perpetrated against Ortensia, nor if Giulia or her father received any compensation in their case against the knights who made noise outside her house. But legal courts were often disproportionately lenient when sentencing violent men who assaulted women. This was particularly true for patrician knights, who had far less to fear than the working classes when it came to criminal sentencing. More often than not, the aristocracy could avoid punishment—if not by the social capital their family name alone afforded, then by simply paying off officials or offering up money for a fine. It is unlikely that the knights received a punishment anywhere near as harsh as the many months Rolando Turco spent languishing in prison for loudly shouting at Maria Maddalena in the Convertite church. Nonetheless, Ortensia's case reveals a legal process where noise was framed as criminal, transgressive, and violent across social classes. Moreover, the recorded details of her case reveal a strong link between physical assault and sonic assault in early modern logic and the deeply gendered and sexualized nature of many sonic assaults. For women like Ortensia, petitioning a legal system riddled with systemic misogyny and predisposed to devaluing the testimonies of women generally, and of sex workers in particular, meant that their cases had to be strategically worded to highlight themes that would resonate with the officials evaluating the incidents.[98] The clear and careful references to "noise" in Ortensia's complaint echo many of the noise complaints made by institutionalized women during this period, and together they reflect the importance Florentines attributed to the soundscape and its gender, class, spatial, and social implications. Women living in institutions and private homes understood the power of noise as a persuasive descriptor and variously described themselves as "disturbed and molested," "defiled," and "scandalized" by the sounds associated with sex workers, rowdy and violent male youths, and aggressive and violent men.[99] In doing so, elite and non elite, cloistered and noncloistered women alike used noise complaints as a means to claim urban space, to defend their social status, to pursue grievances, and to gain the attention of civic and church authorities.

How should we interpret noise complaints created by Florentine women? Many of the noise complaints examined in this chapter were likely genuine in their content. Sex workers and their clients who gathered near the Santa Maria di Candeli convent were probably loud, just as the nuns described. The continual volley of balls and stones lobbed at the Santa Maria di Montedomini convent no doubt disturbed many of the nuns inside. Groups who gathered to play instruments, gamble, sing, and shout near the Convertite were likely an unignorable interruption to the nuns' devotions and the regimes of silence within the institution. But when the Santa Maria di Candeli nuns complained about noisy sex workers in Via Pilastri, they were perhaps primarily concerned about how exposure to the sounds of sex work could blur the boundary distinguishing honorable nuns from "dishonorable" women. Ultimately, the nuns sought to assert their gendered piety and sexual purity against the backdrop of the sounds created by women of the *mala vita*. The categories of *silence* and *noise* served to distinguish two classes of women: quiet, pure and pious nuns and noisy, impure and sinful sex workers. To both perform and preserve their gendered and social status, the Candeli nuns understood it was fundamentally important to sonically separate themselves from women who were labeled as impure and noisy. Sounds, and descriptions of sound, thus parsed and publicized social hierarchies, and noise complaints made and marked the gendered boundaries of sexual, spiritual, and bodily propriety. Florentine women used noise complaints to assert their presence, to perform their honor, and to lay claim to the spaces in and around their institutions and homes.

Talking, shouting, gameplay, stone throwing, aggressive scorning, and the rattling sound of coaches were all regular features of the urban soundscape, and Florentines experienced a noisy reality. Criminal records and noise complaints reveal how urban officials identified women sex workers, male youths, and aggressive men as particularly problematic noisemakers, especially in the spaces near cloistered communities of girls and women. Concerns about the sounds each of these groups made were rooted in persistent anxieties about feminine purity, the poor and working classes, disruptive homosocial gatherings, and transgressive men. Institutions for girls and women were designed to be silent retreats from the city. Yet sonic disruptions were always a lurking possibility, and cloistered women often complained about the sounds that drifted into their institutions. A shout in the night, a lewd word or song, or the drop of a ball all threatened to dissolve the carefully constructed social, spiritual, sexual, and sonic boundaries that institutional and urban officials worked to uphold. To fully understand why various authorities understood noise as criminal, assaulting, and injurious, Chapter 3 examines medical, scientific, and spiritual theories of sound. According to prescriptive health and spiritual writings, sound was a powerful force that profoundly affected the physical body and the environment. Beyond the daily annoyances that shouts, clatter, and urban racket caused, sound was also a powerful agent that could either heal or harm both body and soul.

CHAPTER THREE

Sound: Bodily and Spiritual Health

*I*N HIS 1603 medical treatise *On the Popular Errors of Italy,* the Roman-born physician and Dominican friar Scipione Mercurio described the intensely powerful effects of sound on the human body. Outlining the precautions pregnant women ought to observe to avoid miscarriages, Mercurio warned against attending festivals and loud public gatherings because of the "extreme danger" posed by sensory overload. Unexpected stimuli, he wrote, caused "that sudden fear, that violent terror, that terrible fright; [that] goes to the core of the heart and cools the blood, disturbs the spirits, pales the face, induces fevers, causes passions, produces defect, and agitating the fetus too much, brings it close to death." But, if nothing else, Mercurio explained, "shouting, those sharp screeches, those vehement voices . . . are sufficient to cause fetuses to abort." To drive the point home, Mercurio explained that loud sounds and overwhelming stimuli were "sufficient to pale the face and tremble the heart not only of women, but even of courageous men."[1] Mercurio described a process of maternal imagination in which a pregnant body, and the fetus it carried, bore the signs and effects of surrounding sensory stimuli. Shouting, screeches, and noises not only penetrated the mutable female body but also imprinted on the unborn, with potentially devastating effects.[2]

Mercurio's insistence that sound was a powerful force that impacted the human body, for better or for worse, was echoed by many writers in the sixteenth and seventeenth centuries. A wealth of prescriptive literature from the period expounded on the body's relationship to sensory stimuli in general, and to sound in particular, and offered detailed sensory regimes that reminded readers to carefully monitor the sounds, sights, smells, tastes, and textures that surrounded them in order to maintain humoral balance and bodily health. These writers claimed that noise was not merely an annoyance but rather an invasive and caustic force that degraded bodily and spiritual health. Women, whose bodies, minds, and souls were often assumed to be naturally precarious, weak, and mutable, were identified as particularly vulnerable to this process.[3]

This chapter investigates early modern Italian theories of sound and hearing and explores the relationship between soundscapes, the body, and the soul to better understand the determination with which Florentines sought to regulate girls' and women's soundscapes. A diverse collection of sixteenth- and seventeenth-century writings discussed the physicality of sound and its perceived bodily and environmental effects. These writings range from medical treatises authored by university trained physicians eager to assert expertise on the body, to plague and health manuals that described how sounds could either cleanse or further corrupt plague-infested airs, to poetry and literature that framed the peaceful country villa as a respite from the noisy city, crafting a sonic dichotomy that mirrored the urban and rural boundary. Advice manuals on household management, books of secrets, botanical guides, and recipe books also circulated advice on how to treat various sonic ailments and ear problems. Spiritual treatises written by theologians, friars, and priests expounded on the spiritual effects of sound and the intimate relationship between soundscapes and the soul. The edicts and decrees of Catholic Reformation councils and local synods similarly advocated for a new emphasis on quiet and silence in sacred spaces and oral and aural reform were articulated as important elements of Catholic reform. Taken together, these diverse sources reveal a broad early modern consensus on the profound physicality and materiality of sound, its penetrative and formative nature, and the importance of carefully monitored soundscapes.

Sound and Hearing

To understand the importance Italians invested in sonic regulation it is
necessary to first understand basic early modern theories of sonic production and hearing. Anatomists, body experts, and philosophers were
deeply influenced by Aristotle and medieval writers like Avicenna and Bo-
ethius, who all claimed that sound and hearing were directly linked to
the circulation of air. In 1642 the Roman medic Domenico Panarolo published his text *Aerology: A Discourse and Treatment on Air's Instrumentality
for Health,* which offered a detailed analysis on different airs and their
health implications. Panarolo continually asserted the direct link between
sound and air, explaining that "air universally takes many forms . . . and
many times it is sound."[4] Several decades later in 1680 the Jesuit priest
Daniello Bartoli, author of a popular history of the Jesuit order, published
a text exploring the specifics of sound and hearing titled *On the Sound of
Harmonic Tremors and on Hearing.* Bartoli claimed that sound "is not par-
ticles, not atoms, not tremors, not substance . . . nor anything other than
vibrations, and ripples of the air. . . . This gentle beat of swollen air enters . . . into the ear canal."[5] Early modern writers were clear that sound
was air and that it entered directly into the body via the process of hearing.

According to Aristotle and his early modern interpreters, sound and
hearing were the product of a series of interconnected processes: the creation of a sound by a hard body or object such as a bell that disrupted
the air, the movement of this sound-filled air, and the meeting of sound-
filled "external airs" with the body's own "internal airs" on a sound's entry
into the ears.[6] In 1553 the Florentine academic Bernardo Segni outlined
this basic process in his treatment of Aristotle's *On the Soul,* explaining that
"the auditory sensorium is aerial . . . there would not be hearing if the exterior medium, which is air, did not move into the interior, which is the
sensorium. And from there hearing is born." Segni explained that sound-
filled "exterior air" entered the body via the ears, "where the body's inner
air is animated," and from this "sensation is made."[7] Bartolomeo Traffichetti, a physician and philosopher from Rimini, also drew directly from
Aristotelian thought to explain the mechanics of hearing in his 1565 text
The Art of Preserving Health, in which he asserted that "sound is the frac-
turing of air made from hard bodies [such as bells], and air waves, having
been fractured and broken up, move around."[8] Traffichetti explained that

in order for "the sensory soul" to "sense the sound (which is the goal of hearing) it needs an insertion of air, for which the [ear] cavity is designed and proportioned." According to early modern theorists, once sound-filled airs entered the ears these sonic properties were taken in by the inner sensory faculty, the sensorium or *imaginatio*.[9] It was here that sounds were interpreted, made sense of, and stored within the body and soul. This was the sensory soul that Traffichetti referred to in his description of hearing.[10] According to Avicenna and Galen, the sensory soul was located in the brain, while Aristotle located it at the heart, and described a process where sensory data first traveled to the front of the brain and then to the heart. Mercurio's description of noises that "went to the core of the heart" and then cooled the blood and caused fevers and chills was thus working directly from an Aristotelian model of the *imaginatio* and sensory perception in combination with a Galenic humoral model.[11] The *imaginatio* was considered responsible for the processes of perception and cognition and functioned as the pathway between sensation, intellect, and the physical body. Almost all theorists also agreed that the *imaginatio* could store a simulacrum of a sensed sound, and in this way sounds and their inherent properties continued to reside within the body long after they faded from the external environment. As François Quiviger has noted, scientific illustrations of the period often depicted lines traveling directly from the ears, eyes, tongue, and nose to the front of the brain to visualize the process by which sensory stimuli physically entered the body.[12] Once inside the body, seemingly ephemeral sounds had a protracted and profound impact on both the body and soul. As many early modern writers explained, consequential humoral and bodily shifts were often prompted by the agitation of the sensorium or *imaginatio*.

Medical and scientific theorists were also unanimous in acknowledging the force and materiality of sound-filled airs, often describing sounds as "piercing" and "blunt."[13] Early modern writers variously described sounds as swollen or fractured air, and Aristotle had claimed that echoes were produced when "air is made to bounce back like a ball."[14] All of these discussions highlighted the perceived physicality of sound, which was thought to materially act on bodies and spaces with profound implications. While invisible to the eye, sound had a material presence and impact. Renaissance artists likewise recognized the physicality of sound-filled airs. Amy Bloch has argued that sound is represented as a tangible force in

Figure 3.1. Lorenzo Ghiberti, detail of Joshua Panel (destruction of Jericho) from the *Gates of Paradise,* 1425–1452.

Photograph by the author.

Lorenzo Ghiberti's famed *Gates of Paradise* on Florence's baptistry doors. In particular, Ghiberti's depiction of the book of Joshua shows the walls of Jericho splitting and crumbling from sheer noise as the Israelites shout and blow trumpets. In the bronze cast panel, three Israelites are revealed with their hands raised, gesturing toward the splitting walls and holding out their palms as if grasping the thickened sound-laden air itself (see Figure 3.1).[15] Images like these communicated to viewers the physicality of both sound and air. As Florentines passed by the baptistry, perhaps stopping to take in the stories engraved on one of the city's most important religious and civic sites, they may have been reminded of the power of sound and its profound impact on the environment, on built space, and on individual bodies.

Discourses on sound and its physical effects dovetailed with discussions about the other senses and their bodily impacts. Reforming writers like Gabriele Paleotti, the archbishop of Bologna, expanded on Tridentine decrees on art and discussed the importance of regulating visual cultures and artistic production in his 1582 text *Discourse on Images, Sacred and Profane.* Paleotti repeatedly described the power of images to shape the body, mind, and soul.[16] The Franciscan friar Girolamo Menghi, known for his demonology and exorcism manual, likewise discussed the power of images in his 1609 text *The Heavenly Treasure of the Glorious Mother of God, The Virgin Mary*. The text outlined proper engagement with Marian devotion and imagery in the context of Catholic reform, and Menghi wrote that "there are many effects that arise from [viewing] images, both profane and sacred." He explained that just like sound, sight also stimulated the *imaginatio*, "from which important affections & changes are born and manifest signs are imprinted on these bodies [which take in images]." As evidence, early modern writers like Menghi referenced the biblical tale of Jacob, describing how he influenced the patterning and coloring of the coats of goats and sheep by placing peeled branches in front of them while they copulated, thus producing mottled coats. Menghi also repeated a series of well-known stories that further attested to the power of vision and its bodily effects. Like Mercurio, he was particularly interested in maternal imagination and, referencing Plutarch, described how pregnant women sometimes attempted to mold the physical features of a fetus by gazing on "simulacra and delightful images which they use with their husbands and thus give birth to similar parts." Menghi then referenced a widely circulated story about a Black baby supposedly born to white parents and explained how the mother "had given birth to a son not similar in looks to the father after looking at an image of an Ethiopian."[17] Menghi, and the many writers who circulated similar versions of this story, drew on concepts of visuality, the senses, and maternal imagination as tools of race making and used sensory discourses as a tool to frame "the dark-skinned individual as antithetical, altered, and visibly marked."[18] Much like Mercurio's warnings about how pregnant women needed to avoid "shouting, those sharp screeches, those vehement voices," stories about darker-skinned infants born to lighter-skinned parents served to reinforce the importance of regulating female bodies, and pregnant bodies in particular, and their sensory intake. Moreover, these writers used reproduction as a site to articulate intersecting asymmetries of sex, gender, and race. Both authors agreed that female bodies were highly susceptible to sensory stimuli and that sights, sounds, and the other senses "imprinted on these bodies" with profound consequences.

Taken together, the specifics of sound and hearing as described in scientific, philosophical, and medical writings of the sixteenth and seventeenth centuries continually asserted the intense materiality of sound and the senses. Sounds disrupted the air, moved through space, entered into bodies, and were overwhelmingly characterized by a physicality that extended beyond their seemingly fleeting and immaterial nature. Noises stood to disrupt the humors, prompt fevers, cool the blood, and pale the face; sounds lodged within the body's "sensory soul," and the process of hearing required an intimate mixing of external and internal airs that integrated an individual into the larger environment. Ultimately, sonic production and hearing revealed the profoundly permeable nature of the early modern body and the material power of sound. The direct links between sound and air help to explain why many urban authorities were concerned with regulating soundscapes. When external sounds entered the internal body via the ears, opportunities for bodily corruption or restoration abounded and sound and hearing were intimately linked to health. Sounds could riddle the body with illness and sin, either as a product of unhealthy sounds themselves or by way of the unhealthy airs that carried these sounds into the body. Moreover, impure, noisy, or impious sounds stood to corrupt external airs as they drifted through spaces and communities. Conversely, positive and healthy sounds could uplift the body and spirit, calming and soothing the internal core while also cleansing the larger environment.

Sound and Air Quality

Air pollution and noise pollution were often expressed as interconnected phenomena. General knowledge held that "corrupted" air was a primary vehicle for the transmission of contagions, and early modern Italians were carefully attuned to factors thought to pollute or cleanse the air. Plagues and pandemics in particular were understood to be transmitted primarily through corrupted airs, spreading illness via miasmic haze and the inhalations and exhalations of the sickly.[19] In 1619 Fulvio Giubetti, a magistrate for Florence's Offizie della Sanità (Office of Health), published a short text on the plague, its treatments, and causes. He explained that "plague is a contagious illness born from infected air . . . or rather the plague is a poisonous vapor, concentrated in the air, [and the] enemy of the vital spirit."[20] This theory, in combination with the all but unanimously accepted assertion that sound was air and that external and internal airs mixed together in the body via the process of hearing, produced a sharpened focus on the link between soundscapes, health, and disease.

Internalizing unhealthy airs could be a direct by-product of hearing. It was this logic that lead Bernardo Segni to explain that when "air that enters into the ear is not natural . . . it corrupts."[21] Similarly, Bartolomeo Traffichetti described the importance of ensuring that "air is pure, in order to [properly] receive all the differences of sound" and also explained the importance of treating unhealthy bodily vapors "from throughout body to the head and particularly to the ears, [because] these internal vapors mix with the airs and render them impure and disturbed."[22] Particular sounds were also thought to pollute the air. A 1577 treatise titled *Causes and Remedies of the Plague and of Other Illnesses,* anonymously authored in Florence and dedicated to Grand Duchess Joanna of Austria, claimed that "madrigals, and vile songs . . . and inappropriately intimate conversations" all stood to prompt plagued airs and illness.[23] The negative effects of noise were thus far more profound than the daily annoyances that "vile" songs, shouts, and clatter could elicit; these noises also stood to pollute the environment and to prompt illness.

But while some sounds corrupted, others cleansed. In particular, Italians employed bell ringing, music, and loud artillery firing in an attempt to disperse polluting haze. For example, in Alessandro Petronio's 1592 posthumously published health manual for Roman residents, the physician noted that in Rome "the air is always dense, thick, and like the water of swamps," but he went on to write that urban residents regularly took sensory measures to purify chronically polluted urban airs. Petronio explained that in the city "the air is purged by fire and smoke and by the sounds of bells, and this breaks [the air]," cleansing it.[24] In a 1602 health manual for Genoese residents, the Veronese physician Bartolomeo Paschetti similarly noted how cities were marked by "the sound of bells . . . that lighten and purify the air." Paschetti then asked if the air would "not then be better and more thin in the city than in the country villas" where these sonic practices were less common. Ultimately, Paschetti boasted that "because the air of Genoa and nearby places is completely thin, light, and pure, in that country there is no reason for [cleansing] fires and for the sound of bells, nor for the comparison made of the villa to the city."[25] Paschetti's flattering description of Genoese air is characteristic of a regionalism common to many prescriptive health writings from the period. Authors like Paschetti used health manuals to assert their expertise and to praise the particular region they dedicated their works to.[26] This regional patriotism was contrasted by the generalized knowledge included in many health manuals.

Indeed, a shared set of sonic practices were used to cleanse urban airspace throughout Italy, all of which recognized the power and motility of sound. These practices were particularly important during times of plague, when corrupted air was thought to envelop cities, wreaking havoc. In 1630, when northern Italy was victim to a devastating plague that moved throughout the region over the course of several years, the medic Thomaso Tomai published a plague and health manual in Bologna and described how "the sound of bells is a most convenient remedy, because the noise of bells dissolves the haze and clears the air."[27] The physician Fabritio Ardizzone referenced similar practices in his 1656 text *On the Preservation and Curing of Pestilence*. Ardizzone warned that when urban populations "inhale polluted winds, it is prescribed to close up all windows, raise up the city gates, fire the artillery, and sound the bells."[28] Ardizzone's text was published in Genoa in 1656 when the city was besieged by a plague that claimed approximately fifty-five thousand lives from a population of around seventy-three thousand.[29] Other sources from 1656 reveal how the Genoese put these sonic recommendations into practice, attempting to drive away plague-riddled airs with a citywide symphony of sounds. According to Luca Assarino, editor of the seventeenth-century newspaper *Genova*, "in all the churches of Genoa everyone continued to sing at the same hour alongside the universal roar of all the bells, and then all of the artillery throughout the city and every vessel of the port responded as a second choir."[30] In Naples, Giambattista Della Porta, whose publications ranged from works on alchemy to stage plays, also discussed the environmental impact of sound. In Della Porta's 1562 text *On the Miracles of Nature* he dedicated a section to "when you want to drive away a storm or hail" and explained "of course, bells can do this with their ringing, or even the barrels of artillery, because they break the air with that roar and break up the clouds, which many people think should also be done at the time of plague."[31] In Cesare Crivellati's 1631 *Treatise on Plague* the physician from Viterbo likewise suggested a remedy purportedly advised by Hippocrates that was said to have "liberated [ancient] Athens from plague." Crivellati recommended "making sound" by "ringing all the bells along with all the organs of the churches, alongside hearing devout music throughout the city so that the air is better broken up and renders itself pure and drives away anything that could infect it." Crivellati also recommended a "second remedy" whereby "in every piazza and main street intersection let them have bombards, double muskets, firecrackers, arquebuses, and other similar instruments ... and at the same time let them hear trumpets, drums, and other similar sounds throughout the city, all without stopping the continual sound of bells and organs." Crivellati explained that this collective music making and bell ringing, "in addition to breaking up and purifying the air, which will take place, will also result in people celebrating, which is of no small significance in these [plagued] times."[32]

The curative sound of music was also presented as an antidote for individual bodily ailments. The Veronese writer Lodovico Moscardo described the importance of "instruments and songs" in his 1656 *Memorie* and described how "the music of instruments and of song is not only a remedy for the afflictions of the soul, but moreover for the illnesses of the body, like in those who are bitten by vipers."[33] Likewise, Domenico Panarolo discussed music as a healing remedy in his discourse on air, claiming that "music cures diseases and disturbances not only of the spirit but also of the body, likewise when the quotidian singing of melody is applied it cures fever and even injuries." Panarolo noted that "some patients of other physicians, nearly beyond hope of health, have been healed by the delights of music."[34] These claims drew on a long tradition of Europeans employing "magical songs" to cleanse the soul, heal the body, ward off demons, invoke good weather, and engage with the cosmos. When explaining the power of magical song, Marsilio Ficino wrote that "harmony through its numbers and proportions has a wonderful power to calm, move, and affect our spirit, soul, and body" and explained that "very powerful music," just like "celestial figures," fundamentally impacted the body and environment by "penetrating everything."[35] Remi Chiu has examined the important role of music in the Renaissance "pestilential pharmacopeia" and music's stated ability to shift the humors, organs, and the *imaginatio*. Indeed, plague treatises from the Black Death period consistently prescribed music as a preventative and curative treatment for plague. As Chiu notes, the Florentine writer Tommaso del Garbo advised his readers to "make use of songs and minstrelsy and other pleasurable tales." The French doctor Nicolas de Nancel advised a two-pronged approach that combined quiet and silence interspersed with salubrious music, writing, "Before and immediately following meals, stay quiet and calm; some time after . . . sing sweetly and melodiously some sweet spiritual song, not crass words or songs of villainy that some drunk singers and musicians might belch or vomit up. Or play musical instruments, like I said before, for music greatly refreshes the spirit."[36] Throughout Italy, health writers, philosophers, and urban populations collectively drew on the power of sound in the battle against polluted air, plague, and individual illness. All of these practices recognized sound's intense power. Sounds were thought to profoundly impact the individual body and the environment at large, for better or for worse. Sounds moved through bodies and spaces, both imbibing and altering the attributes of the surrounding environment. This prompted early modern Italians to devote careful attention to classifying and regulating particular sounds and auditory cultures.

The Noisy City and the Quiet Villa

While bells, music, and artillery could cleanse urban airspace, even prompting health writers like Paschetti to wonder if these sonic regimes had the potential to render urban airs healthier than unattended rural airs, most prescriptive writers advised readers to avoid urban cacophony whenever possible. These authors upheld the rural villa as an antidote to the frenetic urban soundscape and its polluted airs. In Senofonte Bindassi's 1582 book *The Pleasure of the Villa,* the Venetian poet praised the peaceful countryside, writing, "In the villa one does not experience the many curses . . . scorns, resentments, the many frenzies . . . brawls . . . sighs, sobs . . . screams and screeches of so many who live in the cities of the world."[37] This sentiment was echoed by Agostino Gallo in his popular 1556 dialogue on the values of living in in the country villa as opposed to the city, *The Thirteen Days of Agriculture and on the Pleasures of the Villa.* The widely published agronomist disparaged noisy urban soundscapes and claimed that upstanding residents were continually assaulted by the sounds of urbanites as they hawked their wares, hustled and begged in the street, and otherwise filled the air with the sounds of desperation or immorality. Describing "the things I hate to hear," Gallo wrote of the "chimney sweeps and cobblers who shout, the porters and wine porters who clatter [down streets], the madams and prostitutes who solicit and ensnare, magicians and charmers who enchant, the soothsayers and witches that foretell . . . and the hypocrites and deceivers that bark." Noble Italians, Gallo argued, did well to flee the barking, shouting, and clattering of the city. He thus advised his readers, "We cannot say enough that it is a health-giving thing to abandon . . . the noises of the city, in order to enjoy the reposes, the joys and the contentments of the villa." He argued that the peace and quiet of the villa was the "most potent remedy for maintaining every happiness and genteel spirit while in residence in the prison of our fragile body."[38]

Free from caustic urban soundscapes, villa literature and health writings described spaces of sensory tranquility and idyllic soundscapes. In Castore Durante's popular 1586 text *The Treasure of Health,* the physician and botanist described one such ideal listening environment, writing, "The man, therefore, who wants to be healthy, frequents the gardens, looking at the vegetables, and pleasant places, and converses with cheerful friends, and [listens to] eloquent instruments and songs, for through these things one restores virtue, and strength grows with food, with wine, with good smells, with tranquility, and with conversation with friends, likewise it confers to listen to great histories, fables, and pleasant arguments, sounds, and songs."[39] In the idealized villa sensorium, positive sounds were not forced to compete with the din and racket of the city. The senses were positively stimulated, and the entire body was placed at ease. Good smells soothed the nose, wine and food satiated, and the eyes were pleased by greenery and gardens. Above all, the country villa was presented as a tended, domesticated, but still natural soundscape. Here Italians could actively choose the sounds that surrounded them, free from the layered and unpredictable human-made sounds of the city.

Villa literature regularly referenced the chirping of birds as a testament to the health-giving properties of the countryside, its healthy airs, and salubrious soundscapes. Agostino Gallo boasted that the city "remains deprived of singing birds, that we see day and night [in the villa]." He claimed that while urbanites could attempt to replicate villa soundscapes by keeping caged birds, this would never fully capture the sweetness of wild birdsong. He wrote "that if we [in the villas] enjoy their singing with their liberty, these [caged urban] prisoners always sing forcefully, fearing to die of starvation if they do not sing. Therefore, it is no wonder that the singing of our birds is more cheerful, more resonant, and sweeter."[40] Birding manuals often included illustrations of joyful musical performances accompanied by birdsong, visualizing the villa soundscape that health writers praised as particularly salubrious (see Figures 3.2 and 3.3). Despite Gallo's claims about the limited benefits of caged birds, both

Figure 3.2. A concert of music to make birds sing. Antonio Valli da Todi, *Il canto de gl'augelli* (Rome: Antonio Tempesti, 1601).

urban and rural Italians kept songbirds in an effort to reap the benefits of their singing and chirping. They built cages and aviaries in which to house them, and referred to their chirping, singing, and calling as healthy, joyful, and positive sounds. In Giovanni Pietro Olina's birding manual the author stated that "we are incredibly delighted by the melody of birds" and claimed that "the study of excellent singers is nowhere better used than to

Figure 3.3. An idyllic villa soundscape with music and birdsong. Giovanni Pietro Olina, *Uccelliera overo discorso della natura e proprieta di diversi uccelli* (Rome: M. Angelo de Rossi, 1684).

resemble birds."[41] Birding manuals such as Cesare Manzini's 1607 text *Instructions for Raising, Grazing, and Caring for Birds Which Are Caged for the Use of Singing* were filled with tips and tools on how to prompt individual species to sing and described in detail the variations and qualities of specific songs.[42] The healthy sound of birdsong was contrasted by many writers' descriptions of the human screeching, cawing, and hooting that so often characterized the urban soundscape. The Perugian writer Leandro Bovanini, a member of the satirical Academy of Fools, criticized men and women who like a flock of geese "go around with a noisy tongue, cawing, croaking and clamoring for air, filling it with nuisance and tedium."[43] It was this same type of clamoring and cawing that lead Gallo to claim that "honorable men and women . . . honest wives, modest widows, decent maidens, and even cloistered brides of Christ" were better off in the countryside, where they were not subject to the dishonest words, gossiping, and slander that supposedly took place "beneath the loggias of the city or in the workshops of artisans."[44] All of these venomous sounds, Gallo claimed, were contrasted by the sweet sounds of rural birdsong, music, and peace and quiet.

The literary practice of expounding on the pleasures of villa life had long been a staple in Italian writing. The villa trope was perhaps most famously adopted by Boccaccio as the setting for the *Decameron,* where birdsong and clean country airs were juxtaposed against the image of a plague-ridden Florence.[45] Durante's and Gallo's writings echoed this comparison but used the explicit language of sonic purity, reflective of a sensory focus that early modern writers took up with vigor. In their writings, villa landscapes became synonymous with positive soundscapes and sound and space emerged as deeply connected categories. Yet access to peaceful villa soundscapes was usually restricted to an extremely privileged group of urbanites.[46] The vast majority of working-class Florentines would have been unable to flee the noisy city for a peaceful country villa. Moreover, hierarchies of class and social status were inherent to the very genre of villa literature. When Gallo presented the villa as an antidote to the grating sounds of the city, he was clear that it was the sounds of the working classes and the impoverished that he found particularly offensive and caustic. The clattering, soliciting, and barking he disparaged were all sounds he attributed to the average folk who labored and socialized in public spaces: street vendors, wine porters, fortune tellers, and sex workers. This classist attitude is also evident in a popular genre of early modern engravings that depict tradespeople and humble folk going about their business. These artworks often show beggars, hawkers, and salespeople in the midst of bellowing cries with grimacing, stretched, and pained facial expressions that were meant to appear humorously grotesque. One such engraving from around 1600 by the Italian artist Francesco Villamena shows a character named Geminano in mid-holler. The accompanying text reads in part, "I am Geminian, the roast chestnut seller, who wants to make my name known to the world, because in shouting I have no equal, with my voice I make the bottom of hell shake" (see Figure 3.4). These were precisely the types of soundscapes and social groups that writers like Gallo so disparaged. The boundary separating healthy sounds from unhealthy noises and the peaceful villa from the noisy city ran parallel to social boundaries that functioned to separate the rich from the poor, the pious from the sinful, and the honorable from the dishonorable. This dualistic sonic model was rooted in moralizing claims that the city's working classes were inherently noisy and troublesome. Praising the peaceful villa soundscape also meant critiquing the urban poor, the working classes, and their associated sounds. Quiet and silence were often a preserve of the wealthy and the peaceful villa was presented as a respite from the shouts, screams, and hollers of the urban working-class majority.

Protecting the Ears: Medical Perspectives

Whether urban or rural, wealthy or working class, a crucial step in preserving sonic and bodily health was protecting the ears. Health manuals discussed how to purge aural impurities and offered treatments for extracting noise that became physically trapped in the ears and body. Healthy living manuals, *ricettari* (recipe books), and medical treatises flooded the early modern Italian print market during the sixteenth and seventeenth centuries. Sandra Cavallo and Tessa Storey have argued that the proliferation of this health literature was fueled by a growing "culture of prevention" that took root in the early modern period.[47] A widespread interest in preventative bodily practices brought a medicalized focus to domestic spaces, produced new material cultures devoted to health, and encouraged the rapid publication of health writings. The competitive nature of medical practice also meant that health writers sought to assert their expertise in a diverse and dynamic medical marketplace by offering authoritative or unique health regimes and, often, by disparaging the advice of other health practitioners; all of which further encouraged the rapid publication of health advice.[48] Mercurio's *On the Popular Errors of*

Io fon quel Geminian caldaroftaro
Che voglio 'l nome mio far noto al mondo.
E perche nel gridar, non trouo paro,   *Miffer Gioanni Orlando mio galante,*
Con mia voce conquaffo à Pluto il fondo.   *Ornato di uertu degna e pregiata.*
            Superio͡g licentia.   *A uoi fol dono quefto bel fembiante.*
                                                      F. Villamena F.

O fufto ben compito, a me fi caro
Ritratto fol per farmi piu giocondo.
Chi effendo hoggi da molti riguardato
Mi glorio fol del mio felice ftato.
            Cum Priuilegio.

Figure 3.4. Francesco Villamena, *Geminiano Caldarostaro Crying Out Holding a Tub,* ca. 1597–1601, engraving, Metropolitan Museum of Art, New York. The inscription reads, in part, "I am Geminiano, the roast chestnut seller, Who wants to make my name known to the world, Because in shouting I have no equal, With my voice I make the bottom of hell shake."

Italy, for example, the same text in which he warned pregnant women against the dangers of noise and overexcitement, was written explicitly as a censure against the shoddy cures and superstitious beliefs peddled by "the charlatan, that is most ignorant." A gendered tone accompanied this corrective work; Mercurio claimed that "because most of these [medical] errors are committed by women, who assume too much in medicine, I write and caution you in order to curb such license and to correct such abuse."[49] Authors like Mercurio claimed unique authority for themselves by way of their university training, but in reality their advice usually repeated knowledge and practice that had long circulated in informal channels and domestic settings where women were the primary health practitioners.[50] Many of these published wellness regimes discussed the body's reaction to sensory stimuli and the importance of sonic health. Examining these sources thus reveals some of the widespread attitudes surrounding aural health that circulated in multiple spheres of bodily practice and medical theory in early modern Italy.

Libri di secreti (books of secrets) and *ricettari* containing pharmaceutical remedies emerged in increasing numbers in mid- to late sixteenth-century Italy. Medieval books of secrets, written in Latin, had long been popular throughout Europe, but the advent of the printing press and a desire for sources in the vernacular fueled the rapid publication of new books. Multiple editions and reprintings of popular *ricettari* quickly circulated across Italy and all of Europe. These texts were far more accessible than the purposefully guarded "secret" recipes in medieval Latin manuscripts, and they were often quickly translated into many languages.[51] A desire for bodily care practices that could be easily adopted and individualized further encouraged the wide circulation of *ricettari*.[52] One of the most popular recipe books was Girolamo Ruscelli's *On the Secrets of the Reverend Alessio Piemontese,* first published in 1558. By 1559 an English translation appeared on the market, and by 1600 the text had been reprinted over forty times, in many languages.[53] Like most *ricettari,* Ruscelli's recipes treated a vast and diverse number of conditions ranging from concoctions for whitening teeth; clearing the face of freckles; lightening the hair; and curing syphilis, gonorrhea, and the plague. Among these were several aural treatments, including a "secret from India" that promised to improve hearing, and a recipe for clearing the sound of "ringing ears."[54] Ruscelli also discussed the many uses of *aqua celestiale,* an herbal water of distilled spices, herbs, and flowers, and recommended how "one drop in the ears in the morning or evening" would heal "every pain and infirmity of the ears and thus also the worms and vermin that are born in the ear."[55] Castore Durante's *New Herbarium* likewise outlined standard and well-known remedies for a wide variety of bodily ailments. Intricate botanical woodcuts by Isabella Parasole, an accomplished engraver, accompanied the 1602 printing of the *Herbarium*.[56] The text contained remedies for quotidian ear problems like deafness, plugged ears, and earaches, recommending a variety of poultices, herbal liquids, and oils to be placed within the ear. Alongside these were more specific sonic remedies. Durante advised, for example, that "the juice of onions mixed with honey . . . mixed into the ear, removes noise."[57] Similarly, in his 1563 medicinal discourses *On Medicinal Matters,* Pietro Andrea Mattioli listed a number of treatments for "noises that are felt in the ears," advising that "cedar oil inside [the ear . . .] dried ground figs with mustard seed and dissolved with some liquor; honey together with finely ground mineral salt, leek juice with incense, vinegar and milk; hot vinegar boiling so that it smokes and that goes inside the ear."[58] Eugenio Raimondi's 1626 book on hunting and villa management, *On Hunting,* likewise noted well-known recipes, explaining how "the juice of radishes instilled in the ears blocks the winds and the noises of the ears."[59] That same year, Francesco Scarioni da Parma published *An Assembly of Political, Chemical, and Natural Secrets.* The text similarly included a recipe for removing "noises in the ear" and directed readers to "extract juice from leeks, boil with honey, place in the ear."[60] It is notable that prescriptions for removing "noise" often directly accompanied instructions on how to remove "vermin" from the ears, suggesting that health writers understood noise, much like worms, vermin, and pests, as an external force that needed to be cleansed and extracted from the body. Like "vermin," noise infiltrated and entrenched itself within the body with adverse consequences and needed to be purged.

Early modern Italians prescribed, crafted, and administered purgative treatments for "noises in the ear" with a keen awareness of how sonic disruption stood to impact the body and soul. Alongside the daily discomfort caused by conditions like tinnitus and other "noises that are felt in the ears," early modern Italians were concerned about what these "trapped" sounds signaled: a body riddled with noise, ringing, and buzzing was in danger of humoral imbalance and illness, which, as Mercurio made clear, could have cascading consequences throughout the body, including fevers, chills, cooled blood, and other dangerous conditions. Purging the ears of noise and other impurities was thus crucial to maintaining health and regulating the body's senses and humors.

Sometimes health writers volleyed competing claims about sound, hearing, and aural treatments back and forth in an effort to assert their prominence. For example, beginning in 1565 Bartolomeo Traffichetti, a widely published physician active in Rimini and Romagna engaged in a protracted debate with Matteo Bruno, another physician from Rimini. The two authors published lengthy treatises responding to the purported "errors" of the other. In his original 1565 text *The Art of Conserving Health,* Traffichetti explained that because the ear is a dry organ, all medicines placed in the ear to treat aural impurities and to purge noise must also be dry to "conserve [the ear's] natural temperature." This was in keeping with Galenic practice, in which medicinal treatments were meant to correspond with the natural temperature and humidity of the body part under treatment. With this in mind, Traffichetti listed a number of "dry" concoctions that could purge the ears of various ailments and impurities, including noises and vermin. He recommended, for example, one dram of white hellebores and castor oil, and a half dram of saltpeter, and directed users to "mix these powders with vinegar . . . and dissolving them with vinegar then pack it into the ear . . . with cotton padding."[61] In 1569 Matteo Bruno responded with the publication of his *Discourses of M. Matteo Bruno Doctor from Rimini on the Errors Made by the Excellent M. Bartolomeo Traffichetti.* Bruno claimed that Traffichetti had failed to satisfactorily outline the importance of the ear and hearing. He then claimed that Traffichetti's aural medications were dangerous and misguided. He chastised Traffichetti, writing, "if you want to use dry medications for the ears, because they are a dry organ, do not then say that one must wait for the concoction [to take effect] to ascertain its final properties [of dryness or wetness]."[62] This, he suggested, was bad practice, and he accused Traffichetti of essentially encouraging his patients to take the undue risk that the final properties of their aural medicines may not align with the natural state of the ear. Traffichetti, unwilling to allow Bruno the last word, published a follow-up in 1572 responding to Bruno's critiques. He bristled at Bruno's suggestion that he had not satisfactorily explained the critical importance of the ears in preserving bodily health and, somewhat testily, claimed, "If I wanted to show the excellence of hearing, [I need only] say that we need it to improve faith and Christian perfection. . . . You in these certain undue ways of speaking are without any respect and I do not want to give any other answer."[63] He then defended his aural medicines, claiming that when mixed together "medications that are applied to the ears, moisten at first, if they are by their nature dry, but by natural heat they will change to fit [the task] and will dry up."[64] In their debate, each medic sought not only to repudiate the other but also to establish himself as an authority on the body and the environment. Focusing on the senses and sensory organs was a persuasive avenue through which to accomplish this, and it reflects a robust medical and health culture of the period that emphasized the central role of the senses in regulating bodily health. No record of a further response by Bruno has been found, but Traffichetti continued to publish health regimes and medical advice. In 1576, his text *Summary of the Way to Conserve Health in the Time of Pestilence* was published in Bologna. Traffichetti advised his readers again on the importance of aural health and repeated many of the regimes he had first outlined in 1565 and later defended in 1572. In particular, Traffichetti's plague treatise once again reminded readers of the primary importance of "purging the ears" in order to protect the body from plague and illness.[65]

The advice disseminated in health manuals and books of secrets reflects the widely shared medical and bodily culture of the early modern period. Physicians like Bruno, Durante, Mercurio, and Traffichetti claimed exclusive authority for themselves by way of their training and publications. However, the recipes and advice reproduced in their books was often drawn from a collective pool of knowledge about health and the senses. Aural treatments were crafted, adopted, and circulated by a wide variety of agents of health: physicians, agronomists, homemakers, and informal healers. The daily practice of bodily care was much more diverse and collaborative than writers like Mercurio, who promulgated narratives of "professionalization," made it out to be.[66] Moreover, despite their claims to be secret or unique, the aural treatments these texts contained were widely circulated. Moreover, almost all of the ingredients listed in recipes for purging noise from the ears were easily available, affordable, and multipurpose. Leeks, honey, vinegar, milk, and similar items were used to prepare a wide variety of foods and medications and were part of a broader "kitchen table" pharmaceutical culture. These sources therefore provide valuable insight into the everyday ways that Italians attended to their sonic and aural health.

Protecting the Ears: Spiritual Perspectives

While health writers discussed how to purge noise from the ears, spiritual writings implored readers to protect themselves from exposure to bad sounds in the first place and discussed the importance of guarding the ears against spiritually corrupting and sinful sounds. Preachers and theologians made direct links between the body, the senses, and the soul. In Onofrio Zarrabini's 1586 text *On Matter and Predictable Subjects,* the Augustinian priest from Cotignola explained that "just as our body has five senses, there are five windows through which death enters into us, this happens when these windows are not well closed, locked, and guarded with diligence."[67] Sonic health—and, by extension, spiritual health—required shielding the ears and carefully monitoring which sounds entered the body. It was this same logic that led Giacomo Affinati d'Acuto, a Dominican prior in Padua, to encourage his readers to "place a lock on your ears." In D'Acuto's 1601 text *The Speaking Mute,* a dialogue treating scriptural passages on silence, he explained that "there is no doubt that the mouth is like a door, and the lips are the entryway to the heart . . . close the door to your mouth and place a lock on your ears." He warned that unguarded ears and loose lips, like an open door, were "wide open . . . bringing forth many evils and [this] is the cause of infinite disorders."[68] Prescriptive spiritual writers described the body and soul as dangerously susceptible to sensory agitation and ailment. Protecting both body and soul thus required a careful regulation of surrounding sensory stimuli.

But locking or blocking the ears, as Affinati and Zarrabini encouraged, was a difficult task. Sound was amorphous, rippling through space in a manner according to Avicenna and his early modern interpreters, much like when "a stone is thrown in water."[69] Unlike sight and vision, where individuals could close or avert their eyes or, better yet, build physical structures to block sight lines, sound was more difficult to control. Sounds could drift into unwittingly open ears rendering the physical body troublingly permeable. Spiritual writers therefore discussed in detail which sounds to let into the ears and which to block out, advocating for constant aural vigilance. In a 1613 sermon in Florence,

Raffaello delle Colombe, the Dominican prior of Santa Maria Novella who denounced Galileo from the pulpit, preached about the importance of carefully guarding one's ears. Colombe acknowledged the usefulness of medical treatments that could purge unhealthy noises from the ears, noting, for example, a commonly used concoction of saltpeter and vinegar poured into the ears to treat those "who suffer from noise and whistling in the ear," and he noted that when this mix is "dripped into the ear if at first it bites, fizzes, and pinches, those who patiently endure recover and [will] have hearing restored." Yet Colombe went on to claim that these bodily treatments did nothing to soothe and calm the soul from sonic discord and he described how, so often, "the sinner is so stunned by the sounds and din of the world that he does not want to hear the harmony of the word of God." As a solution, Colombe claimed that Christians needed to treat their ears like "seashells, which are always closed except when the morning dawn breaks," and he admonished his listeners to similarly "close your ears to gossiping, flattery, and obscenity" and to only open the ears to godly sounds of prayer, preaching, and sacred music.[70]

In Alessandro Sperelli's 1675 pastoral guide, the bishop of Gubbio similarly discussed the importance of blocking out the sound of gossipers and other illicit utterances. He claimed that parishioners could take cues from the classical story of the *Odyssey,* where the hero Ulysses plugged his ears with wax to block out the sirens' call. Sperelli acknowledged that it was possible, and even useful, "to close up your ears with wax so as not to hear murmurings" and claimed that homemade earplugs served "admirably as an antidote and protection from the poison of many grave sins." Ultimately, however, Sperelli suggested that it was best to actively ignore gossipy murmurings, building up an aural and spiritual fortitude that did not require material aids. Consciously ignoring particular sounds, he argued, provided a "more stable and secure lid with which we must close our ears," and he claimed that the Holy Spirit wanted individuals to surround their ears "with a dense and thorny hedge so that murmuring voices cannot penetrate."[71] Sperelli's advice added to a rich genre of antigossip and anti-slander literature that bemoaned the corrosive nature of unmonitored speech. While Sperelli emphasized protecting the ears, other writers focused on punishing the tongue. Erasmus, for example, stated that "if only pills were made of the pounded tongues of slanderers, so that they might aid by this cure those

whom they harmed by their poison."[72] Antigossip tracts and accompanying fantasies of cutting out or pounding up gossiping tongues were
often deeply misogynistic, framing women as venomous gossips who
were uniquely inclined toward unruly and socially corrosive speech. These
authors complained about how "women sin and go against the laws of
nature . . . by loosening their tongues."[73] In reality, women's oral and aural
networks were crucial to the maintenance of community bonds, neighborhood identities, and the transmission of important information.[74] Nonetheless, silencing the tongue and locking the ears were framed as impera-
tive spiritual exercises, especially for women who were considered both
more susceptible to the ill effects of noise and more likely to spread sinful
sounds. Spiritual manuals thus advocated for a willful rejection of potentially sinful and corruptive sounds and called on imagery of walls, seashells, thorny hedges, and locked doors to describe aural or oral fortitude.
This emphasis on locking, guarding, and blocking the ears had distinctly
gendered implications. As Chapter 4 will explore in more detail, sonic discipline was considered uniquely important for the many girls and women
who lived behind physical walls, gates, and doors in cloistered institutions.
Cloistered residents were thought to be especially vulnerable to sensory
agitation and its negative spiritual implications and the physical walls and
gates that enclosed institutions serve as a rich parallel to the metaphors of
thorny hedges, locked doors, and sealed windows that spiritual writers
and preachers used to describe protected ears.

As an antidote to murmurings, gossip, slander, noise, and racket,
theologians and preachers discussed the formative power of silence. In
Jerónimo Gracián's 1600 text *On the Rule of Discipline,* the Spanish Carmelite and spiritual director to Teresa of Avila (1515–1582), articulated
this belief, writing, "silence enriches the heart, purifies the conscience, il-
luminates the spirit, clears the internal body, conserves virtues, generates
humility, and is the first of innumerable goods."[75] Like medical and health
writers of the period, Gracián depicted a porous body that was deeply
affected by sound, noise, and silence and inextricably linked to the
soul. Moreover, he made direct links between silence, the body, and
"virtue." Similar calls for silence and quiet were an important element
of broader Catholic reform. Tridentine decrees (1545–1563) called for
a new emphasis on sonic comportment, banning "profane conversations;
all walking about, noise, and clamor" during church services.[76] These

regulations built on the decrees of earlier assemblies like a 1336 synod in Trent that had ordered church services to "be conducted daily in the said church with dignity, solemnity, and devotion, without any chatting or laughter."[77] Efforts to halt shouting, clamor, and general inattentiveness during sacred rituals continued well into the seventeenth century. The 1619 Florentine Synod once again echoed earlier Tridentine concerns by proclaiming that "all those who go into churches during mass and while celebrating the divine offices to talk with a loud voice . . . or to do anything that gives great scandal, and those who disturb the divine offices, or are dishonest with women, will suffer the penalty of our arbitration."[78] Religious calls for silence and "active listening" were also linked to the broader notions of bodily and sensory comportment that developed in the early modern period, and the emergence of what Andrew Dell'Antonio terms an "elite discourse on listening."[79] Early modern Italians were increasingly encouraged to display their respectability by way of carefully regulated sonic behaviors.[80] Silence and quiet were associated with bodily and social piety, but also with class status and the hazy concept of "decorum." Religious edicts that sought to enforce quiet and silence fused with broader cultural shifts and emerging notions of *civilitas* (civility) so that "religious discipline became the civil discipline of society from the medieval to modern age."[81] By performing sonic decorum, guarding the ears, and surrounding themselves with quiet and silence, Italians enacted entwined notions of health, piety, and social status. It was this type of thinking that prompted writers like Leandro Bovanini and Agostino Gallo to critique the noisy working poor and for Bovanini to disparage those who went "around with a noisy tongue, cawing, croaking and clamoring for air, filling it with nuisance and tedium."[82]

In Florence, calls for quiet and silence were also uniquely linked to the city's rich history of rousing preachers that stretched back to the Observant Movement of the fourteenth and fifteenth centuries. Saint Antoninus (1389–1459), the charismatic fifteenth-century archbishop of Florence, had outlined a dualistic sonic framework in his 1472 posthumously printed confessional manual. Antoninus warned that "you have language for three reasons, first to praise God. . . . Second, to ask and speak of your needs. Third, to instruct pupils with words . . . every other manner of speaking is vain and sinful."[83] Antoninus's warning also applied to

hearing: sounds that did not praise God, express genuine need, or instruct
were dangerous and sinful, worming their way into vulnerable ears much
like the vermin referenced in later health manuals.[84] Religious exhortations about the importance of aural discipline reached new highs later in
the fifteenth century when Florence was gripped by the Savonarolan
movement. Fra Girolamo Savonarola (1452–1498), prior of the Dominican San Marco monastery, briefly seized political and religious control
of Florence when he and his fervent followers sought to establish Florence as the "New Jerusalem." The apocalyptic preacher attracted large
crowds with his fiery sermons and many Tuscans were drawn to his critiques of corruption, gambling, sex work, and other "vanities." In his sermons Savonarola railed against the noisy chaos that so often disrupted
church services, and in a 1495 sermon he outlined new protocols to enforce silence in churches, anticipating reforms that were later issued by
Tridentine reformers.[85] A key element of Savonarola's vision was reform
of Tuscan monasteries and convents. He denounced the comforts and
"worldliness" he claimed had taken root in many religious houses
and preached about the need for spiritual renewal and strict reform. A
1545 printing of Savonarola's sermons included one in which he had disparaged those Christians who "give themselves to all sensual pleasures"
and claimed that nuns and monks in particular "spoiled" religious houses
with their incessant "talking and jabbering." Savonarola went on to claim
that "nuns must remain in silence and solitude because silence is the
father and solitude the mother and when these two couple together, they
generate and give birth to their daughter named prayer and contemplation."[86] Like reformers before and after him, Savonarola identified sound
as a potent actor that shaped both body and soul and was directly linked
to gendered and spiritual purity. Savonarola's rule came to an abrupt halt
in 1498 when he was executed in Florence's Piazza della Signoria.[87] But
the Savonarolan movement had a lasting impact, particularly on women's
spirituality, well into the sixteenth century. Many "Savonarolan sympa-
thizers" streamed into Tuscan nunneries after his death and held to the
reforming zeal he had preached, including the push for pious silence.[88] In
early modern Italy, prescriptive spiritual writings, the decrees of Trent,
local synods, and the lasting influence of charismatic preachers like Colombe and Savonarola coalesced to produce a particular spiritual emphasis on aural discipline and carefully guarded ears.

Despite these repeated calls for quiet and silence, both before and after the Council of Trent, sacred spaces were often noisy. For example, a 1482 contract for singers hired at Florence's San Giovanni church warned the singers to not "make scandal or noise either by speaking or by laughing, under penalty of two soldi for each offence, and for every time."[89] In 1547 the patrician Florentine, Pier Francesco Riccio, wrote a letter to Duke Cosimo I on behalf of the priests at the Cathedral of Santa Maria del Fiore. Riccio implored the duke to take action against a group of noisy troublemakers who had burst into the cathedral stomping their feet, shouting, and making so much clamor that the matins service was canceled.[90] Loud socializing or fighting during church services was by no means unique to Florence. A 1583 chronicle recounted how the bishop of Modena had "ordered that in the cathedral polyphony will not be sung, but instead plainchant, because the priests were indolent and chatted while the singers sang."[91] According to the bishop, polyphonic singing produced troublingly complex soundscapes that allowed parishioners and priests alike opportunities to chat, adding noise to the already layered soundscape that melodic singing created. The bishop's attempt to enforce plainchant aimed to simplify the soundscape, to render it singular, thus making it easier to monitor. In reality, liturgical Tridentine reforms were, at best, sporadically enforced. Nonetheless, persistent calls for quiet and silence and complaints about noise in sacred spaces reveal yet again how idealized sonic decorum was increasingly framed as an important element of Catholic reform.

Italian medical, health, and spiritual writers repeatedly acknowledged the power of sound. Sounds, both healthy and unhealthy, pious and sinful, were thought to physically penetrate the body and to profoundly impact the soul. Sound could purify or pollute the air, heal or harm the body, and fundamentally shape urban and rural experience. Scientific and medical theories about hearing prompted heightened concerns about the corrosive effects of noise, and medical manuals implored readers to purge and protect their ears from sonic impurities. Medical and spiritual writers alike emphasized the importance of sonic regulation and offered a robust portfolio of sonic health practices. Moreover, Italians devoted careful attention to classifying and monitoring the sounds that surrounded them and cataloged the various effects of chirping, ringing, cracking artillery, music, shouting, gossiping, noise, quiet, and silence. Chapter 4 returns to Florence's cloistered communities to consider how sonic regulation was particularly important in and around enclosures for girls and women. Institutional, ecclesiastical, and civic authorities all understood that monitoring the oral and aural experiences of girls and women was crucial to maintaining their health, piety, and purity. In contrast to the "curses . . . scorns, resentments, the many frenzies . . . brawls . . . sighs, sobs . . . screams and screeches of so many who live in the cities of the world," cloistered girls and women were to surround themselves with silence.[92]

CHAPTER FOUR

Silence: Sonic Regulation, Gender, and Reform

*W*HEN THE BISHOP Alessandro Sperelli published a spiritual guide for nuns in the seventeenth century, he made sure to devote ample space to a discussion on the unique importance of silence for women. Sperelli asked, "Do you want to know if a woman is truly good? . . . Her words will be few," and he went on the claim that "silence is the most beautiful ornament of the female sex; indeed, it increases female beauty . . . not only for Christian laywomen but also for brides of Christ."[1] Other Catholic writers similarly discussed the particular importance of silence in cloistered communities. In Domenico Zon's 1615 guide for convent entrants, dedicated to the abbesses of two esteemed Venetian convents, he discussed how every nun must commit herself to the "complete and perfect mortification of her senses." Zon went on to detail how "murmuring, useless and pernicious chattering, and all other distractions of the soul" must be replaced with "sacred silence."[2] For Catholic authorities and institutional officials, silence was not the passive absence of sound but rather a formative agent that was both a privilege and a penance for institutionalized girls and women. Prescriptive writings framed silence as curative and purifying and presented noise as sinful, corrosive, and scandalous. This view, in combination with health writings that emphasized the powerful effects of sound on the body and the particularly porous nature of the female body, resulted in a unique emphasis on sonic regulation in and around communities of girls and women.

Officials faced two key challenges in the pursuit of quiet and silence, however. First was monitoring the sounds institutionalized residents made. Early modern Catholic authorities encouraged new modes of sonic comportment, and through a series of church edicts, decrees, and institutional regulations aimed to curate cloister soundscapes to prioritize quiet and silence. While some enclosed residents embraced silence as a necessary spiritual privilege, many others willfully or inadvertently ignored these rules and found the sonic regimes they encountered in institutions oppressive and untenable. Despite repeated exhortations about the necessity of silence, cloistered girls and women often lived loudly as they chatted, laughed, sang, cried, fought, and shouted. A second challenge was regulating the sounds cloistered residents heard. As we have seen in previous chapters, halting the sounds from nearby streets, squares, and homes from penetrating institutions was easier said than done.

This chapter examines how ecclesiastical, institutional, and civic authorities worked to regulate the sounds cloistered girls and women both made and heard. To begin, I consider in more detail the distinctly gendered meanings associated with silence in Florentine reform houses, charities, and nunneries. Institutional mandates and prescriptive writers expanded on the broadly held early modern focus on sonic regulation to argue that silence was particularly crucial for the cultivation and preservation of feminine honor. These writers drew on long-standing spiritual scripts and monastic traditions to claim that silence was uniquely necessary for both the recovery of sexual honor and the maintenance of gendered piety. However, these sonic ideals were often disrupted by a noisier reality in which cloistered girls and women ignored or subverted sonic rules. Church and civic documents contained repeated exhortations on the importance of quiet and repeatedly expressed annoyance at the chatter and clatter enclosed women made on a day-to-day basis. Examining these records provides a more nuanced view of the internal soundscapes in cloistered spaces. Next, this chapter examines institutional architecture and its role in both ensuring and subverting sonic and sensory regulation. Architecture was increasingly conceptualized as a sonic barrier, and enclosure authorities identified windows, walls, doors, and gates as precarious sites of sonic porosity that required careful design, maintenance, and attention. Yet visitation records from throughout Tuscany reveal how many enclosures shared thin walls with neighboring houses; had gardens that were easily accessible to outsiders; were surrounded by taller buildings with open windows that looked directly into institutional spaces; and had crumbling walls, gates, and doors that were barely monitored. Many authorities expressed urgent concerns about these architectural weaknesses and discussed how sounds, sights, and smells flowed freely in and out of poorly constructed buildings, threatening the integrity of the built structure and its soundscape. Officials responded, in part, by attempting to repair, renovate, and expand cloister architecture in the hopes of blocking unsanctioned sounds and other sensory stimuli from passing in and out of these spaces.

Civic authorities, for their part, responded by enacting laws that aimed to carefully regulate the sounds Florentines made near women's institutions. The final part of this chapter considers an expanding corpus of secular legislation that emerged from roughly the mid-sixteenth century on and that coalesced with the ecclesiastical and institutional pursuit of quiet and silence. These civic regulations were an important element of centralizing Medici urban governance and were linked to the city's shifting political and legal character. In particular, secular legislation articulated new spatial and social boundaries around girls' and women's institutions that aimed to combat perceived noise pollution throughout the city, marking gendered enclosures as key sites of sensory discipline for the broader urban population. Most often this was an ad hoc and reactive process. Civic magistrates responded to the city's continually unfolding soundscape with regulatory efforts that sought to order space, sense, and sociability in distinctly gendered ways. Sonic legislation reveals how the urban soundscape, in both its idealized and everyday forms, was uniquely shaped by the city's many communities of girls and women.

Sacred Silence and Feminine Honor

In the noisy city, silence was a potent marker that distinguished sacred from profane space. It was by way of this sonic dualism that institutional and church authorities aimed to distinguish the cloistered from the non-cloistered, the reformed from the unreformed, and the pious from the impious. The links between silence, gender, reform, and spiritual renewal were explored by the Dominican prior Giacomo Affinati D'Acuto in his 1601 discourse on silence, *The Speaking Mute*. When discussing penitent sex workers, such as the many women who lived in the Convertite and Malmaritate, Affinati wrote, "What is a prostitute if not a sinful soul who has broken faith with God?" He explained the "three things that every sinful penitent soul must do in order to achieve pardon: sit, be silent, and enter into the darkness." He advised sex workers to "retreat with a sweet silence to a solitary place, far from the worldly clamor. Second, one must be silent, to not speak of worldly things." Affinati also drew on biblical and hagiographical motifs to further claim that repentant sex workers ought to enter into "the caves, the horrid deserts . . . sequestered from human interaction."[3] The desert landscape emerged in such spiritual writings as a curative "sensescape" that many urban institutions sought to emulate. Christian writings had framed the desert wilderness as a purifying eremitic space since antiquity.[4] Early Christian saints like Mary of Egypt and the Desert Fathers were said to have retreated to the desert as an act of asceticism, living in caves, mortifying the flesh, facing demons, and ultimately finding spiritual abundance in this sparse, desolate space.

Saint Mary Magdalene, the most common patron saint for women's reform houses and custodial institutions, was upheld as the ideal reformed sex worker and sensory ascetic. Popular medieval and early modern legends surrounding the Magdalene claimed that she had retreated to the desert wilderness in solitude for thirty years to purify herself.[5] The Malmaritate's 1582 book of governance thus opened with a block print of the penitent Magdalene praying in the wilderness. Images of the Magdalene regularly appear in Florence's Convertite records, and Sandro Botticelli's *Pala delle Convertite* hung in the convent church. The painting depicts a penitent Magdalene, patron saint of the Convertite, alongside Saint John, the patron saint of Florence. Botticelli's Magdalene is gaunt and ascetic, and the surrounding landscape is desolate and desertlike, evoking the legends associated with Mary Magdalene. This was the spiritual script repentant Tuscan women were meant to emulate in their penitential practices—a script marked by isolation, retreat, and silence (see Figures 4.1–4.3). Desert legends likewise inspired Pistoia's Convertite

Figure 4.1. Penitent Mary Magdalene praying in the wilderness, frontispiece of a Malmaritate book of regulations: *Sommario de capitoli della venerabile Compagnia di Santa Maria Maddalena sopra le Mal Maritate* (Florence: Bartholomeo Sermartelli, 1583).

Figure 4.2. Penitent Mary Magdalene. Image in Convertite convent records, Florence.
Courtesy of the Ministerio della Cultura della Repubblica Italiana/Archivio di Stato di Firenze.

convent to stipulate that all entrants were required to "purge the heart of all sensual and worldly affection" and that just as Magdalene had fled to the wilderness, so too would the Franciscan nuns of Pistoia's Convertite "retreat to the solitude of the holy religion in this convent dedicated to that Saint [Magdalene] for no other aim but to do penance as is required for your wicked past lives."[6]

But institutional authorities faced a crucial dilemma in their quest to provide this purifying regime of gendered eremitic solitude: how to re-create the reforming and purifying conditions of the early Christian desert within the crowded urban environments of the early modern Italian city. Increasingly, idealized soundscapes stood in for imagined landscapes. In particular, soundscapes of silence aimed to foster internal reform just as the harsh desert landscapes described in Christian hagiographies facili-tated Christian asceticism. The hundreds of women living in Convertite

Figure 4.3. Sandro Botticelli, *Trinity with Saint Mary Magdalene and Saint John the Baptist,* ca. 1491–1494. Courtauld Gallery / Samuel Courtauld Trust, London.

convents and civic reform homes like the Malmaritate were unable to flee the city as Magdalene was believed to have done or, as Affinati encouraged, to go into "the darkness . . . the caves, the horrid desert." But they could participate, or be forced to participate, in the same Christian narratives of redemption and spiritual renewal through enforced silence and strict cloistering, allowing them to flee "worldly clamor" and "purge the heart." Carefully controlled soundscapes of quiet and silence, in both civic and ecclesiastical institutions, thus functioned much like the desert landscapes of the Christian imagination: purging, purifying, and reforming both body and soul. Re-creating the Christian desert in the city, and within institutions, involved imbuing the institutional soundscape with the qualities of these imagined sacred landscapes. Women's cloisters were therefore designed to be bastions of sonic solitude, linking space, sound, and gender together in meaningful ways.

Similar concerns prevailed in the city's many nunneries. The 1619 Florentine Synod, which aimed to enforce Tridentine decrees more fully, published a series of edicts specific to nunneries and highlighted the need for the "good governance of those virgins who are dedicated to the service of God in sacred cloisters."[7] Alongside rules stipulating that nuns' cells should be inspected yearly for any "superfluous" items, the synod also sought to carefully regulate nuns' vocalizations and auditory experiences. When in choir, for example, nuns were banned from making "indecent music and songs, laughter, joking, and anything that is not appropriate."[8] Nuns were also forbidden to "sing or play music in such a manner that they can be heard by laypeople except when saying the divine office" and were warned that "they should only sing sacred motets in Latin, not in Italian."[9] The synod likewise stipulated that when taking the habit and professing their vows, women should undergo the sacred ritual in silence and without them or any audience members creating "tumult or noise"; it also warned that cloistered women were not allowed to speak with anyone at the institutional gate, under the threat of severe penalties.[10] Those who had permission to speak with visitors at the parlor grate had to do so under the careful supervision of the *ascoltatrice*, "who always stays close enough to be able to hear what it said." Nuns who disobeyed this rule were barred access to the grate for three months and forced to subsist only on bread and water for three days.[11]

In diverse institutional contexts, an emphasis on quiet and silence served to create the ideal conditions for girls and women to achieve a level of inwardness and interiority that was thought to bolster individual devotion and deepen pious contemplation.[12] Beyond the individual, silence also functioned to foster "a sense of communal unity" as women from diverse backgrounds came together, or were brought together, to share and preserve silence as part of an ongoing sensory and spiritual project.[13] In this context "silence thus shifts from being something that stops action—a silencer, a structural articulator or a frame—to being the main canvas . . . a primary agent in the narrative while sounds interact over its surface."[14] Silence and quiet were increasingly framed as key features of idealized devotional spaces in both domestic and institutional settings.

For example, in Federico Fregoso's 1543 treatise on prayer, the reforming cardinal focused on domestic devotions, encouraging his readers to pray in private, silent, and even secret places "where vanity, hypocrisy and the titillations of worldly glory cannot enter." Fregoso and many other writers advocated for silent mental prayer in quiet spaces rather than verbal or communal prayer, a recommendation that contributed to changing patterns of domestic devotion through which individuals increasingly prayed alone in bedchambers and with a variety of material aids designed to foster the silent interiority that religious authorities increasingly advocated for.[15] Similarly, in institutional settings a focus on interiority, quiet, and privacy encouraged architectural choices that were "designed to efface, hide, enclose and silence," a topic explored in more detail below.[16] In early modern Florence and Tuscany, the devotional motives that undergirded the pursuit of silence fused with specific institutional mandates of sexual reform and gendered care to promote a particular emphasis on sonic regulation. Enclosed communities and their various authorities strove to create gendered spaces filled with "a sweet silence."[17]

Noisy Nuns and Loud Neighbors

Issuing sonic regulations may have been fairly straightforward, but enforcing these rules proved much more difficult. Many girls and women simply ignored sonic regulations or found the requirement of near perpetual silence unbearable.[18] Ecclesiastical records from throughout Tuscany abound with complaints about women religious who loudly shouted, joked, laughed, and shrieked, and, in the words of convent visitors, broke the cloister silence with "filthy and dishonest words."[19] Others invited their young relatives into the convent or transgressed the cloister by going out and visiting with children.[20] These boys and girls were notoriously loud, producing the same soundscapes that vexed the Orbatello authorities, who complained about how noisy children disturbed institutional "quiet and modesty."[21] The repetitive articulation of rules that forbade chattering, laughing, secular songs, and music suggest that, in fact, enclosed girls and women regularly engaged in these behaviors and that idealized sonic regimes were far from universally applied. It was perhaps frustration at this reality that had lead the fifteenth-century Abbess Scholastica, of Le Murate, to be "vigilant in every regular observance, but especially in the requirement that silence be maintained at all times." In an effort to maintain silence, Abbess Scholastica would lock nuns in their cells in the evening then sneak out of her own cell "by way of that window under the new dormitory stair, using a ladder, and she would go everywhere to see who was talking."[22] Prowling the monastery halls at night, the abbess sought to halt any whispers, late-night chatting, or other utterances that threatened to disrupt the silence she was tasked with preserving. Despite her best efforts, an examination of diverse institutional records reveals that Abbess Scholastica and most other authorities were usually unsuccessful in maintaining perpetual silence.

A detailed investigation from 1571 at the Augustinian convent of Beata Christiana di Santa Croce in Val d'Arno provides a richly detailed account of the sounds that often reverberated throughout cloistered communities. Over the course of July and August, officials from the diocese of Lucca interrogated the nuns, who lived "under the dominion of the grand duke of Tuscany."[23] Of pressing concern were accusations that the convent was in moral free fall, in large part because the Abbess, Suor Ludovica, allegedly made no attempt to enforce the cloister; allowed tensions to fester among the nuns; invited male relatives to eat, sing, dance, and play music in private cells; and regularly allowed men and women of poor repute into the nunnery. Accusations against the confessor similarly claimed that he spent all day chatting and drinking with the nuns and was a poor spiritual guide. Individual nuns and clerics testified to these claims under oath. The vicar claimed he had been assigned to the convent church eight months earlier, only to find its governance was "very bad . . . and likewise I found the cloister was barely observed," a situation that he blamed on the abbess.[24] When questioned "as to whether disorders and disputes among the nuns had arisen in his time in the monastery, and whether other disorders could be found," he described how the previous December nuns had physically fought and shouted at each other in the choir and how Suor Filippa had hurled "injurious words" at Suor Nannina, causing a fight to break out among many of the nuns.[25] He claimed that "when mass is celebrated, the nuns who are there to listen do not keep silent and instead chatter so much and stand about with so little reverence that many, according to my understanding, do not even hear the mass."[26] During celebration of the divine office he similarly claimed that the nuns "stand with such little reverence and devotion and lack of silence, because while one choir sings the others chatter so loudly that it can be heard in the exterior church."[27] Many nuns agreed with these general sentiments. Suor Prudentia testified that "the greatest disorder that I know of in our convent is that the nuns speak very dishonestly, saying words to each other that are filthy and dishonest and are not good even for a prostitute to say, let alone a nun."[28] But Prudentia asserted that she had always known the abbess "to be a good woman and useful for the governance of the house" and claimed that the issues lay primarily with the confessor, "who has never satisfied me in confession and communion and I dislike how he stands at the *ruota* (a turning wheel used to move goods in and out of the cloister) chatting with the nuns so much during confession and at other times."[29] Suor Petronilla, for her part, testified that "a few days ago there were certain words exchanged between Suor Nannina and Suor Eugenia" that then escalated into "such a great uproar that many of the nuns and Suor Niesa ran to ring the bells in alarm to stop the noise."[30] Suor Niesa did not mention this incident while under oath, and instead railed against the abbess claiming that "a short time ago the abbess brought one of her 16- or 18-year-old nephews into the convent, and I heard that they made music and danced in the little church near the garden."[31]

The testimony of Suor Monica corroborated others' claims that it was, in fact, the confessor who was primarily to blame for disorders that gripped the community. She claimed that "the chaplain and confessor is doing very badly and stays at the grate all day with Suor Nannina and Suor Aurelia, chatting and drinking . . . I have seen them bring drinks and *buccellati* [Lucchese sweet breads] and they do nothing but commit evil . . . and I beg your Lordship to remove him from here if you want this convent to be in peace."[32] Other nuns, however, simply denied all accusations of disorder. Suor Brigida stated that "it seems to me that our convent is temporally and spiritually well governed, and I say that the abbess is my sister and in truth it pleases God that before she became abbess the nunnery was so well governed and at present I know nothing of any disorder."[33] Brigida was quick to follow up and say that if there were, in fact, any problems, they were the fault of the confessor and not the abbess. Suor Nannina, who was at the center of so many accusations, outright denied chatting, drinking, and eating cakes with the confessor but did claim that the gardener and greengrocer who came to work in the cloister garden was "a good man but I have heard from many that he is scandalous and has little respect and uses bad language."[34] A young nun named Suor Maria Angela, likely apprehensive at being interrogated by church officials, hoped to avoid being drawn into the controversy and stated, "I am a girl who was a secularist for six years and have been a nun for six more years in the convent." She claimed that, as such, "there is little that I know . . . I have not seen any disorders aside from the words and shouting between some nuns . . . which, like a girl, I flee from so as not to hear them."[35]

Abbess Ludovica gave her testimony after all of the other nuns had been interviewed. She explained that she had been abbess for the past eighteen years and confirmed that "while the divine offices were being celebrated no one observes the proper silence and they stand around with little reverence and some, if called, go over to whoever calls for them."[36] She also said it was true that "in the refectory the nuns eat together, but with little observance of silence."[37] But Abbess Ludovica pushed back at accusations that this noisy reality was solely the result of her poor management. She claimed that it was impossible for her to be everywhere at once and to monitor every exchange and movement, noting, for example, that "most of the nuns come to hear mass in the church but another part go to the oratory where I was unable to see everything because I was in the church."[38] Fights, shouts, chatter, and screams that broke out beyond her purview could hardly be considered her fault, she argued, but she did suggest that "in my opinion it would be good if all the nuns came to hear mass in the church so that I could see [and hear] them all."[39] The abbess said that much of the chaos in the nunnery could be pinned on a few bad apples and stated that "in our monastery there are presently no nuns of bad reputation, *mala fama,* except Suor Stefana, who has always been vicious and scandalous, and there are also some who are not very obedient and have a wicked tongue. . . . Those who have a particularly wicked tongue are Suor Illaria, Suor Lucia, Suor Filippa and Suor Giulia."[40] The abbess was also keen to express her distain for the confessor, saying, "I consider him of little good and scandalous," and she noted that despite Suor Nannina's denials the fact remained that he had "a particular and close friendship with Suor Nannina and Suor Aurelia and is not ashamed to stay all day with them and leaves the *ruota* at one or two in the morning after chatting and whispering with them."[41]

After a lengthy investigation, convent visitors summarized their findings and made a series of recommendations. They confirmed the "great disorder and discord in this convent" and stipulated that in the future the cloister needed to be strictly enforced, with no outsiders coming and going.[42] They also discussed how the nuns needed to "live with greater fear of God and religiosity than they previously have."[43] Alongside reiterating regulations about who could speak to nuns at the parlor grate and under what circumstances, the visitation report also recommended posting a series of written notices throughout the nunnery to explicitly remind the community of these rules. They also stated that going forward, whoever used "injurious or dishonest words" would be "castigated severely" and warned that no nun was to "say injurious words, to scream, or get in altercations nor replicate any of the words or deeds discovered here" and instead were required "to live quietly, with the fear of God, and to obey the abbess."[44] It is unclear how successfully these reforms were implemented or with what rigor the abbess and other authorities worked to enforce quiet and silence after the inspectors left. Above all, the visitation report reveals the void that could separate sonic ideals and sonic realities in cloistered communities.

While the "wicked tongues" at Beata Christiana di Santa Croce drew the attention of church authorities, they were far from unique. The shouting, fighting, and chatter referenced in the visitation report may have been more sustained than in some other communities, but throughout Tuscany nuns and enclosed residents regularly flouted rules of silence. This was particularly the case when forcibly cloistered women loudly resisted their enclosure. Church authorities stipulated that women taking the habit were to undergo the sacred ritual without causing "tumult or noise" and that after formalizing their vows they were to maintain a "sacred silence."[45] But forcibly enclosed girls and women often cried, shouted, and screamed in protest or to express their grief at being enclosed. For example, in 1578 Ginevra di Baccio Perini was placed inside Florence's Le Murate monastery with the hope that she would become a nun. Ginevra was a religious seer whose visions and prophecies had drawn the attention of Grand Duke Francesco I, who, impressed by her spiritual abilities, worked to make her transition into the monastery as comfortable as possible. He gave Le Murate 400 scudi to cover her expenses, provided her with separate living chambers complete with "all the conveniences and necessities possible for a woman's habitation," and even gave permission for Ginevra to come and go from the institution for an initial period, offering

her a flexible cloister that would ease her transition into monastic life.[46]
Ginevra, however, was unwilling to accept this arrangement and had no
true monastic vocation and no desire to live a permanently cloistered life.
She thus held little regard for the monastery's rules, and particularly not
the rule of silence. Sister Giustina Niccolini, author of the Le Murate
chronicle, testily recorded how Ginevra "could neither enjoy the benefits of
this arrangement nor accommodate herself to the religious life" and described how she "deprived everyone of quiet ... tormenting both herself
and us." Over the course of nine months Ginevra's torments, which perhaps included shouting, crying, angry outbursts, willful transgressions of
the cloister, and a rejection of the regime of silence, gripped the nunnery as
she "mocked ... the advantages provided her."[47] Eventually Ginevra's noisy
protests were successful and she was allowed to leave Le Murate, moving
into a house with the support of the grand duke.

A similar despair at being forcibly enclosed sometimes lead other
cloistered women to flee their institutions, but most did not have Ginerva's influence that allowed her to leave Le Murate without severe punishment and even with ducal consent. In 1562 Sandrina da Pistoia was
imprisoned for two years in the Stinche prison for having scaled the
Convertite walls to escape the convent with two other women whom she
was accused of "contaminating" with her plot to escape.[48] A man named
Giovanni Betti was imprisoned on suspicion of acting as an accomplice in
Sandrina's plan and organizing her escape from the outside, though he
claimed he had merely sent his servant Maria to deliver some cherries and
artichokes to Sandrina prior to her escape—a meeting, he claimed, that
had nothing to do with helping her escape from the Convertite.[49] It was
precisely these types of potentially illicit conversations and meetings that
institutional authorities sought to halt by demanding that all encounters
be monitored by the alert ears of an *ascoltatrice*. Sonic regulations prioritized silence and quiet, but also stipulated that any sanctioned vocalizations be closely monitored to avoid disruptions within the institution.

Other sonic transgressions were even more scandalous. In 1559 Andrea Mancinelli, prior of the Orbatello, wrote a letter to the duke reporting
how one of the resident widows could regularly hear two women living
in the apartment below her loudly entertaining men in their room, despite cloister rules that strictly forbade men from entering the community. After further investigation, the women and their guests were caught

"kissing and touching each other dishonestly." To make matters worse, the men were Franciscan friars who had taken vows of chastity. The friars entered the Orbatello "under the guise of giving the women news of their relatives," and Mancinelli described how "if they had not been discovered by the other widow who lives above them, the women may have proceeded further with these men." The prior requested permission to place the apprehended women in the pillory for a morning as "a spectacle to all the other women" and to then "confine them outside of the Orbatello."[50] The ducal office agreed and recommended that Mancinelli report the friars to their superior, who would determine what penalties the men would face. Mancinelli's report hints at the complex social dynamics that prevailed in many institutions. Perhaps the unnamed woman who reported the scandalous affair had been listening to her neighbors for months or even years and had finally had enough of her noisy neighbors. Perhaps there were other resentments at play that prompted her to approach the prior with this information. Perhaps she was genuinely scandalized. Whatever her reasons, the incident reveals the importance of "earwitnessing" in cloistered communities.[51] Alongside oft-repeated rules of silence, institutional authorities relied on rank-and-file residents, as well as *ascoltatrici,* to listen carefully to the institutional soundscape and to report any sonic or social transgressions. This aural vigilance was crucial in monitoring the behaviors of enclosed girls and women and, from the perspective of institutional authorities, to maintaining institutional order. Yet despite the many decrees and regulations issued during this period, institutionalized girls and women regularly broke the silence in their institutions. The shouts, chatter, singing, crying, and sounds of socializing that alarmed institutional authorities reveals the complicated personal and communal experiences of institutionalization and the diverse reactions girls and women had to strict enclosure. Ultimately, regulating the sounds enclosed residents made was easier said than done, and often women's communities were not filled with the sweet silence that authorities strove to attain.

Sound and Space: Doors, Windows, and Walls

Institutional and church authorities also faced persistent challenges ensuring that cloister architecture was sufficiently robust to act as a sonic

barrier—halting any unsanctioned sounds from seeping in or out of institutions. Many enclosures had thin walls, open windows, flimsy doors,
and crumbling structures that eroded efforts at complete sonic enclosure
and meant that sounds flowed in and out of institutions relatively freely.
For example, a 1509 visitation to the San Dalmazio monastery in Volt-
erra had recounted how the Tuscan nuns and their neighbors could easily
hear each other. The visitor's report anxiously noted how "the nuns are
heard and can hear every little word that they [in the neighboring house]
say." In particular, the visitor expressed concern about how most of the
nuns' cells shared a wall with the neighboring house and described how
the wall was "very thin, with windows that meet the garden," allowing
sounds to easily pass through.[52] Issues of sonic permeability and insufficient architecture had long been a point of contention for church authorities. In the fifteenth century, before the Le Murate community moved
into a fortresslike complex near Florence's eastern city walls, the small
community of women had lived in a hermitage on the Rubaconte Bridge,
a busy thoroughfare. By 1424 the women were facing mounting pressure
to leave their home on the bridge and move into a fully walled, and quiet,
environment under direct ecclesiastical authority. The women resisted
and asserted their intention to stay living on the bridge as a largely self-
governed community. In 1424 Dom Gomezio, abbot of the Badia Fiorentina, expressed his frustration at the situation, claiming, "These women
are in the mouths of wolves as regards [to] their bodies, and, as far as their
souls are concerned, in the jaws of Satan." Gomezio continued to bemoan
the "scandal" that resulted from women living "in such a place, where a
person cannot so much as pass by without them hearing," and asked, "Is
the noise and uproar of the people who continually pass there not certain to be a disturbance to their every devotion?"[53] After Gomezio's
alarmist rhetoric, the women eventually bowed to ecclesiastical pressure
and moved into the Le Murate complex, far from the bustling bridge and
its vibrant soundscape. Sonic enclosure framed and facilitated the community's transition from unmonitored to monitored and was central in
church efforts to bring the community of women under direct ecclesiastical supervision. Noise marked a lack of enclosure, while quiet and silence
were presented as evidence of successful cloistering.

   Concerns about sonic enclosure and insufficient architecture became
even more acute during the sixteenth and seventeenth centuries as part

of the Tridentine focus on cloister reform. Tridentine decrees published
in 1564 proclaimed "that the enclosure of nuns be carefully restored,
wheresoever it has been violated, and that it be preserved, wheresoever it
has not been violated."[54] While the decree did not explicitly reference sonic
enclosure, many reformers understood this to be centrally important.
Moreover, the exponential growth of convent populations during this period meant that many institutions had record high populations that
pushed enclosures to the very brink of their capacity limits, an issue
compounded by the fact that many communities needed substantial renovations and refurbishments to bring them in line with Tridentine require-
ments. In 1589 the reforming Roman cardinal, Michele Bonelli, wrote to
the archbishop of Florence, Alessandro de' Medici, then resident in France,
to discuss the "augmented [numbers of] entrants" in nunneries and the
practical problems this posed. Cardinal Bonelli was clear that overcrowded
institutions filled with many unwillingly enclosed girls and women resulted in "the many disorders of nuns and convents and in particular the
nonobservance of the cloister so that it is almost universally violated."[55]
This included the shouts, laughter, secular music, and other unsanctioned
vocalizations that alarmed church authorities. Bonelli noted that Tuscan
nunneries needed to discriminate more carefully whom they accepted to
halt the widespread practice of forced enclosure that resulted in overcrowded institutions with dysfunctional cloisters. In a 1601 letter, Archbishop Alessandro de' Medici likewise discussed the importance of strict
cloistering but focused more explicitly on the architectural weaknesses
that plagued many cloisters. The archbishop outlined the various types of
structural problems convent visitors ought to look for when physically in-
specting women's institutions. He wrote, "I have also in visits had an eye to
check through the convent that there are no holes through which from
the church or from the outside," and he warned how cracks in walls "are
very dangerous, even if they are very small."[56] The archbishop was perhaps
primarily concerned about how crumbling or cracked walls allowed nuns
to pass notes to the outside or allowed outsiders to see into institutions,
but sounds also moved through these cracks, blurring any separation between institutions and the surrounding soundscape.

Indeed, ecclesiastical reports from throughout Tuscany often expressed urgent concern about sounds that drifted into unprotected gardens, through interior walls, out open windows, and over the crumbling

or cracked outer walls of many nunneries.[57] A series of letters sent from the Podestà in Prato to ecclesiastical authorities in Florence in 1551 described how the Dominican nuns of San Vincenzo in Prato were scandalized by a number of windows on the neighboring building that looked directly into their monastery garden. The letters noted how the nuns were easily seen and heard by their neighbors, and vice versa. The convent, which housed Catherine de' Ricci (1522–1590), a Florentine holy woman and Savonarolan sympathizer, considered this a direct threat to their cloister. A convent visitor was dispatched to inspect the situation and confirmed how "the windows lord over the aforementioned [convent] garden"; he encouraged church authorities in Florence "to command on our behalf to Francesco, owner of this [neighboring] house, that by next month in mid-August he will have walled up all the windows that look into the garden of these nuns, all at his own cost."[58] A 1570 letter written by the bishop of Lucca on behalf of the nuns of Castelfranco di Sotto, a small community west of Florence, similarly discussed the nuns' desire to purchase a plot of land adjacent to their convent.[59] The letter explained how a mulberry grove and recently constructed columbarium lorded over the convent's small garden and ground floor, and meant that anyone socializing near the trees or attending to the pigeons in the columbarium could easily see the nuns. Moreover, the bishop noted how "more often than not, because of the gatherings of young men and boys under the mulberry trees, the nuns hear blasphemes and other very scandalous words."[60] The nuns sought ecclesiastical support to offer "a fair price" for purchase of the land, which would allow them to expand their garden and better shield themselves from the intrusive sounds and lurking gaze of youths who gathered in the grove. In this instance, the nuns' exposure to "scandalous words" provided a compelling justification for the convent's expansion and the letter reveals how the pursuit of quiet was central to many of the architectural and spatial issues flagged by cloistered women and ecclesiastical authorities in the Tridentine period.

Other senses were also identified as dangerously penetrative. A series of letters in 1577 and 1578 described the "bad location" of the Santa Maria Nuova monastery in Pescia, noting how it was too close to a busy bridge and a series of troublesome workshops.[61] Most concerning was the fact that a man named Guerra Gelessi and his brothers had purchased a gallery of apartments contiguous to the nunnery from which they were operating a tannery. The pungent smells of tanning seeped directly into the nuns' garden, and according to local officials, "throws such a great stench throughout the convent that the nuns cannot survive."[62] Alongside miasmic airs that were said to be ailing the nuns to the point of death, ecclesiastical visitors and the local vicar, Francesco Strozzi, reported that "what matters most are those neighboring windows, which mean that the nuns cannot go out into their garden without being seen and the windows are also such that one can climb in and out of them with little difficulty."[63] The nuns were so easily accessible to the men who stripped, soaked, and prepared leathers in the neighboring apartments that church authorities alarmingly reported how the tanners could "touch hands and do other problematic things" with the nuns.[64] "In addition to this," the report noted, "there is no manner in which the neighbors can speak so that the nuns do not hear all sorts of words, and more often than not these are dishonest words."[65] The letter concluded by stating that there was "evident danger of great scandal" and the sounds, smells, and sights that circulated freely between the nuns and their neighbors meant it was "as if the nuns are not cloistered" at all.[66] Francesco Strozzi followed up with another letter recommending that the nunnery, with church support, purchase all of the buildings contiguous to the monastery from Gelessi, noting that "there is no other way to secure the cloister."[67] Here again, sensory concerns provided justification for significant institutional expansion.

The struggle to craft impenetrable cloisters only continued as the sixteenth and seventeenth centuries progressed. A 1588 visitation to the recently founded Augustinian convent of Santa Maria del Latte in Montevarchi, part of the Fiesole diocese, reported that when the nuns stood in their garden, they were easily visible to the residents who lived in three homes that shared a wall with the convent. To make matters worse, the report noted how "even more easily these [outsiders] can talk with whomever may be in the garden."[68] The visitation report noted that "in order to resist every scandal" the convent needed to quickly repair its garden walls and issue laws that forbade any outsiders from "going toward or using the walls that hold in the nuns' garden," where they might speak or listen to the nuns.[69] A 1614 letter from the San Paolo convent in Pisa similarly described a neighboring "closed ordinary window correspondent to the garden of the nuns which we do not like."[70] The letter discussed how the window rendered the convent "public" and threatened the integrity of the cloister because of the sounds and sights that easily drifted in and out of the opening. As convent reform was pursued throughout Tuscany, architectural protections were identified as foundational to sonic and sensory enclosure. In many instances, sensory concerns justified a sizable expansion of nunneries and the acquisition of adjacent properties. Much like how nuns in Florence used noise complaints to assert their urban presence and lay claim to the broader neighborhood soundscape, cloistered communities of women throughout Tuscany capitalized on the Tridentine emphasis on strict cloistering and sonic regulation to physically lay claim to surrounding groves, walls, shops, and homes.

Issues of sensory permeability were also a problem in civic institutions in Florence. Although civic houses were not formally bound to the edicts of the Council of Trent, sixteenth- and seventeenth-century lay enclosures likewise took up the task of implementing stricter cloisters and listing the architectural weaknesses that resulted in unmonitored and permeable facilities. In 1543 the Guelf Party identified two problematic apartments "contiguous to the Orbatello from which one could climb into the oratory of the Orbatello."[71] The apartments allowed outsiders to sneak into the institution, and Orbatello residents were both visible and audible to their neighbors. Officials ordered both points of access into the Orbatello to be blocked off within fifteen days and outlined heavy penalties for occupants of said apartments if they did not comply; the occupants also had to agree to cease any use of gardens that backed directly into the Orbatello.[72] To make matters worse, the Orbatello was continually in need of repairs to maintain its own structures. In 1592, institutional officials requested a meager sum of 400 scudi from the city to fund the "restoration of the Orbatello."[73] The institution planned to use the money to buy, among other things, doors, sills, and stone brackets to repair broken windows and doors and to refortify the outer gate.[74] Several decades later, however, the Orbatello was still in need of substantial work. A 1631 letter to Grand Duke Ferdinando II described how the building needed to be "restored more than ever, but it would be necessary to restore . . . door shutters and windows, and other similar things."[75] The Orbatello's run-down state attests to the limited budgets and overburdened finances many Florentine charities faced. Moreover, reports of dilapidated windows, doors, gates, and clandestine entry points were directly linked to broader concerns about cloistering, sensory enclosure, and institutional order. The Orbatello's structural weaknesses were often listed alongside reports of "the many disorders" that plagued the institution: the men and youths who shouted in the street outside the complex, the younger wards who used street-facing windows to chat with outsiders and to invite visitors in, and the men and women who easily sneaked in and out of the complex, either through neighboring apartments or through the poorly policed outer gate.[76] The crumbling physical structure of the Orbatello was seen as a direct reflection of the institution's lax cloister and of the noisy scandals that took place in and around the complex. Efforts to repair the Orbatello aimed to restore the institution's structural integrity and were also part of a larger effort to establish a strict cloister separating the women and children from the city. It was this same logic that prompted Orbatello officials to propose that younger residents be confined to the inner courtyard apartments, while apartments facing the public street and outer door be allocated to "old and more venerable" widows whom they hoped would "remedy or at least report the disorders."[77] The pursuit of silence had practical spatial implications and sensory isolation was increasingly presented as a prerequisite to successful cloistering and institutional reform.

Concerns about windows and doors as sites of sensory exchange recall the architectural language that spiritual and health writers used to describe how sound pierced the body and soul. Preachers like Onofrio Zarrabini warned that the ears, eyes, nose, and mouth were "windows through which death enters into us," and he discussed the disastrous consequences for both body and soul "when these windows are not well closed, locked, and guarded with diligence."[78] Similarly, the preacher Giacomo Affinati d'Acuto claimed that "there is no doubt that the mouth is like a door" and reminded his readers to "close the door to your mouth and place a lock on your ears."[79] Parallels between the architecture of the individual body and the architecture of the cloister no doubt further propelled efforts to fully enclose institutions and to halt unregulated sounds, smells, and sights from flowing in and out of these enclosures. Sounds that penetrated the cloister, drifting through windows and cracked doors, also penetrated the windows and doors of the body and soul and threatened the spiritual and physical integrity of enclosed communities and of individual girls and women. It was this same logic that lead some cloistered women to describe how they were "greatly disturbed and molested" and "defiled" by the sounds that pierced their institutions.[80] Much like how the bishop Alessandro Sperelli advised pious Catholics to build "a dense and thorny hedge" around their ears "so that murmuring voices cannot penetrate," institutional authorities worked to block up problematic windows, patch cracks in walls, and refortify cloister architecture in an attempt to stop unsanctioned sounds from penetrating or escaping women's institutions.[81] Despite these efforts, however, windows, doorways, courtyards, and walls remained "liminal spaces, ones that were both inside-outside and closed-open" and they disrupted any neat distinction between public and private.[82] For many girls and women, these locales facilitated "reversed contacts" as they visually, orally, and aurally engaged with their broader community by way of these liminal sites.[83] As Flora Dennis notes, the flow of sounds, or lack thereof, in and out of domestic spaces both constructed and contested domestic boundaries.[84] For many institutional authorities, the "constantly negotiated" and shifting nature of these sensory sites was a source of contention and anxiety.[85] Creating impenetrable cloisters was an institutional ideal, but rarely a reality.

Civic Legislation

While church authorities conducted institutional visitations in the pursuit of quiet, civic authorities relied on secular legislation. Beginning in the second half of the sixteenth century, government agents in Florence published sonic regulations in and around girls' and women's institutions with new focus. A growing body of secular legislation sought to monitor the urban soundscape by banning shouts, lewd words, music, games, gatherings, and general "noise" in the spaces directly adjacent to girls' and women's institutions. Strict regimes of silence were of little use if the enclosure soundscape continually resonated with urban sounds of sociability. Regulating the sounds that Florentines made in the streets and squares near institutions was thus equally important as regulating the sounds enclosed residents made. Civic legislation coalesced with institutional and ecclesiastical laws to produce a uniquely gendered emphasis on sonic regulation in early modern Florence.

Sonic laws around women's institutions had been articulated by urban officials before the sixteenth and seventeenth centuries. For

example, in the early fifteenth century the Florentine republican government adopted laws that forbade men from approaching convents to talk
with nuns. According to the 1435 law this was a necessary precaution
because nuns, "whose sex is weak and fragile," needed to be "preserved
in security and the convents flourish in liberty."[86] While the law did
not explicitly reference noise, it nevertheless laid the groundwork for
a sonically focused notion of enclosure and highlighted the sounds
of men as a threat to these "weak and fragile" nuns. In the following
decades, similar laws became more explicitly sensorily focused. In 1445,
the city's fifteenth-century governing councils moved to forbid *suonatori
della Signoria* (civic musicians) "from going to play instruments within
50 braccia [30 meters] of the convents of nuns, under penalty of law."[87]
This law was rooted in similar assumptions about the "fragile" nature
of women who were thought to be particularly prone to sensory agitation; the law therefore specifically targeted nuns and made no mention of
male monastic institutions.

Beginning in the mid-sixteenth century, under the princely reforms
of Cosimo I de' Medici and his successors, sonic legislation near institutions and throughout Florence was articulated with new regularity and
urgency. The repetitive publication of sensory legislation roughly corre-
sponds with the protracted "emergence of a bureaucracy" and "negotiated
absolutism" that took place in late sixteenth- and early seventeenth-
century Tuscany.[88] These laws were part of sweeping legislative reforms
enacted by the Medici duke and his successors that sought to stabilize
Medici governance after the assassination of Cosimo I's predecessor,
Alessandro de' Medici, and was part of a larger strategy to mitigate republican mentalities and governmental structures that lingered in Florence. Elena Fasano Guarini has explained that "Cosimo I can in effect be
considered one of the great 'princely legislators' in a period of intense
legislation [across Europe]."[89] From the 1530s onward there was a "repetitive production of rules and regulations" concerning a wide variety
of quotidian issues: public order, sumptuary laws, prohibitions against
betting and games, carrying arms, injurious words, and indecency.[90] The
majority of these laws were created by the Otto di Guardia. As successive
Medici rulers worked to centralize their governance over the sixteenth
and seventeenth centuries, the Otto and many other Tuscan magistracies were restructured, bringing these administrative bodies and their

resources firmly within the orbit of Medici control. From the mid-sixteenth century on, the offices of the Otto were almost always stacked with Medici loyalists. Moreover, while the Otto grew beyond its original number with the creation of new positions and the significant expansion of Medici bureaucratic governance, its financial and legislative independence diminished. These centralizing administrative shifts coincided with a broad legislative push that repeatedly issued regulations for social and sensory behaviors. As a result, sonic regulation emerged as a notable feature of Medici governance in Florence, and the Otto developed as a central branch of civic discipline that remained tightly linked to Medici rule. Sonic laws from this period are thus both a reflection of Florence's changing political framework and a larger history in which early modern rulers with centralizing ambitions were keenly focused on regulating sensory behaviors as a means of consolidating social, civic, and governmental influence.[91]

Many of the laws issued during this period focused on the sociosonic groups identified in previous chapters: noisy sex workers, rowdy youths, and loud, aggressive men. For example, alongside sixteenth century laws that forbade sex workers from riding about in private coaches or living within sixty meters of any nunnery, urban and church authorities consistently reissued and amplified legislation that was designed to limit their movements, presence, and vocalizations. Ecclesiastical decrees from the 1564 Florentine Synod sought to double the sex-work free zones around convents, proclaiming that "prostitutes who are publicly registered with the Onestà . . . cannot live within 120 meters of convents."[92] In 1620, the last year of Cosimo II de' Medici's rule, the Onestà once again sought to limit sex workers' mobility and the sound of rattling coaches by forbidding them from traveling at night without permission, stating that those apprehended would be incarcerated.[93] In 1665 Ferdinando II de' Medici expanded the traditional sixty-meter exclusion zone around nunneries and decreed that "prostitutes who are further than sixty meters from a convent can be removed, if with their insolent life convents suffer the prospect of scandal."[94] Laws against noisy homosocial gatherings and gaming also became particularly pervasive. In 1552 the Otto outlawed "anybody from going into public streets to play games . . . of *palla a maglio* (pall-mall) . . . under penalty of 25 scudi, two lashings, and the arbitration of the magistracy."[95] A 1553 prohibition sought to enforce a "peaceful and quiet life in the city" and banned "any person regardless of status to go from their house, or shop, or any other place where they may be and run to see where there is fighting . . . and to gather or make a racket."[96] A 1554 law similarly banned "anyone from going in public streets or squares of the city to throw stones."[97] Laws from 1566 prohibited "any person regardless of status to play, or prepare to play, or stop to see any card game, dice game, ball game, pall-mall, or throwing games in the piazza and public streets . . . under penalty of 10 scudi or two pulls on the strap."[98]

Girls' and women's institutions were usually central in the articulation and application of these sociosonic regulations. For example, A later *bando* (notice) from 1683 specifically prohibited anyone "to play ball games or handball and other types of noisy games in the street of the Orbatello, beginning from Canto alla Catena and continuing to the cloister of the Orbatello."[99] The law aimed to shield Orbatello residents from tiresome sounds of play and socializing and to protect the cloister, but urban officials also used the institution as justification for regulations that aimed to monitor and discipline the sonic productions of the broader neighborhood. Similar laws around girls' and women's institutions were issued throughout the sixteenth and seventeenth centuries with increasing regularity. In 1561 the Otto forbade "racket of any sort, to play instruments, to sing, or to make other resounding noises, to play with balls or any other kind of game" near the Convertite convent.[100] A 1616 law similarly prohibited "any games and children playing ball or any other sort of game and any noises or singing songs at night surrounding the monastery of the nuns of Le Murate and within 100 braccia [60 meters] of there."[101] All of these laws positioned girls' and women's enclosures as pivot points around which broader urban regulations turned, and civic officials identified women's cloisters as disciplinary centers within the larger Florentine soundscape and social fabric.

From the fifteenth to the late seventeenth centuries an observable pattern emerged whereby the city identified bad sounds with increasing specificity while also labeling sex workers, rowdy youths, and aggressive men as distinct sonic groups. The city then worked to publicly ban these groups and their noisy activities in a growing number of urban spaces while continually referencing an expanding corpus of sonic legislation. Simultaneously, civic and institutional authorities expanded the boundaries of the institutional soundscape, moving their focus outward from the institutional structure proper and into the streets, squares, and churches adjacent to cloisters, marking these spaces as gendered sites of sonic concern that hinged on the presences of enclosed girls and women. These two areas of sonic regulation—civic and institutional—overlapped and bolstered each other. The sonic demands of institutional soundscapes reinforced existing urban gender and class hierarchies, further inscribing them onto the surrounding cityscape. Enclosure soundscapes thus emerged as an important element of larger civic efforts to discipline public space and sound. Moreover, regulating the public soundscape was framed as essential to the successful governance of Florentine enclosures. Civic authorities relied on institutional architecture to frame, justify, and publicize much of this emerging sonic legislation.

From roughly the 1590s on, the Otto began affixing stone plaques to the outer walls of many institutions (see Figures 4.4 and 4.5). These plaques were engraved with laws prohibiting specific activities and the sounds they produced within carefully measured zones. The plaques reveal how sensory regulation emerged as an increasingly publicized element of urban governance in early modern Florence. A typical inscription from the late-seventeenth century was posted on the outer wall of the San Silvestro nunnery in the city's northeastern quarter and proclaimed, "The honorable Signori Otto prohibit any person to play any sort of game, to make racket or tumult, to urinate or to make any other sort of foulness near the church of the monastery of San Silvestro within fifty braccia [twenty meters] under penalty of two scudi on capture. And moreover, they prohibit prostitutes or dishonest women of any kind to stay and live near that convent within 100 braccia in every direction under penalty of 200 lire as per the decree of 9 June 1668."[102]

Two undated plaques near the San Barnaba convent in Florence further illustrate the sonic, spatial, and social dynamics these plaques often referenced. The first banned "prostitutes or similar women around the church and monastery of S. Bernaba within sixty meters according to the 1561 law."[103] The second plaque prohibited "every sort of foulness, games or tumult around the church and walls of the nuns of S. Barnaba."[104] Much of this perceived "tumult" came from sex work. The Carmelite convent had opened in 1508 at the corner of Via Mozza in the northwest end of the city, one of the permissible sex work areas later outlined in 1547 laws and an area that was densely populated with nunneries and civic

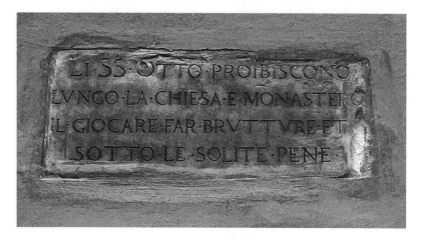

Figure 4.4. Undated Otto di Guardia plaque near the San Pier Martire convent. The inscription reads, "The honorable Sirs of the Otto prohibit any games and filth around the church and monastery under the usual penalties."

Photograph by the author.

charity homes.[105] As sex workers moved into the neighborhood, complaints about noise near the convent rose. In 1572, Onestà records noted how the sex worker Sandra had been "found opposite from the convent of San Barnaba" and was apprehended for "howling and saying dishonest words without respect to the space."[106] A few years later, in 1575, four sex workers were similarly fined for "having made noise" near the convent.[107] In 1576 a sex worker named Menichina di Pistoia who lived in Via Mozza complained that a man named Sanino di Marco "made noise" outside her home during the night after wanting "to sleep with her in spite of her refusal."[108] In 1581 the Onestà reported that Cinzia Monti, Ersilia Romana, and Agnola Siciliana had all been apprehended for loudly fighting in Via Mozza near the convent.[109] And in 1588 a woman named Caterina, "otherwise known as Rondinina the *meretrice* in Via Mozza," was fined for making a noisy uproar in the street.[110] All of these sounds disrupted the San Barnaba cloister and were framed as a threat to the nuns' purity. The Otto di Guardia placed two stone inscriptions near the nunnery in an attempt to delineate a sonic and spatial boundary separating the "dishonorable" sex workers from "honorable" nuns. The plaques were meant to act as a visible bulwark protecting against sonic and social overspill and sought to mediate to complex social demographics of the neighborhood

Figure 4.5. Otto di Guardia stone plaque from 1668 near San Silvestro convent. The inscription reads, in part, "The honorable Sirs of the Otto prohibit any person to play any sort of game, to make racket or tumult . . . near the church of the convent of San Silvestro. . . . And moreover, they prohibit prostitutes or dishonest women of any kind to stay and live near that convent within 100 braccia."

Photograph by the author.

where sex workers and nuns lived in close quarters. Urban officials used sonic legislation and the engraved stone plaques to publicize hierarchies of gender and the senses, inscribing these into the city's walls and claiming that sex workers and their sounds polluted urban space and assaulted cloistered girls and women. Convents like San Barnaba thus served as a disciplinary center that aimed to regulate the oral and aural experiences not only of cloistered residents but also of the sex workers, clients, neighbors, and other Florentines who lived and lingered nearby.

Eighty-six engraved plaques created by the Otto di Guardia have survived in varying conditions, and many can still be seen throughout Florence today.[111] Of this total, approximately eighty-three date to the Medici grand-ducal period (1569–1737).[112] Other plaques were almost certainly posted during the ducal and grand-ducal periods, particularly in the city center where nineteenth-century reconstruction projects remodeled the urban core, demolishing many buildings and their inscriptions (see Figure 4.6).[113] Of the surviving plaques, at least twenty-one were placed on

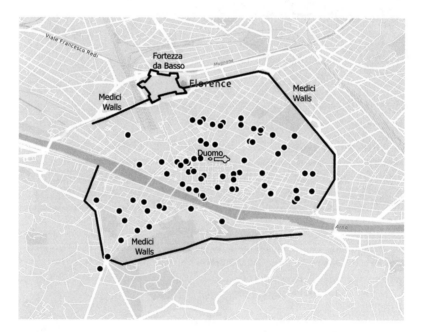

Figure 4.6. Locations of Otto di Guardia stone plaques from the grand-ducal period (ca. 1587–1737).

Map created by Colin Rose.

the side of convent and monastery walls, or directly reference nunneries, and four were placed on or near civic institutions such as the Innocenti foundling home and the Mendicanti poorhouse. Conversely, only three stone plaques explicitly reference male religious institutions.[114] Other common locations for the plaques included on the side of churches, near important civic buildings such as the Palazzo Vecchio or the Bargello, Florence's main policing and judicial site, and in a few instances near the private homes of wealthy noble families.[115] The frequency with which the plaques reference enclosed communities of girls and women once again reveals how central these communities were to the social and spatial topography of Florence.

The surviving Otto di Guardia plaques are all rooted in sensory concerns: the smells of waste and urine, the sight of "dishonorable" individuals, and the sounds of urban din and sociability. Sonic laws are particularly common, however, with explicit prohibitions against "noise," "tumult," "racket," "singing," and "instrument playing" and implicit sonic prohibitions that forbade sex workers, resounding games, and "filth" made by shouts, songs and lewd words (see Table 4.1).[116] The Florentine government consistently identified girls' and women's enclosures as important spaces in the broader social, religious, and political landscape and used these built structures to articulate an expanding corpus of urban sensory legislation. These stone artifacts reference the entwined sensory and spatial histories of early modern Florence and the central position of girls' and women's institutions in shaping the Florentine soundscape.

A particularly valuable element of the Otto plaques are the measured sensory prohibition zones many of the inscriptions include, such as a

Table 4.1. The frequency of sonic prohibitions in Florentine grand-ducal stone plaques, ca. 1587–1737

A. Explicit sonic prohibitions

Prohibition type	Noise (*rumore*)	Tumult (*tumulto*)	Racket (*strepito*)	Singing	Instrument playing	Total
Frequency	5	3	8	6	4	**26**

B. Implicit sonic prohibitions

Prohibition type	Sex work	Gameplay and gambling	Foulness (*bruttura*)	Filth (*sporcitia*)	Street vendors	Carriage traffic	Total
Frequency	10	43	21	11	2	1	**88**

stone plaque placed near the Mendicanti poorhouse from 1696 that prohibited "any person to play any sort of game, to play instruments and to
make racket in any form, during the day or night within 100 braccia of
the house of the Mendicanti under penalty of arbitrament and capture."[117]
These measurements provide insight into how urban officials conceptualized the reach of institutional boundaries and the spread of sounds
through urban space, and they reflect the manner in which spatial boundaries were often negotiated via sensory issues. Measured sensory prohibition zones also expanded over time. The earliest dated plaques from 1596
and 1598 simply prohibited "filth" in the surrounding area but did not
stipulate any specific spatial boundaries in which material or immaterial
filth was prohibited.[118] As the seventeenth and eighteenth centuries progressed, a general trend emerged whereby measured sensory exclusion
zones became more common and encompassed progressively larger areas.
For example, the 1616 plaque near the Le Murate monastery prohibited
noisy ball games, music, and singing "around the convent and within 60
meters."[119] A 1634 plaque outlined a 120-meter area where playing instruments, singing and noisy games were prohibited.[120] A 1635 plaque tri-
pled the traditional 60-meter sex work boundary, stipulating a 180-meter
exclusion zone around the Church of San Salvatore in Ognissanti, in the
city's western quarter, an area densely populated with sex workers and located near numerous nunneries and civic homes.[121] Expanding sensory
measurements culminated in 1700 with an inscription that prohibited
"games and racket" within 480 meters in all directions around the Church
of San Pietro in Gattolino, located in Florence's southernmost corner near
the city gates.[122] This nearly half-kilometer zone encompassed much of
the southern quadrant of the city and even extended beyond the city walls.
At roughly the same time that civic officials were issuing an increasing
number of sonic and sensory laws, they were also expanding the physical
reach of these laws with particular emphasis on the city's sacred spaces
and cloistered communities of girls and women.

But how successful were civic officials in enforcing sonic legislation
and preserving quiet around girls' and women's institutions? While an escalating series of laws emerged during this period that aimed to identify,
locate, and discipline noisemakers, the historical record is clear that urban
officials faced an uphill battle in their efforts to regulate the soundscape
and to discipline "noisy" Florentines. Most often, the stone plaques placed

on or near women's institutions are evidence of the limited application of these laws and of the vibrant soundscapes that resonated throughout the area despite the prohibitions against gaming, noise, music, and loitering detailed in the plaques. For example, almost a century after the Santa Maria di Candeli nuns had first complained in 1568 about the "the shouting, noise, and other dishonest words the nuns experience all night long from their church and dormitory," the Otto di Guardia placed a plaque near the convent that outlined a series of sonic restrictions. The 1664 inscription prohibited "games, songs, and instruments, and other sorts of racket or noise around this convent and within 60 meters in all directions."[123] Despite repeated complaints, laws, decrees, and numerous arrests of individuals who made noise in the area, it would seem that a century later the convent was still surrounded by the same types of sounds that had vexed the community generations earlier. Ultimately, the plaque preserves a record of the continued presence of the very sounds urban officials aimed to limit. Moreover, there is essentially no archival evidence that the Otto consistently monitored the areas around the stone plaques or actively listened for noisemakers in any systematic way. Nor is there evidence that officers of the Otto regularly collected the fines outlined in many of the plaques—fees most Florentines would have been unable to afford in any case.[124] While early modern Florence was a highly policed space with guards stationed at gates, institutional entrances, and civic buildings, the city had a limited number of roaming neighborhood police. The 1632 census listed forty-four *birri* (policemen) but most were assigned exclusively to specific gates and the main market squares.[125] In large part, the Otto likely relied on neighborhood informants and "ear-witnesses" to monitor local soundscapes, a process that explains how many plaques were erected in the first place.[126] Cloistered women in particular listened carefully to the sounds that surrounded them and reported those sounds and the individuals they deemed responsible for them to Florentine officials. Sonic legislation reacted to Florence's vibrant aural life and attempted to enforce quiet and silence, but it was limited in its ability to shape the soundscape. In daily life, many Florentines ignored or were unaware of these sensory laws, and the countless noise complaints and criminal records this study has examined reveal how urbanites continued to shout, laugh, and play music throughout the city despite the best efforts of institutional, ecclesiastical, and civic officials to monitor and regulate these sounds. Ultimately, sonic legislation reflected civic intentions rather than an achieved reality. Yet despite the muted application of these laws, the repetitive production of sonic prohibitions in and around communities of girls and women reflects the Florentine government's investment in the *idea* of sonic regulation as a means to discipline urban space and sociability. These immaterial concerns were made material through the creation of a substantial paper trail and through the memorialization of highly localized sensory tensions in stone.

Enclosure was a sonic project in early modern Florence. Daily regimes that centered around quiet and silence patterned life within the city's many institutions for girls and women. For sex workers and "troubled" women in the Convertite and the Malmaritate, silence and quiet were presented as a curative force that scoured the body and soul of sin and prompted penitence. For vulnerable girls and women in charity homes and conservatories, silence and quiet served to preserve precarious honor and to foster idealized femininities. For nuns, silence was essential to monastic practices, Catholic reform, and the preservation of feminine piety. Institutional, church, and civic authorities all variously worked to establish sonic regulations in and around girls' and women's cloisters as a means of caring for and disciplining these communities. But the repeated calls for silence speak to a louder reality. For many institutionalized residents, rules of silence could be harsh and isolating, and this often lead girls and women to flout sonic regulations or to leave their institutions. Spatial and architectural realities also meant that usually, sensory isolation, quiet, and silence were all but impossible to achieve. Sounds, sights, and smells infiltrated cloistered community as they easily drifted through windows, walls, and doors. Moreover, the Florentines who lived and lingered near women's institutions regularly ignored or were entirely unaware of sonic legislation that aimed to regulate their vocalizations. It seems clear that most people rarely stopped to read the stone plaques that outlined prohibitions against music, socializing, and noise, and if they were aware of the regulations at all, they rarely heeded these proscriptions as they continued to loudly socialize, gather, and conduct business near the city's many enclosures.

Conclusion

$\mathscr{I}$N 1605 the Englishman Robert Dallington published an account of his travels in Tuscany titled *A Survey of the Great Duke's State of Tuscany*. In his highly discursive travel guide, Dallington claimed that Tuscan husbands were particularly prone to take mistresses, to have same-sex relationships, and to seek out the services of sex workers. These behaviors, he claimed, were rooted in the fact that many husbands disliked the sounds and smells their wives made. Dallington explained that "many times the [marriage] match is made before he [the groom-to-be] know eyther how the humour of her braine, or vapour of her stomack will be pleasing to his senses of hearing and smelling." Dallington suggested that women's sounds and smells "may be one chiefe cause why so many husbands dislike [their wives], and of their straying to forbidden fruite." He also claimed that Florence had "some eight thousand Curtizans in the town" to satisfy the sexual appetites of Florentines.[1] While Dallington focused on the sounds and smells of wives, other writers were more concerned with the sensory productions of the many sex workers he referenced. In Agostino Gallo's 1556 dialogue praising the country villa, the Italian agronomist bemoaned the sounds of sex workers who solicited, shouted, and "ensnared" urbanites and claimed that "every passing hour this disease is growing." Gallo violently fantasized about "cutting out the tongue" of every sex worker in order to rid society of the sin and noisy chaos he claimed they wrought on the city and expressed his desire to "exterminate this pestilential seed" from the urban soundscape and social body.[2] We are left to wonder how wives, sex workers, and other women reacted to the sounds their husbands, clients, and other urbanites made. In fact, both authors' neglect of this view reflects a common theme: while women's perspectives were often unaccounted for in normative sensory discourses, female bodies were intense sites of sensory focus, women's activities were framed as particularly sensuous, and both were thought to require careful regulation. Body, sense, and society are intimately linked, and early modern Europeans made sense of sex, gender, and sexuality by way of the sounds, smells, tastes, textures, and sights that surrounded them. Dallington's reference to humors, vapors, and hearing unsettle the priority of sight to reveal a world in which sound shaped bodily and gendered experience.

This book has examined how noise and silence were defined, experienced, and deployed in sixteenth- and seventeenth-century Florence in distinctly gendered ways. In particular, I have considered how "listening for moments of silence and the redefinition of noise and sound can reveal pivotal shifts in the political realm and social structure."[3] In early modern Florence a new emphasis on quiet emerged that associated sonic regulation with bodily, spiritual, gender, and urban order. This sonic shift was directly linked to Florence's emerging religious, political, medical, and social character. Church authorities pursued sonic "decorum" as part of Catholic reform. Church councils and local synods repeatedly emphasized the importance of silence and attentive listening in sacred spaces alongside sporadic efforts to enact restrictions around music and composition in these same spaces. Preachers presented silence as a curative and purifying force that remedied afflictions of the body and the soul and claimed that "noise" was vain, sinful, and spiritually harmful. Catholic reform was sensory reform, and a diverse collection of Catholic thinkers focused on sensory production and experience as central to the deeper questions about spiritual practice that were at the core of early modern Catholic debates. This emphasis on soundscapes and the sensuous coincided with a focus on cloister reform that likewise preoccupied many church authorities. Institutional and ecclesiastical officials strove to discipline and strengthen cloisters, and visitation reports listed the material and immaterial threats to the impregnable enclosures authorities sought to establish. These two aspects of Catholic reform, sonic and cloister reform, coalesced and produced a unique focus on "sensescapes" in diverse communities of girls and women. Enclosure soundscapes emerged as a central axis around which entwined processes of religious reform and dissent took place.

Medical sources likewise discussed the powerful effects of sound on the body and on the environment. Noise was described as a corrosive agent with negative health implications that needed to be purged from the ears, while positive sounds were said to cleanse individual bodies and the environment at large. Metaphors of thorny hedges, locked windows and doors, and sealed seashells described the necessary process of protecting one's ears from dangerous and sinful sounds, and medical manuals repeatedly reminded readers to employ purgative regimes to rid the body of trapped noises and to restore aural health. These sources highlighted the physical and material effects of ephemeral and immaterial senses. Civic authorities and the Medici government, for their part, attempted to regulate and monitor the Florentine soundscape as a means of consolidating political authority and in pursuit of good urban governance. New laws banned particular sounds in precise urban locations, and older laws were repeatedly republicized as part of an iterative effort to combat perceived noise pollution and to quiet noisemakers. The emergence of the centralized grand duchy in Florence and Tuscany was marked by a new focus on sonic regulation.

These religious, health, and civic shifts all intersected with the unprecedented growth, in both number and size, of institutions for girls and women and together produced a unique emphasis on sound in and around the city's dozens of women's enclosures. Cloistered women, and institutional, ecclesiastical, and urban authorities, collectively identified girls' and women's communities as important sonic spaces and established a web of regulations, laws, and edicts that sought to carefully curate the sounds that thousands of enclosed girls and women both made and heard. This had important implications for Florentines living on both sides of the cloister wall, as authorities aimed to regulate not only the oral and aural experiences of enclosed residents but also those of the Florentines who lived, lingered, and labored near their institutions. Girls' and women's enclosures emerged as key sites around which the larger Florentine soundscape was both shaped and contested. The urban soundscape, in its idealized and everyday forms, was uniquely tied to the city's many institutions and communities of women.

Throughout this book, I have endeavored to listen closely to the experiences of girls and women: those who made noise; those who complained about noise; those who pursued silence; those who listened; and those who laughed, shouted, sang, cried, and conversed. Examining these histories reveals the complicated ways that gender shaped the city and its soundscape. In particular, the boundaries of femininity were often constructed, defended, and disrupted alongside parallel boundaries of quiet and noise. When elite nuns complained about noisy sex workers, they used descriptions of sound to enforce hierarchies of gender and class and to assert their sexual, spiritual, and social superiority in contrast to women whom they labeled as noisy. When cloistered women lobbied civic and church authorities with complaints about noisy neighbors who played games, shouted, sang, and socialized near their institutions, they used noise complaints as a compelling tool to assert influence over the streets, squares, and buildings that surrounded their enclosures—spaces they could not physically occupy. Similarly, when women accused the men who harassed or assaulted them of sonic assault, they capitalized on a legal and religious interest in sonic regulation to pursue action against their assailants. When institutionalized women maintained continual silence, they enacted powerful performances of piety, penance, and purity. Conversely, when cloistered girls and women shouted, cried, sang, and loudly socialized, they resisted the intense sonic regimes they often encountered in civic and ecclesiastical institutions. When sex workers moved about the city in rattling coaches or conversed in streets and doorways, they eschewed moralizing efforts to silence them. In all of these ways and more, the Florentine soundscape was profoundly gendered; quotidian sounds mediated complex negotiations of gender, class, and space and reverberated throughout the city.

By placing sound at the center of my analysis, this book offers a unique perspective of early modern Florence and its many institutions. In particular, thinking sonically reveals the profoundly integrated nature of the city's many enclosures for girls and women. Niall Atkinson has

argued that we "cannot afford to ignore the expanding historical dialogue about the sensorial experience of the city, especially since it was the
actual physical arrangement of architectural structures as well as the
very materials from which they were made that determined the particular
sonic imprint of urban spaces."[4] Similarly, we cannot ignore the crucial
role of the senses in shaping cloister spaces and the social experiences of
enclosure. Civic and ecclesiastical institutions were designed, in many
ways, to separate cloistered residents from the broader city, but as this
study has shown, enclosed communities remained intimately enmeshed in the larger urban soundscape and social fabric. As daily sounds
of sociability flowed in and out of enclosures, these ephemeral sonic exchanges served as connective threads that tied institutionalized communities to their neighbors and to the broader city despite the best efforts of many institutional, church, and civic authorities to achieve strict
sensory separation. An impressive roster of scholars have considered the
paradoxical nature of the early modern cloister, showing that while
various authorities worked to enforce strict enclosure, these communities remained central nodes of connectivity. The many references to "porosity" and "permeability" in these works speak to the complex way that
cloistering both separated and connected communities of women—from
their families, from neighborhoods, and from the city. This field of research has been fruitful ground for gender and women's studies, in part
because of how anxieties about the physical cloister paralleled anxieties
about the female body and women's activities in meaningful ways. Many
of these works have focused on material practices of enclosure: institutional walls, gates, and doors and the movement of goods and bodies
in and out of cloisters. My research offers a new focus on immaterial
and ephemeral practices of enclosure, showing how soundscapes inter-
acted with, and were shaped by, the bodies and structures that composed these communities and how these immaterial forces were central
to the institutional shifts that defined early modern Italy. Moreover, previous studies of cloister soundscapes have almost exclusively focused
on music in nunneries—and, indeed, music was a defining feature of
early modern conventual life. But music was just one element of the
soundscape and one variety of sound that acted on the body and on
society. By focusing on silences, racket, din, clatter, and everyday utterances, I have endeavored to expand our understanding of the enclosure

soundscape, the experiences of early modern institutionalization, and the impact of sound on the city and on early modern society.

Thinking sensorially also offers new insights into the constantly negotiated nature of gendered boundaries and their limits.[5] Institutional, civic, and church authorities strove to establish a sonic barrier around institutions, one designed to articulate and enforce particular understandings of feminine purity and of religious and civic order. But sound by its very nature is impossible to fully control. Transgressive sounds, whether willfully produced or not, seeped through cracks, floated over walls, drifted through windows, and pierced the silence in civic and ecclesiastical institutions alike. By working to regulate sound, urban and church authorities were inadvertently acknowledging the very instability of the accompanying gendered boundaries they sought to uphold. Shouts, laughter, chatter, and racket all threatened to disrupt the social and sensory environments institutional authorities aimed to maintain. Ultimately, immaterial histories of sound, noise, and silence offer a unique glimpse into the vibrant and complicated experiences of institutionalization in Florence and the central position of girls' and women's communities in the broader urban soundscape and social geography. In early modern Florence, sound mattered and had material implications; soundscapes shaped and continually reshaped experiences of gender, space, and society.

ABBREVIATIONS

NOTES

BIBLIOGRAPHY

ACKNOWLEDGEMENTS

INDEX

ABBREVIATIONS

A&D	Aquisti e Doni
AAF	Archivio Arcivescovile di Firenze
AOIF	Archivio dell'Istituto degli Innocenti di Firenze
ASF	Archivio di Stato di Firenze
Auditore	Auditore dei Benefici Ecclesiastici poi Segreteria del Regio Diritto
Bigallo	Compagnia Poi Magistrato del Bigallo
BNCF	Biblioteca Natzionale Centrale di Firenze
CPG	Capitani di Parte Guelfa
CRSGF	Corporazioni Religiose Soppresse dal Governo Francese
nn	numeri neri
nr	numeri rossi
Onestà	Ufficiali dell'Onestà
Otto di Guardia	Otto di Guardia e Balia del Principato

NOTES

INTRODUCTION

1. Archivio Arcivescovile di Firenze, Cause Criminale, *Firenze S. Onofrio di Fuligno—Sec. XVII,* no. 1: "Devo sempre come ministra di questo loco sacro ovviare a tutti li scandali e occasioni che possono dare da impiumare male cogitationi. . . . Pero causa di mal' esempio e il sentire tutta la notte mentre siamo in coro tante parole disoneste, rumori, et grida straordinarie di modo che non possiamo dire li divini offici et il tutto deriva dalle qui nominate Meretrici, chi stanno dirimpetto al nostro Monastero . . . non potendo più sopportare che le mie monache habbino restar maculate da tante cattive parole, e sporcizie che si sentono . . . 14 di dicembre 1620."

2. Mark Michael Smith, *Sensing the Past: Seeing, Hearing, Smelling, Tasting, and Touching in History* (Berkeley: University of California Press, 2007), 44; Constance Classen, "Engendering Perception: Gender Ideologies and Sensory Hierarchies in Western History," *Body and Society* 3, no. 2 (1997): 1–19.

3. Archivio di Stato di Firenze (hereafter ASF), Compagnia Poi Magistrato del Bigallo, 1691, fols. 40–41: "Con stare ritirate in silentio."

4. ASF, Fanciulle di Santa Caterina, 7, chap. 6: "in continuo silentio."

5. Giustina Niccolini, *The Chronicle of Le Murate by Sister Giustina Niccolini,* trans. and ed. Saundra Weddle (Toronto: Centre for Reformations and Renaissance Studies, 2011), 118.

6. Gian Rosa, *Le leggi penali sui muri di Firenze* (Florence: Casa Editrice Nerbini, 1911), 97: "Proibiscono che a braccia 150 e a quanto tiene la chiesa e gira il monastero delle rr. monache di s. Orsola che alchuno di qualunque stato e qualsisia non ardisca giocare a palla pallone o altro giocho o fare romori o canti di giorno come di notte alla pena di scudi 4 di cattura e l'arbitrio di lor signori."

7. Sharon Strocchia, "The Nun Apothecaries of Renaissance Florence: Marketing Medicines in the Convent," *Renaissance Studies* 25, no. 5 (2011): 627–647; Melissa Conway, *The Diario of the Printing Press of San Jacopo di Ripoli: 1476–1484; Commentary and Transcription* (Florence: Leo S. Olschki,

1999); Sharon Strocchia, *Nuns and Nunneries in Renaissance Florence* (Baltimore: Johns Hopkins University Press, 2009), 117–139.

8. Daniel M. Zolli and Christopher Brown, "Bell on Trial: The Struggle for Sound after Savonarola," *Renaissance Quarterly* 72, no. 1 (2019): 54–96; David Garrioch, "Sounds of the City: The Soundscapes of Early Modern European Towns," *Urban History* 30, no. 1 (2003): 5–25.

9. ASF, Acquisti e Doni, 293, unpaginated / unfoliated: "Deliberazioni dei Signori e Collegi 15 Febbraio 1445 Si proibisce ai suonatori della Signoria di andare a suonare presso i monasteri di monache a 50 braccia, sotto pena di cassazione dall' ufficio."

10. Niall Atkinson, "Sonic Armatures: Constructing an Acoustic Regime in Renaissance Florence," *The Senses and Society* 7, no. 1 (2012): 39–52.

11. Niall Atkinson, *The Noisy Renaissance: Sound, Architecture, and Florentine Urban Life* (University Park: Pennsylvania State University Press, 2016), 17, 7.

12. R. Murray Schafer, *The Tuning of the World: Toward a Theory of Soundscape Design* (New York: Knopf, 1977).

13. Atkinson, *The Noisy Renaissance,* 185.

14. Atkinson, *The Noisy Renaissance,* 191.

15. Eric Cochrane, *Florence in the Forgotten Centuries 1527–1800: A History of Florence and the Florentines in the Age of the Grand Duke* (Chicago: University of Chicago Press, 1973), 63; Arnaldo D'Addario, *La formazione dello stato moderno in Toscana: Da Cosimo il Vecchio a Cosimo I de' Medici* (Lecce, Italy: Adriatica Editrice Salentina, 1976); Elena Fasano Guarini, *L'Italia moderna e la Toscana dei principi: Discussioni e ricerche storiche* (Florence: Le Monnier, 2008); Luca Mannori, *Lo stato del granduca 1530–1859: Le istituzioni della Toscana moderna in un percorso di testi commentati* (Florence: Pacini, 2016).

16. D'Addario, *La formazione dello stato,* 221–226, 236–245.

17. Elena Fasano Guarini, "Produzione di leggi e disciplinamento nella Toscana granducale tra cinque e seicento: Spunti di ricerca," in *Disciplina dell'anima, disciplina del corpo e disciplina della società tra medioevo ed età moderna,* ed. Paolo Prodi and Carla Penuti (Bologna: Il Mulino, 1994), 664; Julia Rombough, "Regulating Sense and Space in Late Renaissance Florence," *Urban History* 50, no. 1 (2023): 38–57.

18. Emily Cockayne, *Hubbub: Filth, Noise & Stench in England, 1600–1770* (New Haven, CT: Yale University Press, 2007), 147.

19. Nicholas Hammond, *The Power of Sound and Song in Early Modern Paris* (University Park: Pennsylvania State University Press, 2019), 18–27; William Tullet, *Smell in Eighteenth-Century England: A Social Sense* (Oxford: Oxford University Press, 2019), 52; Alexandra Logue, "'Saucy Stink': Smells, Sanitation, and Conflict in Early Modern London," *Renaissance and Reformation / Renaissance et Réforme* 44, no. 2 (2021): 62.

20. Hilde Greefs and Anne Winter, "Introduction: Migration Policies and Materialities of Identification in European Cities: Papers and Gates,

1500–1930s," in *Migration Policies and Materialities of Identification in European Cities: Papers and Gates, 1500–1930s,* ed. Hilde Greefs and Anne Winter (New York: Routledge, 2019), 3–23; Rosa Salzberg, "Controlling and Documenting Migration via Urban "Spaces of Arrival" in Early Modern Venice," in Greefs and Winter, *Migration Policies and Materialities of Identification,* 27–45.

21. Giovanni Battista Baliano, *Trattato della pestilenza, ove si adducono pensieri nuovi in più materie, stampato già l'anno 1547, et hora riveduto et ampliato dall' autore* (Genoa: Benedetto Guasco, 1653), 183: "I poveri habitano in luoghi e stanze più sporche; tengono più succide le proprie vesti, e le proprie persone."

22. Senofonte Bindassi, *Il diporto della villa: Canto di Senofonte Bindassi da Sant'Angelo in Vado* (Venice: Giovachino Brognolo, 1582), 6: "urli, e stridori, in quanti vivono le città del mondo."

23. Between 1551 and 1622 the population of Florence grew by 29 percent, from 59,179 to 76,023. After the plague of 1630–1633 the population had fallen to 66,056 by 1632, but then grew and stabilized in the following decades. R. Burr Litchfield, *Florence Ducal Capitol, 1530–1630* (New York: ACLS Humanities e-book, 2008), chap. 6, para. 273; Carlo M. Cipolla, *I pidocchi e il granduca: Crisi economica e problemi sanitari nella Firenze del '600* (Bologna: Il Mulino, 1979); John Henderson, *Florence under Siege: Surviving Plague in an Early Modern City* (New Haven, CT: Yale University Press, 2019). For population figures in Florence before the Black Death, see W. R. Day Jr., "The Population of Florence before the Black Death: Survey and Synthesis," *Journal of Medieval History* 28, no. 2 (2002): 93–129.

24. Phillip Hahn, "The Reformation of the Soundscape: Bell-Ringing in Early Modern Lutheran Germany," *German History* 33, no. 4 (2015): 529–530. See also Anna Kvicalova, *Listening and Knowledge in Reformation Europe: Hearing, Speaking, and Remembering in Calvin's Geneva* (Cham, Switzerland: Palgrave Macmillan, 2019), 4.

25. John W. O'Malley, "Trent, Sacred Images, and Catholics' Senses of the Sensuous," in *The Sensuous in the Counter-Reformation Church,* ed. Marcia B. Hall and Tracy Elizabeth Cooper (Cambridge: Cambridge University Press, 2013), 37–40; Bette Talvacchia, "The Word Made Flesh: Spiritual Subjects and Carnal Depictions in Renaissance Art," in Hall and Cooper, *The Sensuous in the Counter-Reformation Church,* 49–74.

26. This statement was made in 1567 by Archbishop Sigismondo Saraceno in the parish of Matera (Basilicata) after his return from the Council of Trent; quoted in Robert L. Kendrick, "Music among the Disciplines in Early Modern Catholicism," in *Listening to Early Modern Catholicism: Perspectives from Musicology,* ed. Daniele Filippi and Michael J. Noone (Leiden: Brill, 2017), 38.

27. Kendrick, "Music among the Disciplines," 37.

28. Andrew Dell'Antonio, *Listening as Spiritual Practice in Early Modern Italy* (Berkeley: University of California Press, 2011), 17.

29. *The Canons and Decrees of the Sacred and Ecumenical Council of Trent, Celebrated under the Sovereign Pontiffs Paul III, Julius III, and Pius IV,* trans. Rev. J. Waterworth (London: Burns and Oates, 1888), 161.

30. O'Malley, "Trent, Sacred Images, and Catholics' Senses," 28.

31. Giovanni Domenici, *Regola del governo di cura familiare compilate dal beato Giovanni Dominici fiorentino dell'ordine de' frati predicatori,* ed. Donato Salvi (Florence: Angiolo Garinei Libraio, 1860), 46–54: "Non caggia dalla memoria tua come Eva pericolò per risguardare il pomo"; "gli occhi bassi e fissi nella terra"; "per diletto superfluo"; "Gli orecchi stendi a udire I divini comandamenti, I celestiali consigli, le lode divine, la dottrina santa, la miseria dell'afflitto, le melodie degli uccelli facendo dolci versi al suo signore . . . queste entra il pane dell'anima"; "Non le tenere aperte a favole né a canzoni. Se odi sibillare la lingua serpentina di maldicenti, fuggi, or serra, o tu contradici"; "Offerisci a Dio il sacrificio delle labra tue . . . non bestemmiare, non maledire, non raccordare il demonio . . . non infamare, non mormorare, non parlare de' fatti d'altro se non beve e con verità, non mentire, non parlar doppio . . . non sia lusingatrice, non seminatrice di discorda e men d'errori . . . non parlar disonesto, non motteggiare; però che dicendo, non dire parola oziosa." See also Laura Giannetti, *Food Culture and Literary Imagination in Early Modern Italy: The Renaissance of Taste* (Amsterdam: Amsterdam University Press, 2022), 205.

32. David Gentilcore, *Healers and Healing in Early Modern Italy* (Manchester, UK: Manchester University Press, 1998), 5–7; Luis García Ballester, "On the Origins of the 'Six Non-natural Things' in Galen," in *Galen and Galenism: Theory and Medical Practice from Antiquity to the European Renaissance,* ed. Luis García Ballester, Jon Arrizabalaga, Montserrat Cabré, and Lluís Cifuentes (New York: Routledge, 2002), 105–115; Massimo Montanari, *Gusti del medioevo i prodotti, la cucina, la tavola* (Rome: GLF Editori Laterza, 2014), chap. 1; Galen, *A Translation of Galen's Hygiene (De sanitate tuenda),* ed. and trans. Robert Montraville Green (Springfield, IL: Charles C. Thomas, 1951).

33. Jerome J. Bylebyl, "Galen and the Non-natural Causes of Variation in the Pulse," *Bulletin of the History of Medicine* 53, no. 5 (1971): 482–485.

34. Rudolph E. Siegel, *Galen on Sense Perception: His Doctrines, Observations, and Experiments on Vision, Hearing, Smell, Taste, Touch and Pain and their Historical Sources* (Basel: Karger, 1970); Linda Phillis Austern, "Musical Treatments for Lovesickness: The Early Modern Heritage," in *Music as Medicine: The History of Music Therapy since Antiquity,* ed. Peregrine Horden (New York: Routledge, 2000), 213–248; Herman Roodernburg, ed., *A Cultural History of the Senses in the Renaissance* (London: Bloomsbury, 2014).

35. Evelyn Welch, "Perfumed Buttons and Scented Gloves: Smelling Things in Renaissance Italy," in *Ornamentalism: The Art of Renaissance Accessories,* ed. Bella Mirabella (Ann Arbor: University of Michigan Press, 2011), 19–21;

Holly Dugan, *The Ephemeral History of Perfume: Scent and Sense in Early Modern England* (Baltimore: Johns Hopkins University Press, 2011).

36. Stuart Clark, *Vanities of the Eye: Vision in Early Modern European Culture* (Oxford: Oxford University Press, 2007); Alina Payne, *Vision and Its Instruments: Art, Science, and Technology in Early Modern Europe* (University Park: Pennsylvania State University Press, 2015); Elizabeth D. Harvey, ed., *Sensible Flesh: On Touch in Early Modern Culture* (Philadelphia: University of Pennsylvania Press, 2002).

37. Alessandro Traiano Petronio, *Del viver delli Romani et di conservar la sanità* (Rome: Domenico Basa, 1592), 301: "perche in quelli luoghi è sempre denso, grosso, & come acqua di paludi."

38. Domenico Panarolo, *Aerologia cioè discorso del l'aria trattato utile per la sanità* (Rome: Domenico Marciani, 1642), 89: "et non nullis aliis medicis aegroti pene de speratae salutis musicae oblectamentis curati fuerint."

39. Onofrio Zarrabini, *Delle materie e de soggetti predicabili* (Venice: Battista Somascho, 1586), 373: "Come il corpo nostro ha cinque sense, che sono cinque fenestre; per le quali entra la morte in noi."

40. Castore Durante, *Herbario nuovo di Castore Durante medico, et cittadino romano* (Venice: Li Seffa, 1602), 133: "Il succo delle cipolle messo con mele ne gli occhi, ne leva i fiocchi, & le caligini, & le cateratte, & rischiara la vista; messo nell'orecchia ne leva il romore."

41. Monica Green, "Bodies, Health, Gender, Disease: Recent Work of Medieval Women's Medicine," *Studies in Medieval and Renaissance History* 3, no. 2 (2005): 1–4.

42. Sandra Cavallo and Tessa Storey, *Healthy Living in Renaissance Italy* (Oxford: Oxford University Press, 2013), 7–10.

43. Patricia Crawford, *Blood, Bodies, and Families in Early Modern England* (New York: Routledge, 2004), chaps. 1, 2; Gail Kern Paster, *The Body Embarrassed: Drama and the Disciplines of Shame in Early Modern England* (Ithaca, NY: Cornell University Press, 1993); Lisa Wynne Smith, "The Body Embarrassed?: Rethinking the Leaky Male Body in Eighteenth-Century England and France," *Gender and History* 23, no. 1 (2010): 26–46; Jennifer Evans, "Female Barrenness, Bodily Access and Aromatic Treatments in Seventeenth-Century England," *Historical Research* 87, no. 237 (2014): 423–443.

44. Will Fisher, "The Renaissance Beard: Masculinity in Early Modern England," *Renaissance Quarterly* 54, no. 1 (2001): 155–187; Michael Stolberg, "A Woman Down to Her Bones: The Anatomy of Sexual Difference in Early Modern Europe," *Isis* 94, no. 2 (2003): 274–299.

45. Gianna Pomata, "Menstruating Men: Similarity and Difference of the Sexes in Early Modern Medicine," in *Generation and Degeneration: Tropes of Reproduction in Literature and History from Antiquity to Early Modern Europe,* ed. Valerie Finucci and Kevin Brownlee (Durham, NC: Duke University Press, 2001), 109–152.

46. Kathleen Long, "The Case of Marin le Marcis," in *Trans Historical: Gender Plurality before the Modern,* ed. Greta LaFleur, Masha Raskolnikov, and Anna Klosowska (Ithaca, NY: Cornell University Press, 2021), 68–95; M. W. Bychowski, "The Transgender Turn: Eleanor Ryekner Speaks Back," in LaFleur, Raskolnikov, and Klosowska, *Trans Historical,* 95–113.

47. Ken Albala, *Eating Right in the Renaissance* (Berkeley: University of California Press, 2002).

48. Juliann Vitullo, "Taste and Temptation in Early Modern Italy," *Senses and Society* 5, no. 1 (2010): 107.

49. Vitullo, "Taste and Temptation," 107; Bernardino da Siena, *Le prediche volgari,* ed. Ciro Cannarozzi (Florence: Libreria Editrice Fiorentina, 1934).

50. Scipione Mercurio, *De gli errori popolari d'Italia libri sette divisi in due parti,* vol. 1 (Verona: Francesco Rossi, 1645), 370.

51. Constance Classen, "The Witch's Senses: Sensory Ideologies and Transgressive Femininities from the Renaissance to Modernity," in *Empire of the Senses: The Sensual Culture Reader,* ed. David Howes (Oxford: Bloomsbury, 2005), 75.

52. Strocchia, *Nuns and Nunneries,* 1–2; Jutta Sperling, *Convents and the Body Politic in Late Renaissance Venice* (Chicago: University of Chicago Press, 1999), 18–72; Gabriella Zarri, *Recinti: Donne, clausura e matrimonio nella prima età moderna* (Bologna: Il Mulino, 2000); Francesca Medioli, "To Take or Not to Take the Veil: Selected Italian Case Histories, the Renaissance and After," in *Women in Italian Renaissance Culture and Society,* ed. Letizia Pannizza (Oxford: European Humanities Research Centre, 2000), 122–137; Elisa Novi Chavarria, *Monache e gentildonne: Un labile confine poteri politici e identità religiose nei monasteri napoletani secoli XVI–XVII* (Milan: Franco Angeli, 2001), 56–70.

53. Strocchia, *Nuns and Nunneries,* 2.

54. Peter Spierenburg, *The Prison Experience: Disciplinary Institutions and Their Inmates in Early Modern Europe* (New Brunswick, NJ: Rutgers University Press, 1991), 41–69; Norbert Finzsch and Robert Jutte, eds., *Institutions of Confinement: Hospitals, Asylums, and Prisons in Western Europe and North America, 1500–1950* (Cambridge: Cambridge University Press, 1996); Monica Chojnacka, "Women, Charity and Community in Early Modern Venice: The Casa Delle Zitelle," *Renaissance Quarterly* 51, no. 1 (1998): 68–91; Daniela Lombardi, *Povertà maschile, povertà femminile: L'Ospedale dei Mendicanti nella Firenze dei Medici* (Bologna: Il Mulino, 1988).

55. Silvia Evangelisti, "To Find God in Work? Female Social Stratification in Early Modern Italian Convents," *European History Quarterly* 38, no. 3 (2008): 401.

56. Cecilia Hewlitt, *Rural Communities in Renaissance Tuscany: Religious Identities and Local Loyalties* (Turnhout, Belgium: Brepols, 2008), 162–181, 135–163. For a particular example of a Florentine patrician nun in a rural convent,

see Fra Filippo Guidi, *Vita della venerabile madre suor Caterina de Ricci Fiorentina* (Florence: Bartolommeo Sermartelli, 1622).

57. Evangelisti, "To Find God in Work?," 401–402. More detailed records regarding enslaved girls and women in convents exist in colonial contexts where settler nuns capitalized on enslaved labor and framed it as part of their missionary calling. See also Kathryn Burns, *Colonial Habits: Convents and the Spiritual Economy of Cuzco, Peru* (Durham, NC: Duke University Press, 1999), 113–116. For enslavement in Florence, see Sally McKee, "Domestic Slavery in Renaissance Italy," *Slavery and Abolition* 29, no. 3 (2008): 305–326; and Sergio Tognetti, "The Trade in Black African Slaves in Fifteenth-Century Florence," in *Black Africans in Renaissance Europe,* ed. T. F. Earle and K. J. P. Lowe (Cambridge: Cambridge University Press, 2005), 213–224.

58. ASF, Capitani di Parte Guelfa, numeri rossi, 9, fol. 36v: "Che per l'avenire non possi essere conceduta habitatione in orbatello ad alcuna schiava. Le quali quandunche vene alcuna tutto quello luogo inquietano et perturbano."

59. Nicholas Terpstra, *Cultures of Charity: Women, Politics and the Reform of Poor Relief in Renaissance Italy* (Cambridge, MA: Harvard University Press, 2013), 21–42; Daniel Hickey, *Local Hospitals in Ancien Régime France: Rationalization, Resistance, Renewal, 1530–1789* (Montreal: McGill–Queens University Press, 1997); J. W. Brodman, *Charity and Welfare: Hospitals and the Poor in Medieval Catalonia* (Philadelphia: University of Pennsylvania Press, 1998); Daniela Lombardi, "Poveri a Firenze: Programmi e realizzazioni della politica assistenziale dei Medici tra Cinque e Seicento," in *Timore e carità: I poveri nell'Italia moderna,* ed. Giorgio Politi, Mario Rosa, and Franco Della Peruta (Cremona, Italy: Annali della Biblioteca Statale / Libreria Civica di Cremona, 1982), 164–184, 84–86.

60. *Sommario de capitoli della venerabile Compagnia di Santa Maria Maddalena sopra le mal maritate* (Florence: Bartholomeo Sermartelli, 1583), 16–17: "Le Vecchie non fanno per questo luogo . . . Le inferme non si debbono accettare. . . . Le gravide non s'accettino se non per doppo che haranno partorito . . . cessa l'occasione di dubitare, & di mormorare, come se fussero venute con sinistra intentione."

61. Terpstra, *Cultures of Charity,* 19–55.

62. ASF, Auditore dei Beni Ecclesiastici Poi Segretario del Regio Diritto (hereafter Auditore), 4892, Negozio della Deputazione sopra i Monasteri, 1548–1552, fols. 151r–153r: "Lucrezia Hebrea."

63. Archivio Ospedale degli Innocenti Firenze (hereafter AOIF), 10445, "Libro di nomi delle donne che sono state nel convento di Orbatello, MDCXXXVI," unpaginated.

64. Tamar Herzig, "'For the Salvation of This Girl's Soul': Nuns as Convertors of Jews in Early Modern Italy," *Religions* 8, no. 11 (2017), https://doi.org/10.3390/rel8110252.

65. The first Casa dei Catecumeni opened in Rome in 1543. Others then opened throughout the Italian Peninsula. Kenneth Stow, *Anna and Tranquillo: Catholic Anxiety and Jewish Protest in the Age of Revolutions* (New Haven, CT: Yale University Press, 2016); Natalie E. Rothman, "Becoming Venetian: Conversion and Transformation in the Seventeenth-Century Mediterranean," *Mediterranean Historical Review* 21, no. 1 (2006): 39–75; and Samuela Marconcini, *Per amor del cielo: Farsi cristiani a Firenze tra seicento e settecento* (Florence: Florence University Press, 2016), 71, table 1.

66. *The Canons and Decrees of the Sacred and Ecumenical Council of Trent,* Session 25, Decrees XV, XVII, and XVIII.

67. Sherill Cohen, *The Evolution of Women's Asylums since 1500: From Refuges for Ex-prostitutes to Shelters for Battered Women* (New York: Oxford University Press, 1992), 145–170.

68. Giovanna Paolin, *Lo spazio del silenzio: Monacazioni forzate, clausura e proposte di vita religiose femminile nell' età moderna* (Pordenone, Italy: Biblioteca del l'Immagine, 1996); Francesca Medioli, "Monacazioni forzate: Donne ribelli al proprio destino," *Clio: Trimestrale di Studi Storici* 30, no. 3 (1994): 431–454.

69. Elizabeth Makowski, *Canon Law and Cloistered Women: "Periculoso" and Its Commentators, 1298–1545* (Washington, DC: Catholic University of America Press, 1997), 135.

70. *The Canons and Decrees of the Sacred and Ecumenical Council of Trent,* Session 25, Decree V.

71. ASF, Auditore, 4894, fol. 60r: "Senza paura di nessuna"; Craig Monson, *Nuns Behaving Badly: Tales of Music, Magic, Art, and Arson in the Convents of Italy* (Chicago: University of Chicago Press, 2010), 25–63; Mary Laven, *Virgins of Venice: Broken Vows and Cloistered Lives in the Renaissance Convent* (New York: Penguin, 2004), 8–25.

72. Arcangela Tarabotti, *Paternal Tyranny,* ed. and trans. Letizia Panizza (Chicago: University of Chicago Press, 2004), 59–60; Silvia Evangelisti, "'We Do Not Have It, and We Do Not Want It': Women, Power, and Convent Reform in Florence," *Sixteenth Century Journal* 34, no. 3 (2003): 680–686.

73. Alison More, *Fictive Orders and Feminine Religious Identities,1200–1600* (Oxford: Oxford University Press, 2018), 147.

74. Alison More, "Institutionalization of Disorder: The Franciscan Third Order and Canonical Change in the Sixteenth Century," *Franciscan Studies* 71 (2013): 156–159; Colleen Reardon, *Holy Concord within Sacred Walls: Nuns and Music in Siena, 1575–1700* (Oxford: Oxford University Press 2002), 18–27.

75. Philip Gavitt, *Gender, Honor, and Charity in Late Renaissance Florence* (Cambridge: Cambridge University Press, 2011), 186; John Henderson, "Charity and Welfare in Early Modern Tuscany," in *Health Care and Poor Relief in Counter-Reformation Europe,* ed. Jon Arrizabalaga, Andrew Cunningham, and Ole Peter Grell (New York: Routledge, 2005), 68; Lombardi, "Poveri a Firenze," 168.

76. ASF, Fanciulle di Santa Caterina, 7, chap. 1: "Di mantenere in piedi cosi santa opera et cosi dal Ser.mo Gran Duca ottenuto il sito nella via di San Gallo dell' spedale di Broccando sotto la loggia di Bonifacio si degno quivi a murare un luogo che fusse capace di tante fanciulle, et questo tutto per honore et gloria di Dio. Et conservare tante fanciulle dalle mani del Demonio."

77. Nicholas Terpstra, *Abandoned Children of the Italian Renaissance: Orphan Care in Florence and Bologna* (Baltimore: Johns Hopkins University Press, 2005), 233.

78. AOIF, 10445, "Libro de nome delle donne che sono state nel convent di Orbatello di Firenze dall' anno 1588," unpaginated: "Maddalena di Giovanni fanciulla della Pietà."

79. AOIF, 10445, "Libro de nome delle donne," unpaginated.

80. Constance Classen, David Howes, and Anthony Synnott, *Aroma: The Cultural History of Smell* (New York: Routledge, 1994), 3.

81. Karin Bijsterveld, "Introduction," in *Soundscapes of the Urban Past: Staged Sound as Mediated Cultural Heritage,* ed. Karin Bijsterveld (Bielfeld, Germany: Transcript Verlag, 2013), 14.

82. David Howes, "Introduction: Empires of the Senses," in Howes, *Empire of the Senses,* 3–4.

83. Peter Bailey, *Popular Culture and Performance in the Victorian City* (Cambridge: Cambridge University Press, 1998), 195; Mary Douglas, *Purity and Danger: An Analysis of Concepts of Pollution and Taboo* (London: Routledge, 2002), 50.

84. Hillel Schwartz, "On Noise," in *Hearing History: A Reader,* ed. Mark Michael Smith (Athens: University of Georgia Press, 2004), 52.

85. Classen, "Engendering Perception," 1–19; Mark Michael Smith, *How Race Is Made: Slavery, Segregation, and the Senses* (Chapel Hill: University of North Carolina Press, 2008), 1–32; Alan Hyde, "Offensive Bodies," in *The Smell Culture Reader,* ed. Jim Drobnick (New York: Berg, 2006), 53–58; Schwartz, "On Noise," 53.

86. Mark M. Smith, *A Sensory History Manifesto* (University Park: Pennsylvania State University Press, 2021), 11, 15.

87. "Quest for quiet" is derived from Emily Thompson's use of the phrase in numerous conference papers and interviews. See Emily Thompson, *The Soundscape of Modernity: Architectural Acoustics and the Culture of Listening in America, 1900–1933* (Cambridge, MA: MIT Press, 2004).

88. Schwartz, "On Noise," 52.

89. Smith, *A Sensory History Manifesto,* 65.

CHAPTER ONE ⌒ SPACE

1. Archivio di Stato di Firenze (hereafter ASF), Capitani di Parte Guelfa (hereafter CPG), numeri neri (hereafter nn), 787, fol. 62r: "Havendo Madama

Serissima gusto di sapere in che stato si ritrovi il luogo d'Orbatello in Firenze, et la quantità delle stanze che vi sono, et di che qualità . . . Maggio 1617 [*sf*]."

2. ASF, CPG, nn, 751, fol. 70: "Essendo stati alla visita d'Orbatello secondo il solito, ci haviamo trovato molti disordini causati dalle donne de gl'Innocenti cavate dila . . . di sospetto di pocha honesta et di pochissimo esempio."

3. ASF, CPG, nn, 801, fol. 19: "in desto luogo siano vacanti tredici stanze ciòe otto nella piana strada, e cinque nella seconda, ma del n'è la meta per non se possano abitare . . . sono troppo humide"; ASF, CPG, nn, 801, fol. 71: "Oltre alle predette cinque casine, sono in . . . Orbatello altre 24 casine le quali hanno più bisogno et mai di essere restaurate però sarebbe necessario di rimettervi travi, e correnti tradicci, rifar pulidi e solari, scale, imposte d'usci e di finestre et altre cose simili."

4. ASF, CPG, nn, 698, fol. 13; ASF, CPG, numeri rossi (hereafter nr), fols. 12, 67, 112; ASF, CPG, nn, 698, fol. 38.

5. By 1704 the institution shifted to house young single mothers and pregnant youths. In 1811 the institution became a nursing home for the elderly. Today the Orbatello building houses the art history library of the Università di Firenze.

6. ASF, CPG, nr, fols. 27, 76: "Un luogo tutto intorno, chiamato Orbatello . . . s'entra e esce per una porta sola ch'è di rinpetto alla via della Pergola ed avi dentro una chiesa titolata in Santa Maria d'Orbatello con abituro per prete . . . e in detto luogo à due vie ed avi 27 chase in tre lati tutte con terreno e con palco, le quali si danno a abitare a povere persone per l'amore di Dio e niente se n'à di pigione"; Isabelle Chabot, "Messer Niccolò degli Alberti, 'pater pauperum': Lettura del testamento," in *L'Ospedale dell' Orbatello: Carità e arte a Firenze,* ed. Christina de Benedictis and Carla Miloschi (Florence: Edizioni Polistampa, 2015), 73–81.

7. Lucia Sandri, "Gli Innocenti e Orbatello nel XVIII e XIX secolo: 'Nocentine' e 'gravide occulte' tra progetti e necessità istituzionali," in De Benedictis and Miloschi, *L'Ospedale dell' Orbatello,* 137. The back entrance of the Innocenti was across the street from the front entrance of the Orbatello on Via della Pergola.

8. ASF, CPG, nn, 751, fol. 70: "Che le dette donne delli Innocenti sieno obligate obedire come l'altre al prete sotto pena di privatione della stanza, ne possino loro ne l'altre andare fuori senza sua licentia del medesimo prete."

9. ASF, CPG, nn, 751, fol. 70.

10. ASF, CPG, nn, 701, fols.. 135, 136: "Grachiava"; "Fece hu hu hu hu"; Kate Colleran, "*Scampanata* at the Widows' Windows: A Case-Study of Sound and Ritual Insult in Cinquecento Florence," *Urban History* 36, no. 3 (2009): 359–378.

11. Archivio Ospedale degli Innocenti Firenze (hereafter AOIF), 6218, fol. 452v.

12. ASF, CPG, nn, 751, fol. 70.

13. ASF, CPG, nn, 751, fol. 70: "vecchie più venerande"; "possino remediare al meno referire li disordini."

14. AOIF, 10445, S15 C1 P2, fol. 279: "Libro del Nome delle Donne che sono state nel Convento di Orbatello"; AOIF, 10452: "Filza di mandati delle Donne che sono abitate et abitano nel convento di Orbatello."

15. AOIF, 6218, 452: "non si facia tal' romore che dia impedimento all altre Donne che habitano in detto Convento ò nelle case dove insegnano Maestre et insomma questo si tollerà quando vi si stia con ogni sorte di modestia e di quiete."

16. Leandro Alberti, *Descrittione di tutta Italia, nelle quale si contiene il sito di essa, l'origine et le Signorie delle città et delle castella* (Bologna: Anselmo Giaccarelli, 1550), 41: "Vi sono altri luoghi pietosi & Hospitali, da farne memoria, si come l'Hospitale di S. Maria Nuova . . . supera tutti gli Hospitali d'Italia . . . l'Hospitale delli poveri fanciullini . . . con altri simili pietosi luoghi de quali diconsi esser 37. Et parimenti ritrovansi . . . settanta sei Monasteri di Religiosi fra huomini & donne."

17. David Herlihy and Christiane Klapisch-Zuber, *Les Toscans et leurs familles: Une étude du Catasto Florentin de 1427* (Paris: Presses de la Fondation Nationale des Sciences Politiques, 1978), 157.

18. R. Burr Litchfield, *Florence Ducal Capitol, 1530–1630* (New York: ACLS Humanities e-book, 2008), chap. 3, para. 119.

19. Nicholas Terpstra, *Abandoned Children of the Italian Renaissance: Orphan Care in Florence and Bologna* (Baltimore: Johns Hopkins University Press, 2005), 58.

20. Enrica Viviani Della Robbia, *Nei monasteri fiorentini* (Florence: Sansoni, 1946), 48–50.

21. Daniela Lombardi, *Povertà maschile, povertà femminile: L'Ospedale dei Mendicanti nella Firenze dei Medici* (Bologna: Il Mulino, 1988).

22. Biblioteca Natzionale Centrale di Firenze (hereafter BNCF), Palatino, "Descritione del numero delle case, e delle persone della città di Firenze fatta l'anno MDCXXXII," E.B.15.2.

23. Sharon Strocchia, *Nuns and Nunneries in Renaissance Florence* (Baltimore: Johns Hopkins University Press, 2009), 7. As Strocchia notes, this figure did not include mendicant houses, which accounted for approximately 100 to 150 more women in Florence and its immediate surroundings.

24. Strocchia, *Nuns and Nunneries,* 7–12. Convent population figures vary according to the criteria of inclusion, and scholarly interpretations can be imprecise. These figures, however, reflect general shifts and changes in population over time.

25. Strocchia, *Nuns and Nunneries,* 13; David Herlihy and Christiane Klapisch-Zuber, *Tuscans and Their Families: A Study of the Florentine Catasto of 1427* (New Haven, CT: Yale University Press, 1985), 53.

26. ASF, Auditore dei Beni Ecclesiastici poi Segretario del Regio Diritto (hereafter Auditore), Negozi Della Deputazione sopra i Monasteri, 1548–1552,

4892; Sharon Strocchia and Julia Rombough, "Women behind Walls: Tracking Nuns and Socio-spatial Networks in Sixteenth-Century Florence," in *Mapping Space, Sense, and Movement in Florence: Historical GIS and the Early Modern City,* ed. Nicholas Terpstra and Colin Rose (Abingdon, UK: Routledge, 2016), 86.

27. Litchfield, *Florence Ducal Capitol,* chap. 3, para. 122.

28. Strocchia, *Nuns and Nunneries,* xii; Philip Gavitt, *Gender, Honor, and Charity in Late Renaissance Florence* (Cambridge: Cambridge University Press, 2011), 196.

29. Nicholas Terpstra, "Introduction," in Terpstra and Rose, *Mapping Space, Sense, and Movement,* 3.

30. ASF, Decima Granducale, 3780–3784, fols. 2r, 3r, 4r, 9r, 11r, 18v, 21r, 24r, 26r, 27r, 30r, 31v, 39r, 40r, 45v, 87r, 97r, 112v, 122r, 124r, 126r, 127r, 132v, 143v, 148v, 150v, 153v, 186v; BNCF, Palatino, "Descritione del numero delle case," E.B.15.2, fols. 33v, 42v, 73r, 98r, 114r, 119r, 121r, 124v, 129r, 149v, 181r–v. For additional figures relating to Casa della Pietà, San Niccolò, Santa Caterina, and Santa Maria Vergine, see Terpstra, *Abandoned Children,* 47–63.

31. The 1548–1552 convent census notes at least 675 unprofessed girls and women in various nunneries. These include novices, servants, and child boarders. The actual number was much higher, as many convents did not include this information. ASF, Auditore, Negozi della Deputazione.

32. Carlo M. Cipolla, "The 'Bills of Mortality' of Florence," *Population Studies* 32, no. 3 (1978): 543–548; John Henderson, "Epidemics in Renaissance Florence: Medical Theory and Government Response," in *Maladie et société (XIIe–XVIIIe siècles),* ed. Neithard Bulst and Robert Delort (Paris: Éditions de CNRS, 1989), 165–186.

33. Terpstra, *Abandoned Children,* 46.

34. Carlo M. Cipolla, *I pidocchi e il granduca: Crisi economica e problemi sanitari nella Firenze del '600* (Bologna: Il Mulino, 1979), 33–35.

35. R. Burr Litchfield, *Emergence of a Bureaucracy: The Florentine Patricians, 1530–1790* (Princeton, NJ: Princeton University Press, 1986), 205, 246.

36. Sherill Cohen, *The Evolution of Women's Asylums since 1500: From Refuges for Ex-prostitutes to Shelters for Battered Women* (New York: Oxford University Press, 1992), 41–60; Sandra Cavallo, *Charity and Power in Early Modern Italy: Benefactors and Their Motives in Turin, 1541–1789* (Cambridge: Cambridge University Press, 1995), chap. 4; Monica Chojnacka, "Women, Charity and Community in Early Modern Venice: The Casa Delle Zitelle," *Renaissance Quarterly* 51, no. 1 (1998): 68–91, 71–73.

37. Elena Brizio, "The Role of Women in Their Kin's Economic and Political Life: The Sienese Case (End XIV–Mid XV Century)," in *Creating Women: Representation, Self-Representation, and Agency in the Renaissance,* ed. Manuela Scarci (Toronto: Centre for Reformation and Renaissance Studies, 2013),

169–181; Ann Matchette, "Women, Objects, and Exchange in Early Modern Florence," *Early Modern Women: An Interdisciplinary Journal* 3 (2008): 245–251; Monica Chojnacka, *Working Women of Early Modern Venice* (Baltimore: Johns Hopkins University Press, 2000).

38. Giuliana Albini, "Pauperismo e solidarietà femminile nell' Italia settentrionale (secoli XIII–XIV)," *Storia Delle Donne* 13 (2017): 103–126.

39. Nicholas Terpstra, *Cultures of Charity: Women, Politics and the Reform of Poor Relief in Renaissance Italy* (Cambridge, MA: Harvard University Press, 2013), 62–78.

40. Terpstra, *Cultures of Charity,* 41; Marina Garbellotti, *Per carità: Poveri e politiche assistenziali nel l'Italia moderna* (Rome: Carocci, 2013).

41. Samuel Kline Cohn Jr., *The Laboring Classes in Renaissance Florence* (New York: Academic Press, 1980), 103.

42. ASF, Fanciulle di Santa Caterina, 7, chaps. 7–9.

43. ASF, Fanciulle di Santa Caterina, 25, fol. 134; Nicholas Terpstra, *Lost Girls: Sex and Death in Renaissance Florence* (Baltimore: Johns Hopkins University Press, 2010), 66–80; Francesco Battistini, "La produzione, il commercio e i prezzi della seta grezza nello stato di Firenze 1489-1859," *Rivista di Storia Economica* 21, no. 3 (2005): 242–245; Judith Brown and John Goodman, "Women and Industry in Florence," *Journal of Economic History* 40, no. 1 (1980): 73–80; Nicholas Terpstra, "Mapping Gendered Labour in the Textile Industry of Early Modern Florence," in *Florence in the Early Modern World: New Perspectives,* ed. Nicholas Scott Baker and Brian Jeffrey Maxson (Abingdon, UK: Routledge, 2019), 68–91.

44. ASF, Fanciulle di Santa Caterina, 17.

45. Anthony Molho, *Marriage Alliance in Late Medieval Florence* (Cambridge, MA: Harvard University Press, 1994), 171–172; Jutta Sperling, *Convents and the Body Politic in Late Renaissance Venice* (Chicago: University of Chicago Press, 1999), 18; Elisa Novi Chavarri, *Monache e gentildonne: Un labile confine; Poteri politici e identità religiose nei monasteri napoletani secoli XVI–XVII* (Milan: Franco Angeli, 2001), 31–40; Anthony Molho, *"Tamquam vere mortua:* Le professioni religiose femminili nella Firenze del tardo medioevo," *Storia e Letteratura* 246 (2006): 1.

46. Strocchia, *Nuns and Nunneries,* 29–32.

47. Kelley Harness, *Echoes of Women's Voices: Music, Art, and Female Patronage in Early Modern Florence* (Chicago: University of Chicago Press, 2006), 219–289; Craig Monson, *Nuns Behaving Badly: Tales of Music, Magic, Art, and Arson in the Convents of Italy* (Chicago: University of Chicago Press, 2010), 95–125.

48. Francesca Medioli, "To Take or Not to Take the Veil: Selected Italian Case Histories, the Renaissance and After," in *Women in Italian Renaissance Culture and Society,* ed. Letizia Panizza (Oxford: European Humanities Research Centre, 2000), 122–137.

49. Strocchia, *Nuns and Nunneries,* 31; Tamar Herzig, *Savonarola's Women: Vision and Reform in Renaissance Italy* (Chicago: University of Chicago Press, 2008), 4–6.

50. Elizabeth Makowski, *Canon Law and Cloistered Women: Periculoso and Its Commentators, 1298–1545* (Washington: Catholic University of America Press, 1997); Ulrike Strasser, *State of Virginity: Gender, Religion, and Politics in an Early Modern Catholic State* (Ann Arbor: University of Michigan Press, 2004), 74–77; Silvia Evangelisti, *Nuns: A History of Convent Life, 1450–1700* (Oxford: Oxford University Press, 2007), 45–54.

51. Richard C. Trexler, "A Widows' Asylum of the Renaissance: The Orbatello of Florence," in *Dependence in Context in Renaissance Florence* (Binghamton, NY: Medieval & Renaissance Texts & Studies, 1994), 435. For records of Orbatello petitions to the Guelf Party and salary payments made to the institution, see ASF, CPG, nr, 16.

52. Elena Fasano Guarini, "Potere centrale e comunità soggette nel granducato di Cosimo I," *Rivista Storica Italiana* 89, nos. 3–4 (1997): 490–538; Elena Fasano Guarini, *Lo stato di Cosimo I* (Florence: Sansoni, 1973), 50–60.

53. Nicholas Terpstra, "Competing Visions of the State and Social Welfare: The Medici Dukes, the Bigallo Magistrates, and Local Hospitals in Sixteenth-Century Tuscany," *Renaissance Quarterly* 54, no. 4, pt. 2 (2001): 1319–1355.

54. Lucia Sandri, "L'attività di banco dell'Ospedale degli Innocenti di Firenze: Don Vincenzo Borghini e la 'bancarotta' del 1579," in *L'uso del denaro: Patrimoni e amministrazione nei luoghi pii e negli enti ecclesiastici in Italia (secoli XV–XVIII),* ed. Marina Garbellotti and Alessandro Pastore (Bologna: Il Mulino, 2001), 153–178.

55. Gavitt, *Gender, Honor, and Charity,* 62.

56. Strocchia and Rombough, "Women behind Walls," 90–91.

57. ASF, CPG, nn, 702, fol. 180: "Mona Luchretia gia donna di Buonfiglio Spadaio che ha suplicato a Sua Eccellentia per havere una stanza in Orbatello. La prima cosa è gravida e persona per quanto intendo scandolosa e ha quattro fanciulle e uno fanciullo che ogni giorno daranno fastidio al Magistrato per essere persone supplichievoli."

58. ASF, CPG, nn, 702, fol. 179.

59. Trexler, "A Widows' Asylum," 422–423.

60. AOIF, 10445, Libro de' Nomi delle Donne che sono state nel Convento di Orbatello di Firenze dall' anno 1588, fol. 279.

61. ASF, CPG, nn, 801, fol. 19.

62. ASF, CPG, nn, 701, fol. 94.

63. ASF, CPG, nn, 787, fol. 42: "e aver presidio alla conservazione della sua virginita . . . 2 Marzo 1616 [sf]."

64. ASF, CPG, nn, 787, fol. 42: "Io Fra Benedetto Nacchianti da Monte Varchi, et al presente Confessoro nella chiesa di Santa Croce di Firenze. . . . Fo

fede come la verità e che molt'anni sono ho conosciuto la Lessandra degl'Innocenti e già serva in casa di Francesco Miniati per timora di Dio, e buona fanciulla s'e confessata e communicata spesso e frequenta la Chiesa, che per cio ho fatto la presente di mia propria mano."

65. Terpstra, *Lost Girls,* 140.
66. Stefano D'Amico, "Shameful Mother: Poverty and Prostitution in Seventeenth-Century Milan," *Journal of Family History* 30, no. 1 (2005): 110–111.
67. ASF, Fanciulle di Santa Caterina, 7, chap. 1: "Regnando Don Ferdinando de Medici Gran Duca di Toscana fu per tutta Italia una grandissima carestia onde molte povere fanciulle per la fame si davano a mal' vivere ... molti gentil' huomini timorati di Dio con il favore della Serenissima Gran Duchessa si dettero a raccorre molte povere fanciulle che andavano per le strade."
68. Nicholas Terpstra, "Sex and the Sacred: Negotiating Spatial and Sensory Boundaries in Renaissance Florence," *Radical History Review* 121 (2015): 71–90.
69. John K. Brackett, "The Florentine Onestà and the Control of Prostitution, 1403–1680," *Sixteenth Century Journal* 24, no. 2 (1993): 273–300, 280.
70. ASF, Ufficiali dell'Onestà (hereafter Onestà), 3, "Statuti e leggi 1577–1747," fols. 5r, 15r, 16v, 17r.
71. ASF, Onestà, 5, unpaginated.
72. Brackett, "The Florentine Onestà," 297.
73. ASF, Onestà, 5, unpaginated.
74. Maria Serena Mazzei, *Prostitute e lenoni della Firenze del quattrocento* (Milan: Il Saggiatore,1991), 219–225. For a comparative example from Venice, see Brian Pullan, *Tolerance, Regulation and Rescue: Dishonoured Women and Abandoned Children in Italy, 1300–1800* (Manchester, UK: Manchester University Press, 2016), 50, 61, 100.
75. The modern street name for Via Chiara is Via de' Serragli. The Convertite church is now a Georgian Orthodox church.
76. Cohen, *The Evolution of Women's Asylums,* 18; Craig Monson, *Habitual Offenders: A True Tale of Nuns, Prostitutes, and Murderers in 17th-Century Italy* (Chicago: University of Chicago Press, 2016); Romano Canosa and Isabella Colonnello, *Storia della prostituzione in Italia dal quattrocento al fine del settecento* (Rome: Sapere, 2000), 117–125. The term *convertite* referred to a convert and was especially used to signify a reformed sex worker.
77. ASF, Carte Strozziane, 3rd ser., 233, 34v.
78. ASF, Auditore, Negozi della Deputazione, fol. 209r; Strocchia, *Nuns and Nunneries,* 6; ASF, Corporazione Religiose Soppresse dal Governo Francese (hereafter CRSGF), 126:62, unpaginated: "Nota di tutte le Monache che si trovano questo di primo di Maggio 1620 nel nostro monastero."
79. ASF, CRSGF, 126:81.

80. ASF, Acquisti e Doni (hereafter A&D), 45, *Fondatione dell Monastero delle Convertite della Nostra Compagnia,* unpaginated: "agere penitentiam a Dei Misercordia . . . per perpetuo stent recluse dentro."

81. Cohen, *The Evolution of Women's Asylums,* 62.

82. ASF, Auditore, Negozi della Deputazione, fol. 209r.

83. BNCF, *Pratica universale del Dottor Marc'Antonio Savelli da Modigliana: Estratta in compendio per alfabeto dalle principali leggi, bandi, statuti, ordini, e consuetudini, massime criminali, e miste, che vegliano nella stati del Serenissimo Gran Duca di Toscana . . . al Serenissimo Ferdinando II Gran Duca di Toscana* (Florence, 1675), 254, nos. 45–46.

84. ASF, CRSGF, 126:62, no. 27: "Ma Maddalena di Piero della Torre . . . la quarta parte de sua beni secondo l'uso delle meretrici et della legge fatta l'anno 1533."

85. ASF, Onestà, 1, fols. 39v–40r.

86. ASF, Compagnia Poi Magistrato del Bigallo (hereafter Bigallo), 1691, fol. 11r: "la gran moltitudine di donne di mala vita nella città di Firenze, et che molte ritornerebbono a penitentia se havessero un luogo, dove ritirarsi."

87. ASF, Onestà, 4, fol. 9v: "Christofano di Giovanni Tedesco sarto confinato per un' anno a Livorno . . . per havere scacciato la propria moglie da se per vivere dissolutamente."

88. Cohen, *The Evolution of Women's Asylums,* 40–60; ASF, Bigallo, 1691.

89. It is possible that a plague, house fire, or famine accounted for the population drop; the institution's notoriously bad recordkeeping provide no definitive answer.

90. ASF, Bigallo, 1691, chap. 38; ASF, CRSGF, 143:1, fol. 17: "Numero Cinque stanza a palco compresa la Cucina, piccolo parlatorio e stanza d'ingresso in fondo della quale si passa ad un orticello recinto da alti muri. Montata una branca di scala si trova un piccolo Coro corrispondente in Chiesa e continuando d.a Scala si perviene al Primo Piano composto di Numero tre stanze corrispondenti sull' Orto, e Andito che ammette a No. Cinque stanze a palco due delle quali molto piccole seguitando la Medesima Scala di giunge al Secondo Piano . . . in Numero sette stanze."

91. Cohen, *The Evolution of Women's Asylums,* 41.

92. BNCF, Palatino, "Descritione del numero delle case," E.B.15.2.

93. Terpstra, "Sex and the Sacred," 71.

94. ASF, Onestà, 4.

95. ASF, Onestà, 4, fols. 30v, 76v, 99v: "dato pugna nel viso alla Portia del Piragin"; "per haver percosso malamente la Giulia di Michele sua puttana"; "per havere percosso malamente la Margherita Carissi."

96. ASF, Onestà, 4, fol. 99v.

97. ASF, A&D, 291, "Onestà e meretrice," unpaginated / unfoliated.

98. ASF, A&D, 292, "Partiti degli otto di custodia e balia," unpaginated/unfoliated: "Barbara sia condotta al Monastero delle Convertite di Firenze e non possa uscire per tutto il mese sotto pena di fiorini 21."

99. For a Roman comparative, see Alessandra Camerano, "Assistenza richeste ed assistenza imposta: Il conservatorio di S. Caterina della Rosa di Roma," *Quaderni Storici* 28, no. 82 (1993): 227-260.

100. ASF, Onestà, 4, fol. 8v: "Antonia d'ostro Bolognese . . . non vi potese più ritornare alla pena della frusta e di scudi cinquanta . . . essendo uscita del Monasterio delle Convertite dove haveva presso l'habito monacale e tornata a vita disonesta."

101. ASF, A&D, 291, *Da libri di sentenze del magistrato degli otto,* unpaginated/unfoliated.

102. ASF, A&D, 291, *Onestà e meretrice,* unpaginated/unfoliated: "1586 . . . Caterina da Carniguano chiari fa meretrice, era entrata nelle Malmaritate, e poi uscita e andata a . . . tenere di nuova vita disonesta."

103. *Sommario de capitoli della venerabile Compagnia di Santa Maria Maddalena sopra le Mal Maritate* (Florence: Bartholomeo Sermartelli, 1583), 22: "Il tenere per forza tutte quelle che se ne vogliano andare, causerebbe in casa troppo grande confusione, & spesso bisognerebbe venire a penitente gagliarde."

104. *Sommario de capitoli,* 24: "Et per obviare allo scandalo che ne nasce quando se ne fuggano, acciò con il timore della pena tanto meno pensino a fuggire, vogliamo che quelle che sene fuggano, oltre alle spese per le quali debbono saturare, che per pena habbino da dare a questo santo luogo venti scudi."

105. *Sommario de capitoli,* 19: "anco il sito dell' horto, si conservino li stecchoni sopra le mura dell' horto, poiche non potendosi entrare dentro, senza romperne, quando intervenisse alcun caso, subito sarebbe scoperto, & le nostre sorelle guardino come stanno."

106. ASF, Otto di Guardia e Balia del Principato (hereafter Otto di Guardia), 214, unpaginated, "23 di maggio 1603 [*sf*]."

107. Strocchia, *Nuns and Nunneries,* xii; Mary Laven, *Virgins of Venice: Broken Vows and Cloistered Lives in the Renaissance Convent* (New York: Penguin, 2004), 23–44.

108. For an example of this discourse, see Domenico Ottonelli, *Alcuni buoni avvisi, e casi di coscienza intorno alla pericolosa conversatione, da proporsi a chi conversa poco medestamente* (Florence: Luca Franceschini e Alessandro Logi, 1646), 372–373.

109. Strocchia, *Nuns and Nunneries,* 2. Sperling, *Convents and the Body Politic,* 18–29, notes that by 1582, 53.8 percent of Venetian noblewomen entered into convents; by 1642 the number had risen to 81.58 percent.

110. Strocchia, *Nuns and Nunneries,* 119–120.

111. ASF, Auditore, 4982, fol. 27r. Directly related family members in San Pier Martire included two Acciaiuoli sisters, two Bonsi sisters, two Del Biade sisters, and four Minerbetti women.
112. Strocchia, *Nuns and Nunneries,* 88.
113. ASF, Auditore, 4982, fol. 113r.
114. ASF, CRSGF, 126:62, unpaginated: "Nota di tutte le monache Nobili, et Gentildonne che si ritrovavano nel nostro venerando Monistero . . . dall'anno 1455 insino quasi a questo anno presente 1620."
115. ASF, CRSGF, 126:62, unpaginated; the patrician abbesses listed in the records are "Suora Alessandra di Bartolomeo Lapaccini fu badessa, donna di gran fama di santità e visse in questo santo ufitio circa anni 22 perche stavano a vita. 1455; Suora Clemenza di Bartolomeo Ciacchagnini fu badessa nel 1514; Suora Dianora de Rossi fu badessa nel 1523; Suora Marietta de Rinaldeschi fu badessa 1528; Suora Tommasa Fiorelli fu badessa nel 1539; Suora Aurelia del Milanese fu badessa nel 1564; Suora Innocenza di Antonio Giani fu badessa nel 1583; Suora Cherubina Agolanti fu badessa nel 1592; Suora Agata Vanni badessa nel 1596."
116. This strategy is also discussed in Cohen, *The Evolution of Women's Asylums,* 62.
117. Saint Augustine, *The Rule of St. Augustine,* trans. Russell Robert, OSA, last revised October 6, 2023, http://sourcebooks.fordham.edu/halsall/source/ruleaug.html.
118. Terrence G. Kardong, *Benedict's Rule: A Translation and Commentary* (Collegeville, MN: The Order of St. Benedict, 1996), 79–80.
119. Gabriella Zarri, "Ecclesiastical Institutions and Religious Life in the Observant Century," in *A Companion to Observant Reform in the Late Middle Ages and Beyond,* ed. James D. Mixson and Bert Roest (Leiden: Brill, 2015), 35, 40.
120. Giustina Niccolini, *The Chronicle of Le Murate by Sister Giustina Niccolini,* trans. and ed. Saundra Weddle (Toronto: Centre for Reformations and Renaissance Studies, 2011), 119, 206.
121. Domenico Zon, *Santuario delle monache* (Venice: Fioravante Prati, 1615), 9: "a tutte le Religiose il santo silentio, e si da loro poco tempo di parlare, e di perder il pretioso tempo in parlamenti inutile & otiose."
122. ASF, CRSGF, 191:33, fol. 16v: "Ordiniamo che in Coro et in Chiesa non solo al santissimo Sacrifitio della messa . . . si osservi il debito silenzio, il simile si faccia in refettorio nel tempo della refettione e massime quando si legge et in dormentorio."
123. AOIF, 6855, "Negozi diversi di mons. Vincenzo Borghini circa la clausura dei monasteri dello stato di Firenze: Diverse altre scritture—V," unpaginated/unfoliated: "Il silentio sia osservato in tutti li luoghi . . . [chi] romperà sia tenuta ordinare cinque pater nostri et cinque Ave Marie con le braccia in croce. In refettorio . . . che vada a mangiare. Et se il rompimento fosse disordinato con gridi, et clamori . . . non beva vino la mattina seg-

uente. In coro, in dormitorio in refettorio sempre in questi luoghi si osservi silenzio massime quando si dice messa o il divino officio o si legge le tanie."

124. ASF, Bigallo, 1691, fols. 40, 6: "Con stare ritirate in silentio"; "Nessuna fratello ne offitiale vadia a parlare a nessuna di Casa."

125. ASF, Bigallo, 1691, fol. 41: "Et mentre anco che starano sotto la nostra cura, starano in quiete, scadalose et convertite solo di nome . . . et per più aiuto loro, et per maggior cautela nostra, bisogna che li riduchiamo tutti a memoria quello che le sono state. . . . Nessuno adunque dia orecchio a quanto le dicessero . . . sapendo la natura loro che è di non si contentar mai et di mettere zizania."

126. ASF, Bigallo, 1691, fol. 17: "Et anco perché l'esperienza dimostra che ogni volta che le parlano, stanno poi per il più inquieted."

127. ASF, Fanciulle di Santa Caterina, 7, vol. 1, chap. 6: "La Mattina un hora avanti si dica il santissimo Rosario, come anco il giorno un'altra hora avanti si dica la terza parte del Rosario. In chiesa in continuo silente. In dormentorio quando che è sonata a dormiglione sino alla mattina che è sonato a lavoro. In Refettorio quando che si mangia. Cosi la mattina che si fa la comunione generale sino che sarà d.a la Messa & chi trasgredira a questi ordini vada per una disciplina alla Priora la prima volta, la seconda in terra senza potersi dispensare"; ASF, Bigallo, 1691, 41: "starano in quiete."

128. ASF, Fanciulle Santa Caterina, 7, vol. 2, chap. 8: "avvertisca di parlare cosi forte, che sia udita dall' Ascoltatrice, la quale sara quivi presente. Et se lei vi sarà disetto oltre alla penitenza positive s'intenda essere priva di poter andar alla porta à parlare a parenti ò à altri per sei mesi."

129. ASF, Fanciulle Santa Caterina, 7, vol. 2 "Incomincia la Terza Distintione," chap. 4: "una fanciulla discreta & prudente e modi della quale siano esempio à tutte l'altre. . . . Sia vigilante per tutti i luoghi & e si osservi il silentio."

130. Terpstra, *Lost Girls,* 137.

131. ASF, Fanciulle di Santa Caterina, 7, vol. 1, unpaginated: "non sapendo di che deve fare domandare il Padre. Insegnar a cantare le note o parole del canto fermo mentre che sia in fila la mattina."

132. Alain Corbin, *Village Bells: Sound and Meaning in the Nineteenth-Century French Countryside* (London: Papermac, 1999), x.

133. Carolyn Gianturco, "Caterina Assandra, suora compositrice," in *La musica sacra in Lombardia nella prima metà del seicento: Atti del convegno internazionale di studi,* ed. Alberto Colzani, Andrea Luppi, and Maurizio Padoan (Como, Italy: Antiquae Musicae Italicae Studiosi, 1987), 117–127; Harness, *Echoes of Women's Voices,* 289; Laurie Stras, *Women and Music in Sixteenth-Century Ferrara* (Cambridge: Cambridge University Press, 2018), 18–19.

134. Suzanne Cusick, "He Said, She Said?: Men Hearing Women in Medicean Florence," in *Rethinking Difference in Music Scholarship,* ed. Olivia Bloechl, Melanie Lowe, and Jeffrey Kallberg (New York: Cambridge University Press,

2015), 53–76; Craig Monson, *Disembodied Voices: Music and Culture in an Early Modern Italian Convent* (Berkeley: University of California Press, 1995), 225–239; Robert Kendrick, *Celestial Voices: Nuns and Their Music in Early Modern Milan* (Oxford: Oxford University Press, 1996), 22–27.

135. Gian Lodovico Masetti Zannini, "'Sua vità di canto' e 'purità di cuore': Aspetti della musica nei monasteri femminili romani," in *La cappella musicale nell' Italia della Controriforma: Atti del Convegno Internazionale di Studi nel IV Centenario di Fondazione della Cappella Musicale di S. Biagio di Cento, Cento, 13–15 ottobre 1989,* ed. Oscar Mischiati and Paolo Russo (Florence: Leo S. Olschki, 1993), 137–139; Colleen Reardon, *Holy Concord within Sacred Walls: Nuns and Music in Siena, 1575–1700* (Oxford: Oxford University Press, 2001), 23–24; Oscar Mischiati, "Il Concilio di Trento e la polifonia: Una diversa proposta di lettera e di prospettiva bibliografica," in *Musica e liturgia nella riforma tridenta,* ed. Danilo Curto and Marco Gozzi (Trento, Italy: Provincia Autonoma di Trento, Servizio Beni Librari e Archivistici, 1995), 19–29.

136. Reardon, *Holy Concord within Sacred Walls,* 5–8; Kimberlyn Montford, "Holy Restraint: Religious Reform and Nuns' Music in Early Modern Rome," *Sixteenth Century Journal* 37, no. 4 (2006): 1012; Stras, *Women and Music,* 18–19.

137. Reardon, *Holy Concord within Sacred Walls,* 4.

CHAPTER TWO ∿ NOISE

1. David Rosenthal, *Kings of the Street: Power, Community, and Ritual in Renaissance Florence* (Turnhout, Belgium: Brepols, 2015), 105–106.

2. Gian Rosa, *Le leggi penali sui muri di Firenze: Tratti di corda e penna* (Florence: Casa Editrice Nerbini, 1911), 22; Serena Maria Mazzei, *Prostitute e lenoni nella Firenze del quattrocento* (Milan: Saggiatore, 1991), 226.

3. Rosa, *Le leggi penali,* 22.

4. The Candeli nuns moved into the complex on Via Pilastri in 1365 after ongoing warfare in the fourteenth century pushed the nuns to leave their rural convent and seek shelter within city walls. See Sharon Strocchia, *Nuns and Nunneries in Renaissance Florence* (Baltimore: Johns Hopkins University Press, 2009), 67.

5. Archivio di Stato di Firenze (hereafter ASF), Acquisti e Doni (hereafter A&D), 291, unpaginated/unfoliated: "1560 . . . Giulia napoletana condannata per abitare presso il convento di Candeli."

6. ASF, A&D, 292, unpaginated/unfoliated: "Febbraio 1562 [*sf*] Molti giovani erano di notte andati 'alla casa della Tonina di via dei Pilastri e fattovi baccano e rissa.'"

7. ASF, A&D 291, unpaginated/unfoliated: "1563 . . . Francesca da Pistoia meretrice in via Pilastri andata fuori di notte senza bollettino."

8. ASF, Auditore dei Beni Ecclesiastici poi Segretario del Regio Diritto (hereafter Auditore), 4896, fol. 128: "Le monache di Santa Maria di Candelo es-

pongano come per la grida e rumori oltre alle parole disoneste, che tutta
notte si sentano della lor Chiesa et Dormetorio causate per le meretrice che
habitano nella via de Pilastri et vicine al monastro, sono grandamente disturbate et molestate non solamente quando si trovano in chiesa a far oratione, ma anco nelle proprie celle."

9. ASF, Auditore, 4896, fol. 128: "rumori fatti et di parole che non solamente
danno scandolo a queste ancille di Dio ma anco a molte persone da bene,
et la legge . . . sopra l'habitatione delle meretrici prohibisce che le non possino stare vicine a cento braccia a monasterii"; "sappiamo esser vene molte
che possono . . . dare scandolo a queste monache, comandarli che si
partino."

10. ASF, A&D, 291, unpaginated/unfoliated: "Da Libri di Sentenze del Magistrato degli Otto . . . 1589 Pasquino da Ruota, servitore del Signor Luigi
Dovara per avere con pugnale fatto insulto a Giuliano Chiareschi e fatto
baccano alla stessa in via dei Pilastri et per un terrazzo entratoli in casa per
forza."

11. ASF, Onestà, 4, fol. 6v: "Adi 15 di Luglio 1594 Margherita Brunelleschi meretrice stava nella via di Pilastri condannata scudi di due d'oro da pagarsi
secondo gl'ordini per essere stata trovata vestita da huomo di giorno senza
il bollettino o licenza."

12. Elissa B. Weaver, *Convent Theatre in Early Modern Italy: Spiritual Fun and
Learning for Women* (Cambridge: Cambridge University Press, 2002); Craig
Monson, *Nuns Behaving Badly: Tales of Music, Magic, Art, and Arson in the Con-
vents of Italy* (Chicago: University of Chicago Press, 2010); Mary Laven, *Vir-
gins of Venice: Broken Vows and Cloistered Lives in the Renaissance Convent* (New
York: Penguin, 2004); Anne Jacobson Schutte, *By Force and Fear: Taking and
Breaking Monastic Vows in Early Modern Europe* (Ithaca, NY: Cornell Univer-
sity Press, 2011).

13. ASF, A&D, 292, *Partiti degli Otto Ottobre 1580,* unpaginated: "Pier Francesco
da Diaceto . . . vedendo poi di non potere andare a parlarli a suo modo, aver
cominciato a far baccano al detto monastero e tirar sassi alle finestre."

14. ASF, Compagnia Poi Magistrato del Bigallo, 1691, fol. 11r: "et che molte
ritornerebbono a penitentia se havessero un luogo, dove ritirarsi."

15. Robert Davis, "Stones and Shame in Early Modern Italy," *Acta Histriae* 8,
no. 2 (2000): 449-456; Elizabeth S. Cohen, "Honour and Gender in the
Streets of Early Modern Rome," *Journal of Interdisciplinary History* 22, no. 4
(1992): 597-625.

16. Davis, "Stones and Shame," 450.

17. Archivio Arcivescovile di Firenze (hereafter AAF), Cause Criminale, 36.2, S.
Maria di Montedomini, no. 1: "Le Monache di Montedomini, si querelano
del gran rumore che li fa giorno et sera in sula Piazza della Zeccha con giochi
di Rulle et altre radunate di Gente, et di sassi, et Rulle che sono tirate alla
volta delle loro finestre."

18. ASF, Capitani di Parte Guelfa (hereafter CPG), numeri rossi, 16, fol. 127v: "Qualunque persona di qualsivoglia grado stato o conditione sa sia che per lo avernire non ardisca nella strada d'Orbatello e vincentro a quello ne nelli luoghi che li sono circumstanti et maxime di notte tempo fare o far fare serenate . . . ne sonare o far sonare suoni di sorte alcuna ne cantare o fermarsi audire alcuna delle predette cose sotto pena della nostra indignatione."

19. ASF, Otto di Guardia, 89, fol. 26r: "le Monache del monastario delle Convertite, in torno al loro monastario e chiesa farsi molti bachani di sonare cantare e altri tumulti e ragunare e essere impedito loro la consolatione de li divini offiti."

20. ASF, Otto di Guardia, 89, fol. 26r: "bachano di sorte alcuna. ne sonare o cantare o fare altri strepiti, ne giucare a palla pallottole o altro qual si voglia giuoco, sotto pena del arbitrio del Magistrato."

21. ASF, A&D, 292, unpaginated / unfoliated: "Novembre 1580 Si fa severo bando ad oggetto che nessuno ardisca in modo alcuno andare ne entrare dentro alle porte del nuovo monastero fatto da sua Altezza in via della Scala, dove sono congregato le donne maritate convertite, sotto il titolo della Compagnia di S. M. Maddalena; ne dare o far dare molestia alcuna alle dette convertite . . . parlare o fare parlare in modo alcuno ad alcuna di loro."

22. ASF, Otto di Guardia, 60, fol. 4v: "non possino per l'avinire . . . monastero a braccia 200 giocare . . . cantare, tirare sassi, ragionare o fare altro romori sotto pena di scudi 20."

23. ASF, Otto di Guardia, 62, fol. 120v: "che non . . . per alcune che per l'avenire giochi a giocho alcuno appreso al desta monastero . . . ne farci o dica brutture alcuna o parole inhoneste sotto pena di scudi 20."

24. Strocchia, *Nuns and Nunneries,* 217.

25. ASF, Onestà, 3, fol. 25r: "e dette Monache in l'avvenire non habbino altre disturbi dalle persone inhoneste che habitano vicine al detto loro Monastero da quella parte massime dove esse hanno il loro Dormeatoreo."

26. ASF, Otto di Guardia, 60, fols. 4v, 33r; ASF, Otto di Guardia, 62; ASF, Auditore, 4896, 128; ASF, Otto di Guardia, 64, fols. 62r-v; ASF, Otto di Guardia, 68, fol. 153r; ASF, Otto di Guardia, 72, fols. 10r-v.

27. ASF, Otto di Guardia, 89, fols. 54v–55r: "Monache del Monasterio di S. Piero Maggiore havere fatto reporre che faccendosi in su quella piazza gran baccano ingiucarsi tutto il giorno a cocomeri per il che ne seguita impedimento grandi alli divini offiti, et volendo il Magistrato obviar a tal disordine."

28. ASF, Otto di Guardia, 89, fol. 55r.

29. For a specific example of patrician patronage and familial networks at San Pier Maggiore, see Julia Rombough and Sharon Strocchia, "City of Women: Mapping Movement, Gender, and Enclosure in Renaissance Florence," in *Public Renaissance: Urban Space, Geolocated Apps and Public History,* ed. Fab-

rizio Nevola, David Rosenthal, and Nicholas Terpstra (Abingdon, UK: Routledge, 2022), 169–191.

30. Sharon Strocchia, "When the Bishop Married the Abbess: Masculinity and Power in Florentine Episcopal Entry Rites, 1300–1600," *Gender & History* 19, no. 2 (2007): 351.

31. Strocchia, "When the Bishop Married the Abbess," 361.

32. Strocchia, "When the Bishop Married the Abbess," 359.

33. Paul Rodaway, *Sensuous Geographies: Body, Sense and Place* (London: Routledge, 1994), 89–96.

34. Carole Collier Frick, *Dressing Renaissance Florence: Families, Fortunes, and Fine Clothing* (Baltimore: Johns Hopkins University Press, 2002), 184–185; E[mmanuel] Rodocanachi, *La femme italienne à l'époque de la Renaissance* (Paris: Hachette, 1907), 362; Mazzei, *Prostitute e lenoni nella Firenze,* 121.

35. ASF, A&D, 292, "Febbraio 1564 [*sf*]," unpaginated/unfoliated: "Ed anche dopo questo fatto era tornata a far baccano a quelle donne."

36. ASF, A&D, 292, "Febbraio 1564 [*sf*]," unpaginated/unfoliated: "Giulia meretrice in via Pentolini era andata di notte con alcuni compagni a far baccano a casa della Lucrezia di Jacopo sensale di grani."

37. ASF, A&D, 292, unpaginated/unfoliated.

38. ASF, A&D, 292; 291; ASF, Camera e Auditore Fiscale, 2108.

39. ASF, A&D, 292, unpaginated/unfoliated: "Maggio 1560 Tre giovani tessitori erano processati "'per essere andati di notte in Borgo alla noce a casa la Bita meretrice e spentoli il lume e fattole baccano.'"

40. ASF, A&D, 292, unpaginated/unfoliated: "Luglio 1560 di notte alcuni giovani nobili aveva fatto baccano e baie 'in la via della scala presso alla casa della Cammilla detta la Spiritata.'"

41. ASF, A&D, 291, "Onestà e Meretrice," unpaginated/unfoliated: "1575—Quattro donne di via Mozza aveva fatto baccano alla Mariangiola Spagnuola."

42. ASF, Onestà, 4, fol. 8v; ASF, A&D, 291, unpaginated/unfoliated; ASF, A&D, 292, unpaginated/unfoliated; ASF, A&D 291, "Onestà e meretrice," unpaginated/unfoliated; ASF, Onestà, 5, fols. 5v, 6v, 21r, 31r; Saundra Weddle, "Mobility and Prostitution in Early Modern Venice," *Early Modern Women: An Interdisciplinary Journal* 14, no. 1 (2019): 95–108.

43. ASF, Auditore, 4896, fol. 4: "Le Monache di San Martino in via della Scala insieme con li vicini domandano . . . che la Bruna da Prato di mala fama et in honesta non possi tornare in una casa che l'ha compro vicini al monastero . . . che la legge ultimamente la fatta sopra l'habitationi delle meretrici non lo permette et per ciò . . . le diciamo come la detta casa e vicina alle monache et la Bruna e donna sospetta. . . . Et tornando lei in quell luogo . . . darebbe scandalo alle monache et al'huomini da bene che vi habitano, 20 di Maggio 1562."

44. ASF, Auditore, 4896, fol. 128: "la legge fatta l'anno 1561 sopra l'habitatione delle meretrici prohibisce che le non possino stare vicine a cento braccia a monasterii et piu et meno ad arbitrio de Deputati . . . autorita di poter comandare alle meretrici che si trovassino dare scandolo a monache che fra 15 giorni dovessino partirsi di quel luogo."

45. BNCF, *Estratta in compendio per alfabeto dalle principali leggi bandi, statuti, ordini, e consuetudini, massime criminali, e miste,* 254, no. 2: "Meretrice, e donne disoneste, sciolte, o maritate, paesane, o forestiere non possono abitare per braccia 100 a misura Fiorentina dirimpetto, o appresso alcun Monasterio di Monache che vivano in clausura dentro la Città di Firenze sotto pena di lire 200"; Nicholas Terpstra,"Sex and the Sacred: Negotiating Spatial and Sensory Boundaries in Renaissance Florence," *Radical History Review* 121 (2015): 76-77.

46. Stefano D'Amico, "Shameful Mother: Poverty and Prostitution in Seventeenth-Century Milan," *Journal of Family History* 39, no.1 (2005): 111–112; Tessa Storey, *Carnal Commerce in Counter-Reformation Rome* (Cambridge: Cambridge University Press, 2008), 165-166.

47. Nicholas Terpstra, "Locating the Sex Trade in the Early Modern City: Space, Sense, and Regulation in Sixteenth-Century Florence," in *Mapping Space, Sense, and Movement in Florence: Historical GIS and the Early Modern City,* ed. Nicholas Terpstra and Colin Rose (New York: Rutledge, 2016), 114.

48. ASF, A&D, 291, "Onestà e Meretrice," unpaginated/unfoliated: "e per tutto proibito l'andare di giorno in cocchio carozzo o simile per la città di Fiorenza. . . . Volendo le meretrici usare la carrozza fuor di citta debbano montrare e scendere alla porta della citta ed della carrozza possano valersi durante la notte."

49. ASF, A&D, 291, "Onestà e meretrice," unpaginated/unfoliated: "1577 Monica moglie di Antonio Carbacci, sebbene avesse voluto levarsi dal peccato, vi era ricaduta e viveva disonesta in borgo Santa Croce di consenso del marito."

50. ASF, A&D, 291, "Onestà e meretrice," unpaginated/unfoliated: "1577 passando in cochio per quella strada, lei aveva fatto chiasso e baccano ingiurioso e brutto."

51. Vincenzo Scamozzi, *L'idea della architettura universale di Vincenzo Scamozzi architetto Veneto,* vol. 2 (Venice: Giorgio Valentino, 1615), 359: "Le strade di Roma, e Napoli, e Genova, e Milano, & alcune altre qui in Italia: per non dire della Germania, e della Francia sono selciate parte di pietre dure, & anco ciottoli non molto grossi . . . e selicati di mattoni in coltello, per l'andar de' pedoni, & à questo modo i cavalli, e le ruote delle Carrozze; vi fanno manco rumore."

52. Lorenzo Cantini, *Legislazione toscana: Raccolta e illustrata dal dottore Lorenzo Cantini* (Florence: Albizziniana da S. Maria in Campo, 1804), 131: "Il Serenissimo Gran-Duca di Toscana . . . e degnissimi Signori Otto di Balia della

Città di Firenze ... per ovviare alli disordini, e scandoli che seguono ...
comandano che li Carrozzieri per l'avvenire non scendino mai dalle carrozze, mentre stanno ad aspettare con le carrozze vote"; Giuseppe Pagani,
*Memoriale alfabetico ragionato della legislazione Toscana dalla prima epoca del
principato fino al presente secondo lo stato della medesima* (Florence: Giuseppe
Pagani, 1829), 89-90: "facessero dell' insolenze con accostar troppo le Carrozze al muro, farle correre, levar il posto a chi è avanti, traversare, passare,
o dare indietro in modo da far nascere dei disordini."

53. John M. Hunt, "Carriages, Violence, and Masculinity in Early Modern
Rome," *I Tatti Studies in the Italian Renaissance* 17, no. 2 (2014): 176-177.

54. ASF, A&D, 292, unpaginated / unfoliated: "Maggio 1560 Tre giovani tessitori erano processati 'per essere andati di notte in Borgo alla Noce a casa la
Bita meretrice e spentoli il lume e fattole baccano'"; ASF, A&D, 292, unpaginated / unfoliated: "Febbraio 1564 [*sf*]"; "Ed anche dopo quest fatto era
tornato a far baccano a quelle donne."

55. BNCF, Palatino, E.B.15.2.

56. Nicholas Terpstra, *Abandoned Children of the Italian Renaissance: Orphan Care
in Florence and Bologna* (Baltimore: Johns Hopkins University Press, 2005),
1.

57. Ilaria Taddei, "*Puerizia, Adolescenza* and *Giovinezza*: Images and Conceptions
of Youth in Florentine Society during the Renaissance," in *The Premodern
Teenager: Youth in Society 1150-1650,* ed. Konrad Eisenbichler (Toronto:
Centre for Reformation and Renaissance Studies, 2002), 16-18. Taddei
explains that sometimes *giovani* could even refer to men in their thirties,
though other Florentine records capped the age of the term at eighteen, and
yet others in the mid-twenties; See also Ilaria Taddei, "I giovani alla fine del
medioevo: Rappresentazione e modelli di comportamento," in *I giovani
nel medioevo: Ideali e pratiche di vita,* ed. Isa Lori Sanfilippo and Antonio
Rigon (Rome: Istituto Storico Italiano per il Medioevo, 2014), 11-23.

58. ASF, A&D, 292, unpaginated / unfoliated: "nel marzo 1539 [*sf*] dodici
giovani aveva fatto baccano alla casa della Marietta Sportaina meretrice, ti-
randole sassi alle finestre e cercando di buttarle giù la porta."

59. ASF, A&D, 292, unpaginated / unfoliated: "Settembre 1539 Certi giovani
aveva fatto baccano alla Moretta concubina alla porta Romana."

60. ASF, A&D, 292, unpaginated / unfoliated: "Dicembre 1558 Alcuni giovani
erano processati ... per avere con armi fatto baccano alla casa della Caterina
Seragostini."

61. ASF, A&D, 292, unpaginated / unfoliated: "Aprile 1558 Molti giovani eran
querelati "perche di febbraio di notte tempo in la via dell'Agnolo facendosi
veglia e recitandosi una commedia in casa di Piero di Tommaso lacciolo essendo l'uscio serrato essi con calci e fischi e sassi feciono baccano e tanto
percossone l'uscio che per forza l'aprirono, et entrando dentro, dove erano
molte donne e altra brigata, feciono impeto e tumulto mescolandosi

insieme, traendo alla lumiera più pezzi di seggiola per spegnerla e stracciarono un panno d'arazzo."

62. Anne E. C. McCants, *Civic Charity in a Golden Age: Orphan Care in Early Modern Amsterdam* (Urbana: University of Illinois Press, 1997); Thomas Max Safley, *Charity and Economy in the Orphanages of Early Modern Augsburg* (Atlantic Highlands, NJ: Humanities Press, 1997); Ilaria Taddei, *Fanciulli e giovani: Crescere a Firenze nel rinascimento* (Florence: Leo S. Olschki, 2001), 161; Maria Fabini Leuzzi, *"Dell'allogare le fanciulle degli Innocenti": Un problema culturale ed economico, 1577–1652* (Bologna: Il Mulino, 1995); Terpstra, *Abandoned Children*, 5–9.

63. BNCF, Palatino E.B.15.2, fol. 129r: eighty-two boys under the age of fifteen lived in the Innocenti in 1632, and 132 boys over the age of fifteen.

64. BNCF, Palatino E.B.15.2.

65. BNCF, Palatino E.B.15.2, fols. 104r, 106r.

66. Hugh Matthews, Melanie Limb, and Mark Taylor, "The 'Street as Thirdspace,'" in *Children's Geographies: Playing, Living, Learning,* ed. Sarah L. Holloway and Gill Valentine (New York: Routledge, 2004), 55; Ruth Karras Mazo, *From Boys to Men: Formations of Masculinity in Late Medieval Europe* (Philadelphia: University of Pennsylvania Press, 2003).

67. Ottavia Niccoli, "Rituals of Youth: Love, Play, and Violence in Tridentine Bologna," in *The Premodern Teenager: Youth in Society 1150–1650,* ed. Konrad Eisenbichler (Toronto: Centre for Reformation and Renaissance Studies, 2002), 75–94; Konrad Eisenbichler, *Boys of the Archangel Raphael: A Youth Confraternity in Florence, 1411–1785* (Toronto: University of Toronto Press, 1998), 65.

68. ASF, CPG, numeri neri (hereafter nn), 702, fol. 45: "Li Giovani che vengono in Orbatello sono li infra scritti."

69. ASF, CPG, nn, 702, fol. 45: "Dua servitor di Monastario d'alto Pascio, che portano l'arme e il piu delle volte con altri compagni quali non conosco . . . Matteo tessitore di panni lini, sta in via nuova Con' altro giovane che non so il nome che lo dicono quello dello scorbacchia. Cosi molti altro de quali non so il nome, Piero fornaio nella via dei servi."

70. ASF, CPG, nn, 701, fol. 45: "Le Fanciulle che mi pare a me celi tirino sono queste La Camilla di Mona Pippa, La Marietta di mona. Ermellina, La Luchretia di mona Maddalena, La Masa di mona. Luchretia, La Piera de monzino."

71. ASF, CPG, nn, 751, fol. 70.

72. ASF, CPG, nn, 701, fol. 135: "gracchiando"; "fece hu hu hu"; Kate Colleran, *"Scampanata* at the Widows' Windows: A Case-Study of Sound and Ritual Insult in Cinquecento Florence," *Urban History* 36, no. 3 (2009): 359–362.

73. ASF, A&D, 291, "Onestà e meretrice," unpaginated/unfoliated: "Onestà 1572 Sandra . . . trovata di rimpetto al monastero di San Barnaba con due giovani a far baie a dire parole disoneste senza rispetto al luogo."

74. ASF, A&D, 292, "Negozi degli otto anno 1629," unpaginated/unfoliated: "Quattro giovani erano stato catturati di notte vicino al monastero di San Giuliano in Firenze, che suonavano la chitarra e cantavano alla casa di una meretrice."

75. ASF, Otto, 64, fols. 62r-v: "le monache dell monastero di Santa Maria degli Angioli in borgo San Friano et Monastero di San Friano havere . . . per li giochi di palla et altri giochi si fanno in torno ad monasteri."

76. ASF, Otto, 64, fols. 62r-v: "in torno ad monastero a passi 200 giuchar a giocho di palla o altri giochi sotto pena di scudi 10 per . . . e di 2 tratti di fume per uno."

77. Michael Flannery, "The Rules for Playing Pall-Mall (c. 1655)," in *Sport and Culture in Early Modern Europe,* ed. John McClelland and Brian Merrilees (Toronto: Centre for Reformation and Renaissance Studies, 2009), 183–198; Wolfgang Behringer, "The Invention of Sports: Early Modern Ball Games," in *Sports and Physical Exercise in Early Modern Culture: New Perspectives on the History of Sports and Motion,* ed. Rebecca von Mallinckrodt and Angela Schattner (New York: Routledge, 2016), 22–47.

78. ASF, Otto di Guardia, 89, fols. 54v–55r; AAF, Cause Criminale, 36.2–S. Maria di Montedomini, no. 1: "le Monache di Montedomini, si querelano del gran rumore che li fa giorno et sera in sula Piazza della Zeccha con giochi di Rulle et altre radunate di Gente, et di sassi, et Rulle che sono tirate alla volta delle loro finestre."

79. David Rosenthal, "Owning the Corner: The 'Powers' of Florence and the Question of Agency," *I Tatti Studies in the Italian Renaissance* 16, no. 1 (2013): 181–196.

80. Kelli Woods, "Balls on Walls, Feet on Streets: Subversive Play in Grand Ducal Florence," *Renaissance Quarterly* 32, no. 3 (2018): 365–372.

81. John K Brackett, *Criminal Justice and Crime in Late Renaissance Florence, 1537–1609* (Cambridge: Cambridge University Press, 1992), 10–12.

82. AAF, Cause Criminale, 34.5, 7, unpaginated.

83. Once determined guilty, Rolando was unable to pay the required pecuniary fine and was thus incarcerated in the civic prison as a debtor. See Guy Geltner, *The Medieval Prison: A Social History* (Princeton, NJ: Princeton University Press, 2008), 58; and Brackett, *Criminal Justice and Crime,* 44–56.

84. AAF, Cause Criminale, 34.5, 7, unpaginated: "Io dissi parole in questa chiesa impertinenti, et di grande scandolo."

85. Trevor Dean, "Gender and Insult in an Italian City: Bologna in the Later Middle Ages," *Social History* 29, no. 2 (May 2004): 217–231; Elizabeth Horodowich, "Body Politics and the Tongue in Sixteenth-Century Venice," in *The Body in Early Modern Italy,* ed. Julia L. Hairston and Walter Stephens (Baltimore: Johns Hopkins University Press, 2010), 198; Donald Weinstein, "Fighting or Flyting?: Verbal Duelling in Mid-Sixteenth Century Italy," in *Crime, Society, and the Law in Renaissance Italy,* ed. Trevor Dean and

K. J. P. Lowe (Cambridge: Cambridge University Press, 1994), 204–220; Annamaria Nada Patrone, *Il messaggio dell'ingiuria nel Piemonte del tardo medioevo* (Cavallermaggiore, Italy: Gribaudo, 1993), 21–22; Renzo Derosas, "Moralità e giustizia a Venezia nel '500–'600: Gli esecutori contro la bestemmia," in *Tato, società e giustizia nella repubblica veneta (secolo XV–XVIII)*, vol. 1, ed. Gaetano Cozzi (Rome: Jouvence, 1981), 431–528.

86. AAF, Cause Criminale, 34.5., vol. 7, unpaginated: "alta et intelligibile voce"; "perche questa actione . . . incorsideratamente . . . dette scandalo al popolo, humilmente"; "segui grande disordine et mormorio."

87. Guido Ruggiero, "Mean Streets, Familiar Streets, or the Fat Woodcarver and the Masculine Spaces of Renaissance Florence," in *Renaissance Florence: A Social History*, ed. Roger Crum and John Paoletti (Cambridge: Cambridge University Press, 2006), 295–310.

88. AAF, "Editto di quello che devono osservare li secolari per il sinodo dell'anno 1619," 5: "Quelli che dentro alle Chiese vicino alle porte di esse & alle pile dell'acqua benedetta, o fuori delle Chiese vicino alle porte, o nelli portici & antiporti delle Chiese parleranno con mal fine alle donne che alle dette Chiese vengano, o da quelle si partano, saranno puniti con pena di scomunica."

89. Anna Agostini, *Pistoia sul mare: Il cavalieri di Santo Stefano e Pistoia* (Pistoia, Italy: Settegiorni Editore, 2008); Gino Guarnieri, *L'ordine di S. Stefano nei suoi aspetti organizzativi interni sotto il gran magistero mediceo*, 4 vols. (Pisa: Giardini, 1966).

90. Eleonora Baldasseroni, *Le cavaliere dell'ordine di Santo Stefano: Le monache della santissima concezione di Firenze* (Pisa: Plus, 2008); Elisa Goudriaan, *Florentine Patricians and Their Networks: Structures behind the Cultural Success and Political Representation of the Medici Court (1600–1660)* (Leiden: Brill, 2018), 35–36; Henk Van Veen, "Princes and Patriotism: The Self-Representation of Florentine Patricians in the Late Renaissance," in *Princes and Princely Culture 1450–1650*, vol. 2, ed. Martin Gosman, Alasdair Macdonald, and Arjo Vanderjagt (Leiden: Brill, 2005), 63–78; Richard A. Goldthwaite, *Private Wealth in Renaissance Florence: A Study of Four Families* (Princeton, NJ: Princeton University Press, 1968), 252–275.

91. ASF, A&D, 292, unpaginated / unfoliated: "Ottobre 1567 Tre gentiluomini di notte aveva fatto baccano alla casa della Caterina de Arno meretrice spagnola, rompendole con sassi le finestre."

92. ASF, A&D, 291, "Processi di Cavalieri 1569," unpaginated / unfoliated: "Cancelleri Fiorino Fiorini e dice che da circa due settimane ha ripreso in casa la Giulia sua figlia donna di Niccolo Baroncelli: in questo tempo più volte fra Guidetto Guidetti 'cavaliere di san Giovanni' con altri ariunti di spada e andato a fargli baccano."

93. Cohen, "Honour and Gender," 597; Francisca Loetz, *A New Approach to the History of Violence: "Sexual Assault" and "Sexual Abuse" in Europe, 1500–1850* (Leiden: Brill, 2015), 7–9.

94. ASF, A&D, 291, "Onesta e meretrice," unpaginated/unfoliated: "Carlo Bonsi Fiorentino, Leandro Flori d'Arezzo e Pasquino da Oliveto descritto per imputazione di avere notte fatto baccano alla casa della Ortensia meretrice et entratoli in casa per forza insieme con altri cavalieri di Santo Stefano e fattoli violenza et con li pomi della spade e pugnali percossola e minacciatola se ne parlava."

95. ASF, Onestà, 3, "Statuti e leggi 1577-1747," fol. 15v: "Qualunque molesterà o in qualsivoglia modo."

96. ASF, Onestà, 3, "Statuti e leggi 1577-1747," fol. 15v: "noiera o ingiuvera alcuna di dette Meretrici"; "Magistrato considerata l'offesa la molestia o baccano che sarà stato fatto." Emphasis in the translation is my own.

97. Antonio Maria Cospi, *Il giudice criminalista* (Florence: Zanobi Pignoni, 1643), 401–411: "Delli delitti corporei Cap. VI. . . . E per questo diciamo I delitti nati dalla voce, come le bestemmie, l'ingiurie di parole, e simili incorporei derivanti da' corpi. . . . Le cose corporei sono quelle, che sono sottoposte al senso del tatto, del gusto, a talora del vedere, e dell'odorato, e dell'udito . . . & medesimo possiamo dire del suno, rumore, o voce, mentre si presuppone, che derive da cose coporea perche l'instrumento causante suono o voce sarà materiale, e corporeo."

98. Thomas V. Cohen and Elizabeth S. Cohen, *Words and Deeds in Renaissance Rome: Trials before the Papal Magistrates* (Toronto: University of Toronto Press, 1993), 15–20; William Naphy, *Sex Crimes from Renaissance to Enlightenment* (Stroud, UK: Tempus, 2002), 79; Mary Elizabeth Perry, *Gender and Disorder in Early Modern Seville* (Princeton, NJ: Princeton University Press, 1990), 119–121; Manon van der Heijden, "Women as Victims of Sexual and Domestic Violence in Seventeenth-Century Holland: Criminal Cases of Rape, Incest, and Maltreatment in Rotterdam and Delft," *Journal of Social History* 33, no. 3 (2000): 623–644.

99. ASF, Auditore, 4896, fols. 128r-v: "sono grandamente disturbate et molestate"; AAF, Cause Criminale, "Firenze S. Onofrio di Fuligno—sec XVII," no. 1: "restar maculate"; AAF, Cause Criminale, 34.5, 7, unfoliated: "grande scandolo."

CHAPTER THREE ∾ SOUND

1. Scipione Mercurio, *De gli errori popolari d'Italia libri sette* (Verona: Francesco Rossi, 1645), 370–371: "possono condur le Gravide in estremo pericolo"; "quella subita paura; quel violento terore; quel terribil spavento; core al cuore, e raffredda il sangue, turba gli spiriti, impallidisce il volto, induce febri, causa passioni, produce deliquii, & agitando la creatura sopra modo la precipta quasi nella morte"; "che quel gridare, quei stridori acuti, quelle voci vehementi . . . son bastanti a far disperder le creature"; "bastanti

non solo alle donne, ma sin a gl' huomini coraggiosi di far impallidir il volto, e tremar il cuore."

2. Valeria Finucci, "Maternal Imagination and Monstrous Birth: Tasso's *Gerusalemme liberata*," in *Generation and Degeneration: Tropes of Reproduction in Literature and History from Antiquity through Early Modern Europe*, ed. Valeria Finucci and Kevin Brownless (Durham, NC: Duke University Press, 2001), 54–55; Jacqueline Marie Musacchio, *The Art and Ritual of Childbirth in Renaissance Italy* (New Haven, CT: Yale University Press, 1999), 113; Mary Elizabeth Fissell, *Vernacular Bodies: The Politics of Reproduction in Early Modern England* (Oxford: Oxford University Press, 2004), 207–235.

3. Tara Pedersen, "Bodies by the Book: Remapping Reputation in the Account of Anne Greene and Shakespeare's *Much Ado about Nothing*," in *Mapping Gendered Routes and Spaces in the Early Modern World*, ed. Merry E. Wiesner-Hanks (New York: Routledge, 2015), 117–131; Sara Read, *Menstruation and the Female Body in Early Modern England* (New York: Palgrave, 2013), 156–157.

4. Domenico Panarolo, *Aerologia cioè discorso dell'aria trattato utile per la sanità* (Rome: Domenico Marciani, 1642), 14: "L'Aere universalmente tiene molti significati, essendo che spesso per esso s'intenda il vento, altre volte il terremoto, molte volte il suono."

5. Daniel Bartoli, *Del suono de' tremori armonici e del l'udito* (Bologna: G. Bilancioni 1680), 40: "Finalmente, per non andare in ciò più a lungo; non particelle, non atomi, non tremori, non qualità, ne specie intentionali, ne null'altro che vibrationi, e increspamenti dell' aria, pare oggidì a moltissimi che sia tutto l'esser del suono. Questo gentil battimento dell'aria cosi ondeggiato, entrando con essa nel canal dell'orecchio, percuote, dicono, e solletica il timpano dell'udito."

6. Aristotle, *De anima*, 419b16.

7. Bernardo Segni, *Il trattato sopra i libri dell' Anima d'Aristotile* (Florence: Giorgio Marescotti, 1553), 89: "E il sensorio uditivo aereo, si come e il mezo di questa sensazione; perche altrimenti ella non si sarebbe, se dal mezzo esteriore, che e l'aria, non fosse mossa l'interiore, che e il sensorio. E di qui nasce, che l'Animale non ode da ogni parte del corpo; perche l'aria esteriore percossa non va a trovare, se non quella parte del corpo, dove l'aria interiore animata, che riceve la spezie del suono e fa la sensazione. E adunche lo strumento uditivo areo."

8. Bartolomeo Traffichetti, *L'arte di conservare la sanità* (Pesaro, Italy: Gieronimo Concordia, 1565), 183: "L'instrumento di questa facoltà dove si celebra l'udito deve essere aereo, e quieto, & acciocché l'anima sensitiva potesse sentire il suono (il quale propriamente e oggetto dell' udito) havea bisogno d'un inserimento aereo, il quale fosse atto, e proportionato a ricevere le spetie del suono. E perche il suono e frattione del l'aere, fatta da noi corpi duri, onde l'aere fratto e spezzato si move in giro."

9. Remi Chiu, "Music for the Times of Pestilence, 1420–1600" (PhD diss., McGill University, 2012), 23–37.

10. Traffichetti, *L'arte di conservare sanità,* 183.

11. Mercurio, *Errori popolari,* 371.

12. François Quiviger, *The Sensory World of Italian Renaissance Art* (London: Reaktion Books, 2010), 17–18; Lodovico Dolce, *Nel quale si ragiona del modo di accrescere e conservar la memoria* (Venice: Giovanni Battista e Marchio Sessa, 1562), 5.

13. Charles Burnett, "Perceiving Sound in the Middle Ages," in *Hearing History: A Reader,* ed. Mark Michael Smith (Athens: University of Georgia Press, 2004), 74.

14. Aristotle, *De anima,* 419b25–26; Angelico Buonriccio, *Paraphrasi sopra i tre libri dell' Anima d'Aristotile* (Venice: Andrea Arrivabene, 1565), 82.

15. Amy R. Bloch, *Lorenzo Ghiberti's Gates of Paradise: Humanism, History, and Artistic Philosophy in the Italian Renaissance* (Cambridge: Cambridge University Press, 2016), 214–215.

16. Gabriele Paleotti, *Discorso intorno alle imagini sacre et profane* (Bologna: Alessandro Benacci, 1582), 9–10.

17. Girolamo Menghi, *Celeste thesoro della gloriosa madre di Dio, Maria Vergina: Nel quale si ragiona del vero culto, & adoratione, che si deve alle sacrosante imagini* (Bologna: Giovanni Battista Pulciani, 1609), book 1, chap. 11, 55–56: "Molto sono gli effetti quali nascono dall'imagini, cosi profane, come sacre"; "che indi nascono affettioni & mutationi nù di poca importanza & da quelle in esi corpi s'imprimono segni manifesti"; "Plutarco scrive, che certe donne tenevano simulacra, & imagini delitiose & che usando co i loro mariti partorivano simili parti"; "il che molti esempii da scrittori culti si dichiarano, fra quali si pone quello di una matrona, la quale haveva partorito un' figliuolo non simile al Padre col mirare in una imagine d'uno Etiopo." See also Finucci, "Maternal Imagination and Monstrous Birth," 54–55; Wendy Doniger, "The Symbolism of Black and White Babies in the Myth of Parental Impression," *Social Research* 70, no. 1 (2003): 1–44; and Anu Korhonen, "Washing the Ethiopian White: Conceptualising Black Skin in Renaissance England," in *Black Africans in Renaissance Europe,* ed. T. F. Earle and K. J. P. Lowe (Cambridge: Cambridge University Press, 2005), 109.

18. Grace Harpster, "The Color of Salvation: The Materiality of Blackness in Alonso de Sandoval's *De instauranda Aethiopum salute,*" in *Envisioning Others: Race, Color, and the Visual in Iberia and Latin America,* ed. Pamela A. Patton (Leiden: Brill, 2015), 85.

19. John Henderson, "Coping with Epidemics in Renaissance Italy: Plague and the Great Pox," in *The Fifteenth Century,* vol. 12, *Society in an Age of Plague,* ed. Linda Clark and Carole Rawcliffe (Woodbridge, UK: Boydell, 2013), 179–194.

20. Fulvio Giubetti, *Il cancelliero di sanità da Fulvio Giubetti cancelliere all' Offizie della Sanità della città di Firenze* (Florence: Zanobi Pignoni, 1629), 3: "Che la Peste e un male contagioso cagionato da infezzione d'aria . . . o vero che la Peste e un vapore velenoso, concreato nell'aria, inimico dello spirito vitale."

21. Segni, *Il trattato sopra i libri dell' Anima,* 90: "Quando dentro' al l'orecchio non è l'aria connaturale, e quando ella è mobile, allora si corrompe la sensazione."

22. Traffichetti, *L'arte di conservare la sanità,* 184: "e bisogna procurare insieme che quest'aere sia puro, acciocché posso ricevere tutte le differenze del suono però bisogna haver cura che non si facciano soverchie vaporationi o dallo stomaco, o dal fegato, o da altri membri particolari, o da tutto il corpo alla testa ovvero alle orecchie, li quali si mescolassero con questo aere, e lo rendessero impuro, & inquieto."

23. *Cause et rimedii della peste, et d'altre infermità* (Florence: Apresso i Giunti, 1577), 29: "dishonesti ragionamenti i Madrigali, et canzioni infami, le danze lascive, il conversare insieme con indecent familiarita."

24. Alessandro Traiano Petronio, *Del viver delli Romani et di conservar la sanità* (Rome: Domenico Basa, 1592), 301: "perche in quelli luoghi è sempre denso, grosso, & come acqua di paludi"; "questo si purga da fuochi delle case, da suoni della campane, & si rompe."

25. Bartolomeo Paschetti, *Del conservare la sanità e del vivere de' genovesi* (Genoa: Giuseppe Pavoni, 1602), 128, 129: "del suono delle Campane . . . che rischiarano, & purificano l'aria"; "non sarà egli miglior, & più sottile aere nella Città, che nelle ville?"; "ma perche l'aere di Genova, & dei luoghi vicini egli è tutto sottile, leggiero, & puro, non vale in quella Patria la ragione detta dei fuochi, & del suono delle campane, ne il paragone fatto delle ville alla Città."

26. David Gentilcore, *Food and Health in Early Modern Europe: Diet, Medicine and Society, 1450–1800* (London: Bloomsbury Academic, 2016), 78.

27. Tomaso Thomai, *Discorso del vero modo di preservare gli huomini dalla peste di Tomaso Thomai medico da Ravenna* (Bologna: Clemente Ferroni, 1630), 8–9: "Il suono ancora delle campane . . . esser convenientissimo rimedio, perché dal rumore di quelle si dissolvono le nubi, e sichiarisica l'aria: onde s'è molte volte veduto le grandissime tempeste, in un' instate per il suono delle campane essersi quetate"; Carlo M. Cipolla, *Fighting the Plague in Seventeenth-Century Italy* (Madison: University of Wisconsin Press, 1981), 51.

28. Fabritio Ardizzone, *Ricordi di Fabritio Ardizzone fisico intorno al preservarsi e curarsi dalla peste* (Genoa: G. Maria Farroni, 1656), 26–27: "ove inspirano i venti ammorbati, ordinare che sichiudano le finestre, che s'alzino le mura, si sparino artiglierie, suoni di campane."

29. Carlo M. Cipolla, "The Plague and the Pre-Malthus Malthusians," *Journal of European Economic History* 3, no. 2 (1974): 279.

30. Romano da Calice, *La grande peste: Genova 1656–1657* (La Spezia, Italy: Co-operativa di solidarietà sociale Egidio Bullesi, 1992), 80: "e seguendosi a cantare nella medesima hora in tutte le chiesa di Genova col rimbombo universal di tutte le campane; l'artiglieria di tutti li posti della città e tutti i vascelli del porto rispose come secondocoro."

31. Paolo Piccari, *Giovan Battista Della Porta: Il filosofo, il retore, lo scienziato* (Milan: Franco Angeli, 2007), 21–23; Giambattista Della Porta, *De i miracoli et maravigliosi effetti dalla natura prodotti*, vol. 3 (Venice: Lodovico Avanzo, 1562), 87: "Quando vorrai scacciare la tempesta, ò la grandine. . . . Piu naturalmente il possano fare le campane, con il lor sonare, o pur le botte dell'artiglieria, perciocché rompano con quell strepito l'aria, e rompano le nugole, laqual cosa molti pensano che si debbi fare ancho al tempo della peste: accioche le nugole troppo lente non si fermino."

32. Cesare Crivellati, *Trattato di peste, nel quale breuemente si scuopre la sua natura con quella del contagio, manifestandosi insieme le cagioni, I segni da conoscerla, & il modo da preservarsi, e liberarsi da quella* (Viterbo, Italy: Bernardino Diot'allevi, 1631), 23: "Remedio con il quale Hipp. con tanta sua gloria liberò Atene dalla peste . . . il far sonar per qualche spati di tempo unitamente tutte le Campane, con tutti gl'Organi delle chiese, con far sentir per la città musiche divote, accio l'aere meglio si dirompa e si renda pura e si discacci da quelle qualsivoglia cosa, che infettar la potesse"; "Il secondo remedio sarà che in ogni piazza e capo di strada si faccino porre bombarde, moschetoni, mortaretti, Archibugi, e altri instrumenti simili . . . e nell'istesso tempo si faccino sentir Trombe, Tamburri, e altro simili per tutta la città, non lasciando il continuare il suono delle Campane e de gl'Organi quando vi siano, con le già dette musiche, che oltre al dirompere e il purificare dell'aere, che si sarà, si terrà anche il popolo in festa, cosa di non piccola importanza in simili tempi."

33. Conte Ludovico Moscardo, *Note ovvero memorie del museo di Ludovico Moscardo nobile Veronese* (Padua: Paulo Frambotto, 1656), 298: "Il suono de gl'instrumenti & il canto, non è rimedio solamente alle afflizioni dell'animo, ma giova ancora alle infermità del corpo, come è quelli che sono morsi dalle vipere, e similmente a frenetici."

34. Panarolo, *Aerologia*, 89: "neque solum perturbationibus animorum sed etiam corporis medetur morbis musica modulatio cum febrem quoque ac vulneera Cantiones quotidie adhibeantur"; "et non nullis aliis medicis aegroti pene de speratae salutis musicae oblectamentis curati fuerint."

35. Gary Tomlinson, *Music in Renaissance Magic: Toward a Historiography of Others* (Chicago: University of Chicago Press, 1993), 131.

36. Remi Chiu, *Plague and Music in the Renaissance* (Cambridge: Cambridge University Press, 2017), 12, 16, 17.

37. Senofonte Bindassi, *Il diporto della villa* (Venice: Giovachino Brognolo, 1582), 6: "in villa non si sentono tanti inganni, tante insidie, e agnati,

tanti danni, tanti sdegni, e rancor, tanti furori, crudeli inimicitie, risse, affanni, singulti, pranti, urli, e stridori, in quanti vivono le città del mondo."

38. Agostino Gallo, *Le tredici giornate della vera agricoltura & de piaceri della villa* (Venice: Nicolo Bevilacqua, 1556), 267, 317: "Piu cose odio da sentire . . . spazzacamini & zavattini che gridano, facchini & brentatori che urlino, ruffiane & meretrice che inveschino, malefici & incantatori che fascino, arioli & fitonesse che indovinino, marivoli & tagliaborse che truffino, & manco hippocriti & gabbadei che abbarrino"; "Non tanto possiamo dire che egli è cosa salutifera l'abbandonare gl'Intrichi, i travagli, & rumori delle Città, per godere i riposi, le allegrie, & le contentezza delle ville. . . . Perciochè questa virtù sono la corona di tutti li altri piaceri della Villa, & più potenti per mantener lieto ogni spirito gentile, mentre che dimora nella prigionia del nostro fragile corpo."

39. Castore Durante, *Il tesoro della sanità nel quale si da il modo da conservar la sanità, & prolungar la vita & si tratta della natura de cibi, e dei rimedii de i nocumenti loro* (Rome: Francesco Zannetti, 1586), 45–46: "L'huomo adunque, che vuole esser sano, pratichi per i giardini, guardi le verdure, & luoghi ameni, & conversi con amici giocondi, & facondi, con suoni, & canti, che per queste cose si ristora la virtù, & la forza si accrescono col cibo, col vino, con buoni odori, con tranquillità, & allegrezza, col lasciar le cose, che attristano, & col conversar con gl'amici; cosi parimenti conferisce ascoltare historie grate, favole, & ragionamenti piacevoli, con suoni, & canti, & con dilettevol lettione"; Carole Rawcliffe, "'Delectable Sightes and Fragrant Smelles': Gardens and Health in Late Medieval and Early Modern England," *Garden History* 36, no. 1 (2008): 1–21.

40. Gallo, *Le tredici giornata,* 287: "Le quali la nostra Città con tutta la sua magnificenza non può vedere & manco gustare cosi compiutamente come noi facciamo. Oltra che essa resta priva del cantar de gli uccelli, che noi vediamo giorno, & notte. Et se pur vi è chi desideri udir cantar uccello alcuno li convien tenerlo in gabbia, & darli da beccare & bere: Onde, si come noi fruimo il cantar de nostro con libertà loro, cosi quei prigionieri sempre cantano sforzatemene, temendo di morir di fame se non cantassero. Per tanto, non è maraviglia se' l cantar de nostri è più allegro, più sonoro, & più suave."

41. Giovanni Pietro Olina, *Uccelliera overo discorso della natura e proprieta di diversi uccelli* (Rome: Andrea Fei, 1684), 15, viii: "il suo canto è dilettevole in conserto d'altr'uccelli ma solo, avendo userò assai corto e replicando del continuo l'istesso non è di tutta satisfaction"; "che lo sforzo e lo studio degl'eccellenti Cantori non è altrove maggiormente impiegato, che nel e i movimenti, i riposi, le fughe, i passaggi, le dimore, i rompimenti, le sospensioni, i ripiegamenti, i giri, le tirate, i precipitii, il variare del mormorante, chiaro, fosco, pieno, sottile, acuto, grave, basso, mezano, elevato, frettoloso, lento, frizzante, e dimesso tuono, e l'alterar di tutti i detti movimenti insieme, onde incredibilmente ci diletta la melodia degl'Uccelli e di

quelli massimamente, che nel seguente discorso sono apressi." See also Suzanne Butters, "Natural Magic, Artificial Music and Birds at Francesco de' Medici's Pratolino," in *Sense and the Senses in Early Modern Art and Cultural Practice*, ed. Alice E. Sanger and Siv Tove Kulbrandstad Walker (New York: Routledge, 2017), 31–63.

42. Cesare Manzini, *Ammaestramenti per allevare, pascere, e curare uccelli li quali s'ingabbino ad cantare* (Brescia, Italy: Pietro Maria Marchetti, 1607).

43. Leandro Bovarini, *Del silentio opportuno* (Perugia: Vincenzio Colombara, 1603), 8: "le quali come che con lingua strepitosa, & crocitante vadano tal'hora gracchiando, & romoreggiando per l'aria, empiendo di noia."

44. Gallo, *Le tredici giornata*, 267.

45. Giovanni Boccaccio, *Decamerone* (Florence: San Jacopo di Ripoli, 1483), 30–42.

46. Raffaella Fabiani Giannetto, *Medici Gardens: From Making to Design* (Philadelphia: University of Pennsylvania Press, 2008); Amanda Lillie, *Florentine Villas in the Fifteenth Century: An Architectural and Social History* (Cambridge: Cambridge University Press, 2005).

47. Sandra Cavallo and Tessa Storey, *Healthy Living in Renaissance Italy* (Oxford: Oxford University Press, 2013), 48–70.

48. David Gentilcore, *Medical Charlatanism in Early Modern Italy* (Oxford: Oxford University Press, 2006); Dino Carpanetto, *Scienza e arte del guarire: Cultura, formazione universitaria e professioni mediche a Torino tra sei e settecento* (Turin: Deputazione Subalpina di Storia Patria, 1998); Giorgio Cosmacini, *Ciarlataneria e medicina: Cure, maschere, carle* (Milan: Cortina, 1998); George McClure, *The Culture of Profession in Late Renaissance Italy* (Toronto: University of Toronto Press, 2004), 10–22; Monica Green, *Making Women's Medicine Masculine: The Rise of Male Authority in Pre-modern Gynaecology* (Oxford: Oxford University Press, 2008), 204–246.

49. Mercurio, *Errori popolari*, 268, 1: "Il ciarlatano, che è ignorantissimo"; "Et perché per lo più tali errori sono commessi da donne, le quali troppo presumono nella medicina, Io scrivere & fare avvertite sarà un porre freno a tanta licenza e corregga tal abuso."

50. Montserrat Cabré, "Women or Healers? Household Practices and the Categories of Health Care in Late Medieval Iberia," *Bulletin of the History of Medicine* 82, no. 1 (2008): 18–51; Marina D'Amelia, "Una lettera a settimana: Geronima Veralli Malatesta al Signor Fratello 1572–1622," *Quaderni Storici*, n.s., 28, no. 83 (1993): 381–413; Marina D'Amelia "La presenza delle madri nel l'Italia medievale e moderna," in *Storia della maternità*, ed. Marina D'Amelia (Bari, Italy: Laterza, 1997); Sharon Strocchia, *Forgotten Healers: Women and the Pursuit of Health in Late Renaissance Italy* (Cambridge, MA: Harvard University Press, 2019).

51. Tessa Storey, "Italian Book of Secrets Database," March 3, 2009, https://hdl .handle.net/2381/4335; William Eamon, *Science and the Secrets of Nature:*

Books of Secrets in Medieval and Early Modern Culture (Princeton, NJ: Princeton University Press, 1994), 94–96.

52. Elaine Leong and Alisa Rankin, "Introduction," in *Secrets and Knowledge in Medicine and Science, 1500–1800* (New York: Routledge, 2016), 1–11.

53. It is generally agreed that Alessio Piemontese was the pseudonym of Girolamo Ruscelli; see Danilo Zardin, "Libri e biblioteche negli ambienti monastici dell'Italia del primo seicento," in *Donne, filosofia e cultura nel seicento,* ed. Pina Totaro (Rome: Consiglio nazionale della ricerca, 1999), 376–377.

54. Girolamo Ruscelli, *De' secreti del Reverendo Donno Alessio Piemontese* (Lyon, France: Theobaldo Pagano, 1558), 47–48, 55; Elena Camillo, "Ancora su Donno Alessio Piemontese: Il libro di segreti tra popolarità ed accademia," *Giornale Storico della Letterature Italiana* 162, no. 520 (1985): 539–553.

55. Girolamo Ruscelli, *De' secreti,* 106: "Mettendone una goccia nell' orecchio la sera o la mattina sana ogni dolor e infirmità d'orrecchia e cosi a vermi che nascono in esse."

56. Femke Speelbery, *Fashion and Virtue: Textile Patterns and the Print Revolution, 1520–1620* (New York: Metropolitan Museum of Art, 2016), 44–46.

57. Castore Durante, *Herbario nuovo di Castore Durante medico, et cittadino romano* (Venice: Li Seffa, 1602), 133: "Il succo delle cipolle messo con mele ne gli occhi, ne leva i fiocchi, & le caligini, & le cateratte, & rischiara la vista; messo nell'orecchia ne leva il romore."

58. Pietro Andrea Mattioli, *Della materia medicinale* (Venice: Vincenzo Valgrisi, 1563), 329–330: "Cedria messa dentro. Succhio di bacche di lavro con vino vecchio, & olio rosato. Fichi secchi triti con senape, & dissolti con qualche liquore. Fiele di Toro messovi tepido. Mele insieme con sale minerale ben trito Sugo di porri con incenso, aceto, et latte. Sugo di cipolla applicato nel modo medesimo Senape trita insieme con fichi secchi. Aceto caldo tormentato di forte che il fumo vada dentro."

59. Eugenio Raimondi, *Delle caccie* (Brescia, Italy: Giovanni Battista Catani, 1626), 558: "*ravanello/radice* Il succo della loro radice 'nstillato nell'orecchie ferma i venti, e romori dell'orecchie."

60. Francesco Scarioni, *Centuria di secreti politici, cimichi, e naturali* (Venice: Niccolò Tebaldini, 1626), 39.

61. Traffichetti, *L'arte di conservare la sanità,* 184: "Imperoche disse Galeno che senso l'orecchia membro di sua natura secco, che ha anche bisogno per la conservazione sua, di medicamente molto secchi"; "s'impastino queste polvere con aceto, e se ministrino con aceto . . . e dissolvendo gli con aceto . . . e ponghisi nel l'orecchie con bombace."

62. Matteo Bruno, *Discorsi di M. Matteo Bruno medico ariminese sopra gli errori fatti dal l'eccellente M. Bartolomeo Traffichetti da Bertinoro nell arte sua di conservar la sanità tutt' intiera* (Venice: Andrea Arrivabene, 1569), 128: "se volete usar i medicamenti secchi all' orecchie, perche sono membri secchi, non dite poi

di voler aspettare la concottione per conoscer questa lor similitudine in fine."

63. Bartolomeo Traffichetti, *Idea del l'arte di conservar la sanità . . . et hora per il medesimo diffeso dalle false oppositioni di M. Matteo Bruni* (Venice: Francesco Gasparo Bindoni e Fratelli, 1572), 127: "Volend'io demonstrate l'eccellenza del l'udito, dissi, che ci serve in acquistare la fede, e la perfection chirstiana. . . . Voi in questo con certi modi indebiti traparlate, senza alcuna rispetto. E io non voglio dare altra risposta."

64. Traffichetti, *Idea del l'arte di conservar la sanità*, 127: "I medicamente, che si applicano al l'orecchie, possono humettare al primo occorso, se saranno humid attualmente . . . ma, quando da calor naturale saranno ridotti al proprio atto, seccaranno."

65. Bartolomeo Traffichetti, *Somma del modo di conservars la sanità in tempo pestilente* (Bologna: Alessandro Benacci, 1576), 37, 30.

66. Green, *Making Women's Medicine Masculine*, 204-246; Gianna Pomata, *Contracting a Cure: Patients, Healers, and the Law in Early Modern Bologna*, trans. Gianna Pomata with Rosemarie Foy and Anna Taraboletti-Segre (Baltimore: Johns Hopkins University Press, 1998), 51; McClure, *The Culture of Profession*, 111-115.

67. Onofrio Zarrabini, *Delle materie e de soggetti predicabili* (Venice: Battista Somascho, 1586), 373: "Come il corpo nostro ha cinque sense, che sono cinque fenestre; per le quali entra lamorte in noi; quando egli avviene, che non siano ben chiuse, ferrate, & custodite con diligenza. . . . *Qui se abstinet ab illicito visu & abstineat ab illicito auditu, ab illicito odoratu & ab illicito gustu; ab illicito tactu* (dice Santo Agostino *de verbis Domini*) *propter ipsam integritatem.*"

68. Giacomo Affinati, *Il muto che parla, dialogo ove si tratta dell'eccellenze e de difetti della lingua humana, e si spiegano più di 190: Concetti scritturali sopra il silentio* (Venice: Marc Antonio Zaltieri, 1606), 379-380: "Non v'e dubbio, che la bocca e a guisa d'una porta, le cui labbra sono l'uscio . . . fa la porta alla tua bocca & alle tue orecchie ponigli la serratura"; "e spalancata e v'entra ogni imminenza, proferisce molti mali & e cagione d'infinti disordini."

69. Avicenna, *Liber de anima*, II.5.163.

70. Raffaello Delle Colombe, *Delle prediche sopra tutti gli evangeli dell'anno*, vol. 1 (Florence: Bartolommeo Sermartelli e Fratelli, 1613), 368, 369, 370: "Dice adunque che Galeno nel terzo de medicamenti locali, insegna medicar chi pate il frastuono o fischio nell'orecchie col nitro e aceto misto insieme e stillato nell'orecchio il qual se ben da principio morde, frizza, e pizzica; chi sopporta pazientemente riha l'udito e risanasi"; "il peccatore è tanto stordito da suoni, e frastuoni del Mondo, che non vuole udir l'armonia della parola di Dio"; "Sono le orecchie humane simili alle conchiglie marine, le quali sempre stan chiuse eccetto la mattina allo spurtar dell'aurora . . . Chiudetevi orecchi alle mormorazioni all'adulazioni, all'oscenità."

71. Allessandro Sperelli Vescovo di Gubbio, *Ragionamenti pastorali di Monsignor Allessandro Sperelli Vescovo di Gubbio, prelate domestic del sommo pontefice & assistente Fatti al Clero, alle Monache & al Popolo in tre parti distinti*, vol. 3, *Ragionamenti fatti al popolo* (Venice: Paolo Baglioni, 1675), 114: "e serve mirabilmente per antidoto, per preservativo dal veleno di molti e gravi paccati. Anzi ne meno basta di serrar con la cera l'orecchie per non sentire le mormorationi"; "Ma qual sarà questo piu stabile e piu sicuro coperchio con cui serrar dobbiamo l'orecchie contra la lingua mormoratrice? Lo Spirito Santo nelle parole dame proposte ce l'insegna: vuole che con una folta e spinosa siepe le circondiamo siche cola dentro la voce mormoratore penetrar non possa."

72. Carla Mazzio, "Sins of the Tongue in Early Modern England," *Modern Language Studies* 28, no. 3 (1998): 103.

73. Elizabeth Horodowich, "The Gossiping Tongue: Oral Networks, Public Life and Political Culture in Early Modern Venice," *Renaissance Studies* 19, no. 1 (2005): 26.

74. Horodowich, "The Gossiping Tongue," 23–28; Elizabeth S. Cohen and Thomas V. Cohen, "Camilla the Go-Between: The Politics of Gender in a Roman Household (1559)," *Continuity and Change* 4, no. 1 (1989): 67.

75. Jerónimo Gracián, *Della disciplina regolare* (Venice: R. P. del Carmine, 1600), 256: "Il silentio arrichisse il cuore, purifica la conscienza, illumina lo spirito, rasserena l'interiore, conserva le virtù, genera humilità, et è principio di innumerabili beni."

76. *The Canons and Decrees of the Sacred and Ecumenical Council of Trent, Celebrated under the Sovereign Pontiffs Paul III, Julius III, and Pius IV,* trans. Rev. J. Waterworth (London: Burns and Oates, 1888), 161; John O'Malley, *Trent: What Happened at the Council* (Cambridge, MA: Belknap Press of Harvard University Press, 2013), 14–21.

77. Benedetto Bonelli, *Notizie istorico-critiche intorno al B. M Adelpreto vescovo e comprotettore della chiesa di Trento* (Trento, Italy: Gianbattista Monauni, 1761), 676: "Preterea ordinamus et volumus ut per eos Divinum Officium oneste solemniter et devote omni cessante confabulatione vel risu . . . nec ulla interim fiat altercacio inter eos." See also Marco Gozzi, "Liturgical Music and Liturgical Experience in Early Modern Italy," in *Listening to Early Modern Catholicism,* ed. Daniele Filippi and Michael J. Noone (Boston: Brill, 2017), 55–78.

78. Archivio Arcivescovile di Firenze, *Editto di quello che devono osservare li secolari per il sinodo dell' anno 1619,* Sinodi Fiorentini 16o secolo, no. 4: "Tutti quelli, che ardiranno nelle chiese mente quivi di dice messa, e si celebrano gl' offizii divini . . . parlare con voce alta . . . o fare qualsivoglia altra cosa che dia grande scandolo, e che perturbi gli sacri offizii . . . e inhonesti con donne, sosterrano la pena del nostro arbitrio."

79. Andrew Dell'Antonio, *Listening as Spiritual Practice in Early Modern Italy* (Berkeley: University of California Press, 2011), 17.

80. For a broader discussion, see Norbert Elias, *The History of Manners*, trans. Edmund Jephcott (New York: Pantheon Books, 1978).

81. Dilwyn Knox, "Disciplina: Le origini monastiche e clericali del buon comportamento nell' Europa cattolica del cinquecento e del primo seicento," in *Disciplina dell'anima, disciplina del corpo e disciplina della società tra medioevo ed età moderna*, ed. Paolo Prodi and Carla Penuti (Bologna: Il Mulino, 1994), 6965: "la disciplina religiosa diventò disciplina civile della società tra medioevo ad età moderna."

82. Bovarini, *Del silentio opportuno*, 8.

83. *Confessionale de Santo Antonino arcivescovo de Firenze dell'ordine di predicatori* (Venice: Don Ipolito 1543), fol. 76v: "tu ha la lingua per tre ragioni, prima per laudar Dio.... Secondo per dimandar e per parlar de li tuoi bisogni. Tertio per amaestrare il prossimo... ogni altro parlamento e vano & peccato"; Peter Howard, *Creating Magnificence in Renaissance Florence* (Toronto: Centre for Reformation and Renaissance Studies, 2012).

84. Howard, *Creating Magnificence*, 20.

85. Donald Weinstein, *Savonarola: The Rise and Fall of a Renaissance Prophet* (New Haven, CT: Yale University Press, 2011), 183.

86. Girolamo Savonarola, *Prediche sopra iob del R.P.F Hieronimo Savonarola da Ferrara. Fatte in Firenze l'anno 1494* (Venice: Niccolo Bascarini, 1545), 56: "darsi a tutti e piaceri sensuali, et fare ogni male ... come donne religiose & non è cosa che guasti e moasterii piu, che fa questi parlari & cicalamenti"; "Debbono ... le buone Monache stare in silentio & in solitudine: perche el silentio si dice essere il padre, et la solitudine la madre si chiama: & da questi due copulati insieme si genera & parturisce una loro figliuola chiamata oratione & contemplation."

87. Lauro Martines, *Fire in the City: Savonarola and the Struggle for the Soul of Renaissance Florence* (Oxford: Oxford University Press, 2006).

88. Tamar Herzig, *Savonarola's Women: Vision and Reform in Renaissance Italy* (Chicago: University of Chicago Press, 2008), 19; Lorenzo Polizzotto, "When Saints Fall Out: Women and the Savonarolan Reform in Early Sixteenth-Century Florence," *Renaissance Quarterly* 46, no. 3 (1993): 486–525; Patrick Macey, "*Infiamma il mio cor:* Savonarolan Laude by and for Domincan Nuns in Tuscany," in *The Crannied Wall: Women, Religion, and the Arts in Early Modern Europe*, ed. Craig Monson (Ann Arbor: University of Michigan Press, 1992), 161–189.

89. Gozzi, "Liturgical Music and Liturgical Experience," 57.

90. Medici Archive Project, Doc ID# 18005, vol. 613, fol. 37, Pier Francesco Riccio to Cosimo I de' Medici, June 6, 1547.

91. Gozzi, "Liturgical Music and Liturgical Experience," 60: "El reverendissimo monsignor vescovo de Modena messer Zohane Moron ha ordenato che in el duomo non se ge cantasse canto figurato, ma canto firmo, perche li preti stavano ociosi e zanzaravano mentre li cantori cantavano."

92. Bindassi, *Il diporto della villa,* 6: "in villa non si sentono tanti inganni, tante insidie, e agnati, tanti danni, tanti sdegni, e rancor, tanti furori, crudeli inimicitie, risse, affanni, singulti, pranti, urli, e stridori, in quanti vivono le città del mondo."

CHAPTER 4 ∾ SILENCE

1. Alessandro Sperelli, *Ragionamenti pastorali di Monsignor Alessandro Sperelli Vescovo di Gubbio, prelate domestic del sommo pontefice & assistente al clero, alle monache & al popolo, in tre parti distinti,* vol. 2, *Ragionamenti fatti alle monache* (Rome: Guglielmo Halle Libraro, 1664), 179–180: "Volete conoscere una donna se veramente sia buona? Eccovene il contrasegno, diceva Epicarmo, pochissime saranno le sue parole . . . il silentio esser un bellissimo ornamento del sesso feminile; anzi accresce anche la loro bellezza . . . mirate qunto havrebbono detto non solatemnte alle donne Christiane, ma alle spose di Christo, s'eglino havessero havvuto la vera fede." Here Sperellu is echoing the classical Greek playwright and moralist Epicharmus.

2. Domenico Zon, *Santuario delle monache* (Venice: Fioravante Prati, 1615), 7: "La vita della Religiosa deve essere una intiera, e perfetta mortification di tutti li suoi sensi . . . a tutte le Religiose il santo silentio, e si da loro poco tempo di parlare, e di perder il pretioso tempo in parlamenti inutile & otiose."

3. Giacomo Affinati, *Il muto che parla, dialogo ove si tratta dell'eccellenze e de difetti della lingua humana, e si spiegano più di 190: Concetti scritturali sopra il silentio* (Venice: Marc Antonio Zaltieri, 1606), 224–225: "Qual è questa meretrice, se non l'anima peccatrice . . . perche tre cose deve fare ogni anima peccatrice penitente per conseguir perdono: sedere, tacere, e entrare nella tenebre. Sedere per quiete della mente . . . e con un dolce silenzio ritirarsi in luoghi . . . lonatani da strepiti mondani. Secondariamente bisogna tacere, non favellare delle cose mondane. . . . Tertio, deve entrare nelle tenebre . . . le spelonche, gli sorridi deserti . . . sequestrandosi dall'umano consortio."

4. Jitse Dijkstra and Mathilde van Dijk, eds., *The Encroaching Desert: Egyptian Hagiography and the Medieval West* (Leiden: Brill, 2006); David Brakke, *Demons and the Making of the Monk: Spiritual Combat in Early Christianity* (Cambridge: Cambridge University Press, 2006).

5. Katherine Ludwig Jansen, *The Making of the Magdalen: Preaching and Popular Devotion in the Later Middle Ages* (Princeton, NJ: Princeton University Press, 2000), 203–239.

6. Archivio di Stato di Firenze (hereafter ASF), Corporazione Religiose Soppresse dal Governo Francese, 191:33, fols. 3v–5r. "E necesseario primo purgare l'intesso cuore da ogni affetto sensuale e Mondano"; "ritirate alla solitudine della Santa Religione in questo Monasterio dedicato ad essa

Santa, non con altro fine che di far penitenza come ben vi si richiedeva per la vostra mala vita passata."

7. *Raccolata di alcune cose appartenenti alle monache stabilite nel sinodo diecesano fatto in Firenze il di 14 e 15 di maggio MDCXIX per ordine dell'illustriss. & reverendiss. Alessandro Marzi Medici Arcivescovo di Firenze* (Florence: Bartolommeo Sermartelli e Fratelli, 1619), preface: "Se bene nel sacro Concilio di Trento e nelli Sino di passata e altri editti nostri e de nostri antecessori è stato provvisto a quasi tutto quello che è necessario per il buono governo di quelli vergini che ne sacri chiostri sis ono dedicate al servizio a Iddio."

8. *Raccolata di alcune cose appartenenti alle monache,* no. 9: "Si sbandischino da chori delle Monache i suoni & I canti indecenti, le risa, le burle e tutto quell oche non convien fare davanti alla Divina Maestra con cui parlano salmeggiando."

9. *Raccolata di alcune cose appartenenti alle monache,* no. 28: "Non cantino ne suonino le Monache in modo che possino essere senti e da secolari . . . canteranno solamente mottetti sacri, in latino, non in Italiano."

10. *Raccolata di alcune cose appartenenti alle monache,* nos. 4, 24: "Titolo del Sinodo di quest'anno, e si facia il vestimento senza tumulto e romore;" "Alle porte de monasteri ne si mangi ne si parli ancora con parenti strettissimi tanto donne quanto huomini sotto pena di non potere andare a parlare a forestieri."

11. *Raccolata di alcune cose appartenenti alle monache,* no. 27: "sotto pena di privazione di voce attiva e passive datale una ascoltatrice che stia sempre vicina in mod ache possa udire. . . . Che quelle Monache che saranno disobediente a quanto si ordina sian prive di andare a grate per tre mesi e digiunino tre di in pane & acqua."

12. Beth Williamson, "Sensory Experience in Medieval Devotion: Sound and Vision, Invisibility and Silence," *Speculum* 88, no. 1 (2013): 1.

13. Williamson, "Sensory Experience in Medieval Devotion," 31; Emma Hornby, "Preliminary Thoughts about Silence in Early Western Chant," in *Silence, Music, Silent Music,* ed. Nicky Losseff and Jenny Doctor (Aldershot, UK: Ashgate, 2007), 141-154.

14. Jenny Doctor, "The Texture of Silence," in Losseff and Doctor, *Silence, Music, Silent Music,* 27-28.

15. Abigail Brundin, Deborah Howard, and Mary Laven, *The Sacred Home in Renaissance Italy* (Oxford: Oxford University Press, 2018), 103, 105-106.

16. Hellen Hills, "The Housing of Institutional Architecture: Searching for a Domestic Holy in Post-Tridentine Italian Convents," in *Domestic Institutional Interiors in Early Modern Europe,* ed. Sandra Cavallo and Silvia Evangelisti (New York: Routledge, 2016), 135.

17. Affinati, *Il muto che parla,* 224: "Un dolce silenzio."

18. Giovanna Paolin, *Lo spazio del silenzio: Monacazioni forzate, clausura e proposte di vita religioso femminile nell' eta moderna* (Pordenone, Italy: Biblioteca dell' Immagine, 1996), 17.

19. ASF, Auditore dei Beni Ecclesiastici poi Segretario del Regio Diritto (hereafter Auditore), 4894, fols. 319r–320v: "parole brutti e disoneste." See also Craig Monson, *Divas in the Convent: Nuns, Music, and Defiance in Seventeenth-Century Italy* (Chicago: University of Chicago Press, 2012), chap. 4.

20. ASF, Auditore, 4894, fols. 125r–v: "fanciulli e fanciulle dentro la clausura, et essendo usciti fuori della porta interiore."

21. Archivio Ospedale degli Innocenti Firenze (hereafter AOIF), 6218, 452.

22. Giustina Niccolini, *The Chronicle of Le Murate by Sister Giustina Niccolini*, trans. and ed. Saundra Weddle (Toronto: Centre for Reformations and Renaissance Studies, 2011), 114.

23. ASF, Auditore, 4893, fol. 469r: "Monache et munistero della Beata Christiana di Santa Croce di val d'arno di sotto dominio del Serenissimo Granduca di Toscana diocese di Lucca existente in nella terra di Santa Croce."

24. ASF, Auditore, 4893, fol. 469r: "Sono circa octo mesi che io sono venuto alla cura di detto munistero et circa al governo io l'ho trovato molto male."

25. ASF, Auditore, 4893, fols. 469v, 470r: "Interrogato che disordini et dispareri siano nati a tempo suo nel detto munistero tra le Monache di esso, et che altri disordini si trovino in esso munistero rispuose"; "Del mese di dicembre passato in coro farno parole della precesenza del luogo fra Suor Giulia et sor Madalena diche ne nacqueno dopoi parole et romori . . . vi corsono parole inguiriose ditte da suor Filippa verso di Suor Nannina et ci corsono Suor Maria per Suor Giulia et Suor Nannina per Suor Madalena."

26. ASF, Auditore, 4893, fol. 470r: "disse quando si celebra la messa le Monache che sono ad ascoltarla non fanno silentio et cicarlano assai et stanno con poco riverenza et molte segondo io ho inteso non vengano ad udirla."

27. ASF, Auditore, 4893, fol. 470r: "et quando che celebrano gli offitii divini stanno stanno con poca riverentia et devotione et manco silentio perche mentre che l'uno coro canta l'altra cicarla tanto forte che si sente sella chiesa di fuori."

28. ASF, Auditore, 4893, fol. 471v: "Il maggior disordine che io cognoschi in questo nostro monistero e che le Monache parlano molto dishonestamente et si dicano l'una al altra parole brute et dishoneste et che non stanno bene a meretrice non che alle Monache."

29. ASF, Auditore, 4893, fol. 471v: "a quanto alla Badessa io la ho sempre conosciuta donna di bene et utile per il governo della casa et quanto al confessore a me non ha mai satisfatto circa alla confessione at alla communnione et mi dispiace il suo stare alla ruota a cicalare tanto ne i tempi della confessione quanto in altro tempi."

30. ASF, Auditore, 4893, fol. 472v: "giorni passata furno certe parole tra Suor Nannina et Suor Eugenia per conto del prete secondo ho inteso che non mi ci trovai dove fu gran romore et ci concorseno molte Monache et Suor Niesa per far cessare il rumore o per altro corse a sonare la campane a Martello."

31. ASF, Auditore, 4893, fol. 473r: "et poco tempo fa la Badessa intromisse in munistero un suo nipote di 16 or 18 anni et intesi dire che sonorno et ballorno in chiesina presso al horto."

32. ASF, Auditore, 4893, fol. 474r: "Disse il cappellano et confessore procede assai male et sta tutto il giorno alle grate con Suor Nannina et Suor Aurelia a cicalare et a bere et ci ha bevuto fino alle uvova fresche per quanto ho inteso sire li ho ben visto portare da bere et de buccellati et non attende ad altro che a commettere male sia le Monache et prego la S.V. che lo levi di qui se vuole che questo munisterio stia in pace."

33. ASF, Auditore, 4893, fol. 475v: "Quanto a me mi pare che il nostro munistero sia in temporale et spirituale ben governato et io tutto che la Badessa sia mia sorella io dico cio per la verità et piacessa a Dio che avanti che lei fasse Badessa fasse stato cosi ben governato et al presente non vi conosco disordine alcuno."

34. ASF, Auditore, 4893, fols. 486r–v: "homo da bene ma ho inteso da molte che e scandaloso et mala lingua et che habbia poco rispetto."

35. ASF, Auditore, 4893, fol. 505r: "Io sono fanciulla e sono stata sei anni seculara et sei monaca in questo munistero et per quello poco che io conosco . . . non ci ho visto ci sia altro disordine che le parole et gride ache hanno insieme alcune Monache che vi sono concede altre vi debbe esser stato ditto et io le fuggo come fanciulla per non urdirle."

36. ASF, Auditore, 4893, fol. 508r: "mentre si celebrando I divini offiti non si osserva da alcuna il debito silentio et stavisi con poca devotioni et alcune se sono domandate vanna a chi le domanda."

37. ASF, Auditore, 4893, fol. 508r: "Disse in refettorio si sta a vitto commune ma poco si oserva il silentio."

38. ASF, Auditore, 4893, fol. 508r: "Disse le Monache la maggior parte vengano a udir messa in chiesa et un altra parte vanno in oratorio che io non posse essendo io in chiesa veder tutto."

39. ASF, Auditore, 4893, fol. 508r: "pero a mio giuditio sare bene che tutte a udire messa veni sieno in chiesa che io le potessi vedere."

40. ASF, Auditore, 4893, fol. 501r: "Disse nel nostro munistero non vi sono Monache alcune di mala fama al presente excetto Suor Stefana la quale e stata sempre vitiosa et scandalosa et ci sono poi alcune che sono poco ubidiente et hanno cattiva lingua . . . et quelle che hanno cattiva lingua in particulare sono Suor Illaria Suor Lucia et Suor Filippa et Suor Giulia."

41. ASF, Auditore, 4893, fol. 501r: "Disse il confessore io l'ho per persona poco da bene et scandalosa et it suo procedure ne fa segno et ha preso particulare

et stretta amicitia con Suor Nannina et Suor Aurelia et non si vergogna a stare tutto il giorno con loro et partise a una et due hore di notte alla ruota a cicalare et besbigliare con loro."

42. ASF, Auditore, 4893, fol. 513v: "Haveva trovato di molto disordini et discordie in esso munistero."

43. ASF, Auditore, 4893, fol. 513v: "a vivere ad un' altro modo et con piu timor di Dio et da religiose che non havevano fanno."

44. ASF, Auditore, 4893, fol. 514r: "per l'advenire non usasse piu parole ingiuriose ne dihoneste notificandoli che contra facendo sacra casticata severamente . . . in modo alcuno l'una contra del'altra dir parole ingiuriose o dishoneste ne altercare et griddare o replicare cosa alcuna in ditti o in fatti delle cose fino a giu passate . . . vivere quietamente et con il timor di Dio et ubidire alla Badessa."

45. *Raccolata di alcune cose appartenenti alle monache,* nos. 4, 24.

46. Niccolini, *The Chronicle of Le Murate,* 240; K. J. P. Lowe, *Nuns Chronicles and Convent Culture in Renaissance and Counter-Reformation Italy* (Cambridge: Cambridge University Press, 2003), 183.

47. Niccolini, *The Chronicle of Le Murate,* 240.

48. ASF, Acquisti e Doni (hereafter A&D), 293, unpaginated / unfoliated: "Otto Suppliche 2241. . . . Nel 1562 d'agosto Sandrina da Pistoia fu confinata per due anni nelle Stinche "per avere scalalo el "monastero delle Convertite et fuggitasene et contaminato altre che quios erono che ne n'uscissono."

49. ASF, A&D, 292, unpaginated / unfoliated: "Maggio 1562 Giovanni Betti era carcerato per sospetto della fuga della Sandrina da Pistoia e della Petrina dei Castellani, fuggite insieme con un altra del monestero delle Convertite che non si prova altro "che avere mandato a della Sandrina qualche presentuzzo di ricolte ciliegie e carciofi per la Maria sua serva."

50. ASF, Capitani di Parte Guelfa (hereafter CPG), numeri neri (hereafter nn), 707, no. 104: "insieme basciandosi al tocandosi dishonestamente"; "sott' ombra di darli nuove di certi lor parenti"; "et se non che se amiddono essere stato scoperti da un altra vedova che habita sopra loro per avventura harebbono proceduto più oltea"; "farle stare una mattina in gogna in orbatello serrale le porte di quel luogo accio che sia un spectaculo a tutte l'altre donne et in oltre privarle del luogo confinandole imperperro fuori d' Orbatello."

51. Keith M. Botelho, *Renaissance Earwitnesses: Rumor and Early Modern Masculinity* (New York: Palgrave Macmillan, 2009), 2-3.

52. ASF, Auditore, 4897, unpaginated: "lato al loro Monastario e una casa che . . . le mura che tocca . . . le monache sono sentite et possono udire ogni minima parola che si dica: . . . che la maggior parte della stanze del Monastario hanno il muro commune con della casa et in alcuni luoghi molto sottile e finestre che rispondono nell'horto."

53. Saundra Weddle, "'Women in Wolves' Mouths': Nuns' Reputations, Enclosure and Architecture at the Convent of Le Murate in Florence," in *Architecture and the Politics of Gender in Early Modern Europe*, ed. Helen Hills (Burlington, VT: Ashgate, 2003), 117-118.

54. *The Canons and Decrees of the Sacred and Ecumenical Council of Trent, Celebrated under the Sovereign Pontiffs Paul III, Julius III, and Pius IV*, trans. Rev. J. Waterworth (London: Burns and Oates, 1888), Session 25, Decree V.

55. ASF, Auditore, 4894, fols. 177r-v: "Circa le Monache . . . & Augumentazione delle loro entrate"; "I molti disordini de i Monasteri di Monache, & in particolare l'inosservanza della clausura quasi universalmente violata."

56. Biblioteca Natzionale Centrale di Firenze (hereafter BNCF), Alessandro de' Medici, *Trattato sopra il governo de' monasteri*, Mss Gino Capponi, CIV, 16.

57. ASF, Auditore, 4894, fols. 170r-v, 286r-v, 319r, 320r-v, 336r, 383r-v. For an examination of convent architecture and discussion of Alessandro de' Medici's letter, see Helen Hills, "The Veiled Body: Within the Folds of Early Modern Neapolitan Convent Architecture," *Oxford Art Journal* 27, no. 3 (2004): 271-290.

58. ASF, Auditore, 4889, no. 61: "dette finestre signioreggiano il detto orto et trovato che cosi sia fatto comandamento per parte nostra a Francesco padrone di detta casa che tutte sue spese per di qui a mezo il mese d'Agosto prossimo futuro habbia rimurato tutte quelle che risguardono nel'orto di dette suore."

59. The report does not specify which convent it is referencing, but it was likely the Franciscan Santa Chiara community. Later in the seventeenth century the Florentine Albizi family funded the establishment of the Augustinian San Matteo convent in Castelfranco di Sotto. The Strozzi family also had notable business interested in the area. See Giovan Francesco Franceschini, *Castelfranco di Sotto illustrato* (Castelfranco di Sotto: Biblioteca Communale di Castelfranco di Sotto, 1980), iv, iii, vv, 145, 103.

60. ASF, Auditore, 4894, fols. 382r-v: "è stata fatta una colombara, la quale perimente signoregga il detto horto et il terrazzo di esso monastero, onde quelle poveresse monache tanto per cagione de i gelsi come della detta colombara possono poco praticare che non siano viste et il piu delle volte per il concorso de i giovani et ragazzi che si fa sotto li stessi gelsi, sentono biasteme et altre parole a loro di molto sacndalo."

61. ASF, Auditore, 4894, fols. 370r-v, 371r-v, 372r-v, 376r-v.

62. ASF, Auditore, 4894, fol. 368r: "quelle conce sono pervitiosise e per quell luogo, perche le rispondono in su i loro orto e gettono si gran fetore per tutto il convento che non si puo vivere."

63. ASF, Auditore, 4894, fol. 368r: "ma quell che importa piu sono signioreggiate di maniera da quelle finestre, che non possono uscire in detto orto che non sieno veduta."

64. ASF, Auditore, 4894, fol. 368v: "le Monache non possono andare per il loro orto che non li vedi et esser da loro vedute, et di li si puol toccare la mano e fare altre cose incovenienti."

65. ASF, Auditore, 4894, no. 368r: "e oltre a questo non possono parlare che dette Monache non sentino ogni sorte di parole, e forse il più delle volte disoneste."

66. ASF, Auditore, 4894, no. 368v: "et ci è pericolo evidente di qualche grande scandalo, perche ci e comodita come li ho detto e del parlare et potersi toccare e scendere e in conclusione sono come se non fussino in clausura."

67. ASF, Auditore, 4894, fol. 369r: "non possono altrimenti assicurarsi della clausura."

68. ASF, Auditore, 4896, fol. 296r: "Che quelle monache andando o stando nel horto loro potevano facilmente essere vedute dalle habitatoni di tre case appoggiate alle mura . . . et più che facimente . . . parlare a chi fusse nel horto."

69. ASF, Auditore, 4896, fol. 296r: "per occuare a ogni sandolo"; "che non si possa andare o usare le mura castellane per quanto tiene l'horto delle monache."

70. ASF, Auditore, 4889, fol. 391r: "c'è una finestra serrata ordinaria che risponde nell' orto delle monache la quale a noi non piace."

71. ASF, CPG, numeri rossi (hereafter nr), 15, fol. 67v.

72. ASF, CPG, nr, 15, fol. 67v.

73. ASF, CPG, nn, 801, n.p.: "conto de bisogni per la resturatione delle case d'Orbetello."

74. ASF, CPG, nn, 801, n.p.: "calcine, pietre lavoro cotto, paioli, embrici . . . soglie, scaglioni di Pietra, et altro de danari del Magistrato la somma di scudi 386.4.2.6."

75. ASF, CPG, nn, 801, no. 71: "Orbatello . . . le quali hanno più bisogno et mai di essere restaurate pero sarebbe necessario di rimettervi travi . . . scale, imposte d'usci e di finestre et altre cose simili."

76. ASF, CPG, nn, 751, no. 70: "Essendo stati alla visita d' Orbatello secondo il solito, ci haviamo trovato molti disordini."

77. ASF, CPG, nn, 751, no. 70: "vecchie più venerande"; "possino remediare al meno referire li disordini."

78. Onofrio Zarrabini, *Delle materie e de soggetti predicabili* (Venice: Giovanni Battista Somascho, 1586), 373: "Come il corpo nostro ha cinque sensi, che sono cinque fenestre; per le quali entra lamorte in noi; quando egli avviene, che non siano ben chiuse, serrate, & custodite con diligenza."

79. Affinati, *Il muto che parla*, 379–380: "Non v'e dubbio, che la bocca e a guisa d'una porta, le cui labbra sono l'uscio . . . ferma la porta alla tua bocca & alle tue orecchie ponigli la serratura."

80. ASF, Auditore, 4896, fols. 128r-v; Archivio Arcivescovile di Firenze (hereafter AAF), Cause Criminale, "Firenze S. Onofrio di Fuligno—sec XVII."

81. Sperelli, *Ragionamenti pastorali,* 114.

82. Natalie Tomas, "Did Women Have a Space?," in *Renaissance Florence: A Social History,* ed. Rodger J. Crum and John T. Paoletti (New York: Cambridge University Press, 2006), 313.

83. Danielle van den Heuvel, "Gender in the Streets of the Premodern City," *Journal of Urban History* 45, no. 4 (2019): 699; Elizabeth S. Cohen, "To Pray, to Work, to Hear, to Speak: Women in Roman Streets, c. 1600," *Journal of Early Modern History* 12, no. 3 (2008): 289-311.

84. Flora Dennis, "Sound and Domestic Space in Fifteenth- and Sixteenth-Century Italy," *Studies in the Decorative Arts* 16, no. 1 (2008-2009): 8-10.

85. Van den Heuvel, "Gender in the Streets," 701. For a broader discussion of gender and public and private space in Florence, see Julia Rombough and Sharon Strocchia, "City of Women: Mapping Movement, Gender, and Enclosure in Renaissance Florence," in *Public Renaissance: Urban Space, Geolocated Apps and Public History,* ed. Fabrizio Nevola, David Rosenthal, and Nicholas Terpstra (Abingdon, UK: Routledge, 2022), 169-191.

86. ASF, Ufficiali di Notte e Conservatori dell' Onestà dei Monasteri, 79:2, fols. 68r-69r. Translation from "Chapter 5: The Surveillance of the Convents," in *The Society of Renaissance Florence: A Documentary Study,* ed. Gene Brucker (Toronto: University of Toronto Press, 2001), 207.

87. ASF, A&D, 293, *Deliberazioni dei signori e colleghi,* unpaginated / unfoliated: "Si proibisce ai suonatori della Signoria di andare a suonare presso i monasteri di monache a 50 braccia, sotto pena di cassazione dall' ufficio."

88. R. Burr Litchfield, *Emergence of a Bureaucracy: The Florentine Patricians 1530-1790* (Princeton, NJ: Princeton University Press, 1986), 86; Nicholas Terpstra, "Competing Visions of the State and Social Welfare: The Medici Dukes, the Bigallo Magistrates, and Local Hospitals in Sixteenth-Century Tuscany," *Renaissance Quarterly* 54, no. 4, pt. 2 (2001): 1352.

89. Elena Fasano Guarini, "Produzione di leggi e disciplinamento nella Toscana granducale tra cinque e seicento: Spunti di ricerca," in *Disciplina dell'anima, disciplina del corpo e disciplina della società tra medioevo ed età moderna,* ed. Paolo Prodi and Carla Penuti (Bologna: Il Mulino, 1994), 664.

90. Fasano Guarini, "Produzione di leggi e disciplinamento nella Toscana granducale," 668.

91. John K Brackett, *Criminal Justice and Crime in Late Renaissance Florence, 1537-1609* (Cambridge: Cambridge University Press, 1992), 20-21, 95-96.

92. AAF, Sinodi Fiorentini, 16o secolo, fasc. 7: "Le meretrici descritte publicamente all Offizio dell' Onestà . . . le quali non possono abitare vicino a monasterii a dugento braccia." Despite this decree civic officials almost always favored the one hundred braccia law first established in 1547.

93. ASF, Onestà, 3, fols. 14r-v. This was a reissued sixteenth-century law.

94. BNCF, *Estratta in compendio per Alfabeto dalle principali leggi, bandi, statuti, ordini, e consuetudini, massime criminali, e miste, che vegliano nella stati del serenissimo*

Gran Duca di Toscana, 254, no. 2: "Meretrici lontane da Monasteri anno più di braccia 100 se con la loro insolente vita, o con prospetto soffre di scandalo, o impedimento a Monasteri, o persone Religiose possono essere rimosse."

95. ASF, Otto di Guardia, 61, fols. 62r–v: "Adi 4 di giugno 1552 . . . Li Sp.li di . . . otto di guardia e Balia . . . Chi si facci pubblico bando per li che non . . . si voglia grado . . . che per l'avenire non ardisce in modo alcuno per le strade pubbliche . . . giuchare al gioco che si di . . . palla a Maglio . . . sotto pena di scudi 25 e di 2 tratti di fune e arbitrio del magistrato."

96. BNCF, 15.3.125, no. 59, *Bando che non si faccino ragunate, ne si corra alle quistioni, publiciti adi 13 di novembre 1553, in Fiorenza nella stamperia di Giorgio Marescotti:* "per pacifico & quieto vivere di detta città. . . . Che per l'avvenire non sia persona alcuna di qual si voglia stato, o conditione, etiam ecclesiastica, che ardisca, o in alcun modo presumma uscire di loro case, o botteghe o altro luoghi dove stessi, per correre dove si facessino tali risse, o quistioni, per fare adunate, o tumulto."

97. BNCF, 15.3.125, no. 66, *Bando per conto delle frombe et scaglie pubblicato dai 25 di ottobre. 1554. in Fiorenza, nella stamperia di Giorgio Marescotti:* "Pero nuovamente fanno pubblicamente bandire, & espressamente comandare a ogni, & qualche persona di qual si voglia stato, grado, o conditione si sia etiam che fossi di età minore non ardisca in modo alcuno per l'avvenire per le strade, o piazze pubblicamente della Citta tirarre sassi con scaglie."

98. BNCF, *Estratta in compendio per alfabeto dalle principali leggi, bandi, statuti, ordini, e consuetudini, massime criminali, e miste, che vegliano nella stati del serenissimo Gran Duca di Toscana,* 204, no. 8: "La predetta legge della 23 Agosto 1566 proibisce a qualsivoglia persona quantunque privilegiata il giuocare o far giuocare o fermarsi a vedere ad alcun giuoco di carte, dadi, pallottole, palla a maglio, o tirare forme, e girelle nelle piazza, e strade pubbliche . . . sotto pena di scudi dieci, o vero due tratti di fune per ciascuno."

99. AOIF, 10445, S15 P2, no. 279, "Bando del giuoco ad 29 aprile 1683": "proibire a qualscia persona di quasia stato, grado, o condone . . . di giuocare alle Palla Pilotta o Palottole e qualsisia altro giuoco strepitoso nella via d'Orbatello principiando dal canto alla Catena suo a dove estende la clausura d'Orbatello."

100. ASF, Otto di Guardia, 89, fol. 26r: "bachano di sorte alcuna. ne sonare o cantare o fare altri strepiti, ne giucare a palla pallottole o altro qual si voglia giuoco, sotto pena del arbitrio del Magistrato."

101. Roberto Ciabani, *Le leggi di pietra: Bandi dei signori Otto di Guardia e Balia della città di Firenze* (Florence: Cantini Edizioni d'Arte, 1984), 179: "A di xvii giugno MDCXVI li Spl. SS. Otto di balia della città di Firenze proibiscono che intorno al monastero delle monache delle murate et vicino a quello a braccia cento ne vi si giochi per alcuno et fanciulli alla palla ne a qualsivoglia altro gioco et di notte non vi si soni ne canti canzone."

102. Gian Rosa, *Le leggi penali sui muri di Firenze: Tratti di corda e penna* (Florence: Casa Editrice Nerbini, 1911), 94: "gli spettabili signori otto proibiscono a qualunque persona il giocare a ogni sorte giuoco. Far rumore o tumulto. Orinare. Il fare il dire qualsivoglia altra sorte di sprocizie vicino alla chiesa del monastero di S. Silvestro a braccia 50 sotto pena di scudi dua di cattura e di piu proibiscono alle meretrici o donne disoneste di alcuna sorte il stare et abitare vicino al detto monastero a braccia 100 per ogni verso sotto pena di lire 200 come per decreto de 9 giugno 1668."

103. Rosa, *Le leggi penali*, 27: "Signori otto proibscono intorno alla chiesa e monastero di S. Bernaba a braccia 50 farvi sporcitie ne giocare sotto pena di scudi 2 di cattura e a braccia 100 non vi stiano meretrice o simili secondo la legge del 1561 pena lire 200."

104. Rosa, *Le leggi penali*, 39: "li ss otto anno proibito ogni sorte di sporcizio giuochi tumulti intorno alla chiesa mura del convento delle monache di S. Bernaba sotto pena di scudi dua odi tratti di fune oltra alla cattura e larbitrio di lor ss."

105. Stefano Possanzini, "Il monastero fiorentino delle Carmelitane in San Barnaba," *Carmelus* 43 (1996): 123-145. Today Via Mozza is called Via San Zanobi.

106. ASF, A&D, 291, unpaginated/unfoliated: "Sandra . . . trovata di rimpitto al monestero di San Barnaba al con due giovani a far baie e a dire parole disoneste senza rispetto al luogo."

107. ASF, A&D, 291, unpaginated/unfoliated: "1575—Quattro donne di via Mozza aveva fatto baccano."

108. ASF, A&D, 292, unpaginated/unfoliated: "Ottobre 1576 La Menichina di Pistoia meretrice in via Mozza aveva querelato certo Sanino di Marco di averle fatto baccano di notte per volere dormire con lei a suo dispetto."

109. ASF, A&D, 291, "Onestà e meretrice," unpaginated/unfoliated: "1581 Cinzia Monti, Agnola siciliana ed Ersilia romana aveva fatto rissa in via Mozza."

110. ASF, A&D, 292, unpaginated/unfoliated: "Settembre 1588 La Caterina alias Rondinina meretrice in via Mozza era processata per essersi trovata a certo baccano."

111. These figures reflect an exploration of Florence's modern streets and the Otto di Guardia archives in conjunction with Francesco Bigazzi's 1886 record of public inscriptions, Gian Rosa's 1911 transcription of the stone plaques, and Roberto Ciabani's 1984 photographic collection of surviving plaques. See Francesco Bigazzi, *Iscrizioni e memorie della città di Firenze* (Florence: Pei Tipi dell'Arte della Stampa, 1886).

112. Creating a precise chronology of the stone plaques is difficult because only thirty-nine plaques bear dates. The forty-four remaining plaques can be attributed to three general periods of grand-ducal rule based on content, reference to specific legislation, and similarity in content and quality to

dated plaques. These three periods are 1587 to 1621 (the reigns of Ferdinando I de' Medici, r. 1587–1609, and Cosimo II de' Medici, r. 1609–1621); 1621 to 1670 (the reign of Ferdinando II de' Medici); and 1670 to 1737 (the reigns of Cosimo III de' Medici, r. 1670–1723, and Gian Gastone de' Medici, r. 1723–1737). For more detail, see Julia Rombough, "Regulating Sense and Space in Late Renaissance Florence." *Urban History* 50, no. 1 (2023): 38–57.

113. Vincenzo Giannetti, *"A vita nuova": Ricordi e vicende della grande operazione urbanistica che distrusse il centro storico di Firenze* (Florence: Cassa di Risparmio di Firenze, 1995); Bigazzi, *Iscrizioni e memorie,* preface.

114. Rosa, *Le leggi penali,* 28, 66, 68. One is at the monastery of Santa Maria degli Angeli, which housed a renowned scriptorium; one references the Badia, one of Florence's most important male monasteries; and one references the Oratory of San Carlo, a residence of unvowed priests.

115. Notable locations of the stone plaque and their frequency are as follows: near or referencing churches, 35 plaques; near or referencing government buildings, 3 plaques; near or referencing private homes, 7 plaques; near or referencing civic institutions, 5 plaques; near or referencing nunneries, 21 plaques; near or referencing male monasteries, 3 plaques; no direct reference to a specific site, 18 plaques.

116. Rosa, *Le leggi penali,* 67, 75, 90, 94, 71, 22: "fare romori," "strepitoso," "tumulti," "suoni et altre sorte di strepiti o rumori," "non vi suoni ne canti canzone," "meretrice," "giocare a ogni sorte giuoco," "brutture."

117. Rosa, *Le leggi penali,* 67: "Proibiscono a qualsia persona giocare a qual sorte di giuoco, onare e fare strepito in qual si sia modo, tanto di giorno che di notte vicino al convento de mendicanti a braccia cento sotto pena dell'arbitrio, et cattura."

118. Rosa, *Le leggi penali,* 37–38: "I signori otto hanno proibito farce bruttura."

119. Rosa, *Le leggi penali,* 75: "Prohibiscono che intorno al monastero delle monache della murate et vicino a quella a braccia cento ne vi giochi per alcuno et fanciulli alla palla ne a qualisivoglia altra gioco et di notte non vi si soni ne canti canzone loro."

120. Rosa, *Le leggi penali,* 93.

121. Rosa, *Le leggi penali,* 20. "Fatto decreto sotto il di 26 di settembre 1635 che vicino a 300 braccia a questa chiesa dogni non habitino donne di mala vita con pena a chi non obbedisce."

122. Rosa, *Le leggi penali,* 63.

123. Rosa, *Le leggi penali,* 95: "Proibiscono giuochi, canti, suoni, et altre sorte di strepiti or romori intorno a questa monastero e vicino a quello abbraccia cento per ogni verso."

124. Brackett, *Criminal Justice and Crime,* 28–29.

125. BNCF, Palatino, *Descritione del numero delle case,* E.B.15.2, fols. 85v–86r.

126. Brackett, *Criminal Justice and Crime,* 37.

CONCLUSION

1. Robert Dallington, *A Survey of the Great Duke's State of Tuscany in the Yeare of our Lord 1596* (London: E. Blount, 1605), 65–66, 48.
2. Agostino Gallo, *Le tredici giornate della vera agricoltura & de piaceri della villa* (Venice: Nicolo Bevilacqua, 1556), 168: "esterminare questa pestisera semenza ... cosi alla infame maritata, si debbono cavar gli occhi, tagliar la lingua, e troncar le mani, o piu tosto, per leverla dal mondo, abbrusciarla viva."
3. Mark Michael Smith, *Sensing the Past: Seeing, Hearing, Smelling, Tasting, and Touching in History* (Berkeley: University of California Press, 2007), 50.
4. Niall Atkinson, *The Noisy Renaissance: Sound, Architecture, and Florentine Urban Life* (University Park: Pennsylvania State University Press, 2016), 3–4.
5. Paul Stoller, *Sensuous Scholarship* (Philadelphia: University of Pennsylvania Press, 1997).

BIBLIOGRAPHY

PRIMARY SOURCES

Affinati, Giacomo. *Il muto che parla, dialogo ove si tratta dell'eccellenze e de difetti della lingua humana, e si spiegano più di 190: Concetti scritturali sopra il silentio.* Venice: Marc Antonio Zaltieri, 1606.

Alberti, Leandro. *Descrittione di tutta Italia, nelle quale si contiene il sito di essa, l'origine et le signorie delle città et delle castella.* Bologna: Anselmo Giaccarelli, 1550.

Ardizzone, Fabritio. *Ricordi di Fabritio Ardizzone fisico intorno al preservarsi e curarsi dalla peste.* Genoa: G. Maria Farroni, 1656.

Augustine, Saint. *The Rule of St. Augustine.* Translated by Russell Robert, OSA. Last revised October 6, 2023. http://sourcebooks.fordham.edu/halsall/source/ruleaug.html.

Baliano, Giovanni Battista. *Trattato della pestilenza, ove si adducono pensieri nuovi in più materie, stampato già l'anno 1547, et hora riveduto et ampliato dall' autore.* Genoa: Benedetto Guasco, 1653.

Bartoli, Daniel. *Del suono de' tremori armonici e dell' udito.* Bologna: G. Bilancioni, 1680.

Bernardino da Siena. *Le prediche volgari.* Edited by Ciro Cannarozzi. Florence: Libreria editrice Fiorentina, 1934.

Bindassi, Senofonte. *Il diporto della villa: Canto di Senofonte Bindassi da Sant'Angelo in Vado.* Venice: Giovachino Brognolo, 1582.

Boccaccio, Giovanni. *Decamerone.* Florence: San Jacopo di Ripoli, 1483.

Bovarini, Leandro. *Del silentio opportuno.* Perugia: Vincenzio Colombara, 1603.

Bruno, Matteo. *Discorsi di M. Matteo Bruno medico ariminese sopra gli errori fatti dall' eccellente M. Bartolomeo Traffichetti da Bertinoro nell' arte sua di conservar la sanità tutt' intiera.* Venice: Andrea Arrivabene, 1569.

Buonriccio, Angelico. *Paraphrasi sopra i tre libri dell' Anima d'Aristotile.* Venice: Andrea Arrivabene, 1565.

The Canons and Decrees of the Sacred and Ecumenical Council of Trent, Celebrated under the Sovereign Pontiffs Paul III, Julius III, and Pius IV. Translated by Rev. J. Waterworth. London: Burns and Oates, 1888.

Cause et rimedii della peste, et d'altre infermità. Florence: Apresso i Giunti, 1577.

Confessionale de Santo Antonino arcivescovo de Firenze dell'ordine di predicatori. Venice: Don Ipolito, 1543.

Cospi, Antonio Maria. *Il giudice criminalista.* Florence: Zanobi Pignoni, 1643.

Crivellati, Cesare. *Trattato di peste, nel quale breuemente si scuopre la sua natura con quella del contagio, manifestandosi insieme le cagioni, i segni da conoscerla, & il modo da preservarsi, e liberarsi da quella.* Viterbo: Bernardino Diot'allevi, 1631.

Dallington, Robert. *A Survey of the Great Duke's State of Tuscany in the Yeare of Our Lord 1596.* London: E. Blount, 1605.

Della Porta, Giambattista. *De i miracoli et maravigliosi effetti dalla natura prodotti.* Vol. 3. Venice: Lodovico Avanzo, 1562.

Delle Colombe, Raffaello. *Delle prediche sopra tutti gli evangeli dell'anno.* Vol. 1. Florence: Bartolommeo Sermartelli e Fratelli, 1613.

Dolce, Lodovico. *Nel quale si ragiona del modo di accrescere e conservar la memoria.* Venice: Giovanni Battista e Marchio Sessa, 1562.

Domenici, Giovanni. *Regola del governo di cura familiare compilate dal beato Giovanni Dominici fiorentino dell'ordine de' frati predicatori.* Edited by Donato Salvi. Florence: Angiolo Garinei Libraio, 1860.

Durante, Castore. *Herbario Nuovo di Castore Durante medico, et cittadino romano.* Venice: Li Seffa, 1602.

———. *Il tesoro della sanità nel quale si da il modo da conservar la sanità, & prolungar la vita & si tratta della natura della cibi, e di rimedio de i nocumenti loro.* Rome: Francesco Zannetti, 1586.

Florio, John. *Queen Anna's New World of Words, or Dictionarie of the Italian and English Tongues, Collected and Newly Much Augmented by John Florio.* London: Melch, Bradwood, 1611.

Galen. *A Translation of Galen's Hygiene, De sanitate tuenda.* Translated and edited by Robert Montraville Green. Springfield, IL: Thomas, 1951.

Gallo, Agostino. *Le tredici giornate della vera agricoltura & de piaceri della villa.* Venice: Nicolo Bevilacqua, 1556.

Giubetti, Fulvio. *Il cancelliero di sanità da Fuluio Giubetti cancelliere all'Offizie della Sanità della città di Firenze.* Florence: Zanobi Pignoni, 1619.

Gracián, Jerónimo. *Della disciplina regolare.* Venice: R. P. del Carmine, 1600.

Guidi, Fra Filippo. *Vita della venerabile madre suor Caterina de Ricci fiorentina.* Florence: Bartolommeo Sermartelli, 1622.

Laroon, Marcellus. *The Cryes of the City of London Drawne after the Life.* London: Pierce Tempest, 1688.

Manzini, Cesare. *Ammaestramenti per allevare, pascere, e curare uccelli li quali s'ingabbino ad cantare.* Brescia: Pietro Maria Marchetti, 1607.

Mattioli, Pietro Andrea. *Delle materia medicinale.* Venice: Vincenzo Valgrisi, 1563.

Menghi, Girolamo. *Celeste thesoro della gloriosa madre di Dio, Maria Vergina: Nel quale si ragiona del vero culto, & adoratione, che si deve alla sacroscante imagini.* Bologna: Giovanni Battista Pulciani, 1609.

Mercurio, Scipione. *De gli errori popolari d'Italia libri sette.* Verona: Francesco Rossi, 1645.

Moscardo, Conte Ludovico. *Note ovvero memorie del museo di Ludovico Moscardo nobile veronese.* Padua: Paulo Frambotto, 1656.

Niccolini, Giustina. *The Chronicle of Le Murate by Sister Giustina Niccolini.* Translated and edited by Saundra Weddle. Toronto: Centre for Reformation and Renaissance Studies, 2011.

Olina, Giovanni Pietro. *Uccelliera overo discorso della natura e proprietà di diversi uccelli.* Rome: Andrea Fei, 1684.

Ottonelli, Domenico. *Alcuni buoni avvisi, e casi di coscienza intorno alla pericolosa conversatione, da proporsi a chi conversa poco medestamente.* Florence: Luca Franceschini & Alessandro Logi, 1646.

Paleotti, Gabriele. *Discorso intorno alle imagini sacre et profane.* Bologna: Alessandro Benacci, 1582.

Panarolo, Domenico. *Aerologia cioè discorso dell' aria trattato utile per la sanità.* Rome: Domenico Marciani, 1642.

Paschetti, Bartolomeo. *Del conservare la sanità e del vivere de' genovesi.* Genoa: Giuseppe Pavoni, 1602.

Petronio, Alessandro Traiano. *Del viver delli Romani et di conservar la sanità.* Rome: Domenico Basa, 1592.

Raccolata di alcune cose appartenenti alle monache stabilite nel sinodo diecesano fatto in Firenze il di 14 e 15 di maggio MDCXIX per ordine dell'illustriss. & reverendiss. Alessandro Marzi Medici Arcivescovo di Firenze. Florence: Bartolommeo Sermartelli e Fratelli, 1619.

Raimondi, Eugenio. *Delle caccie.* Brescia: Giovanni Battista Catani, 1626.

Ruscelli, Girolamo. *De' secreti del Reverendo Donno Alessio Piemontese.* Lyon, France: Theobaldo Pagano, 1558.

Savonarola, Girolamo. *Prediche sopra iob del R.P.F Hieronimo Savonarola da Ferrara: Fatte in Firenze l'anno 1494.* Venice: Niccolo Bascarini, 1545.

Scamozzi, Vincenzo. *L'idea della architettura universale di Vincenzo Scamozzi architetto Veneto.* Vol. 2. Venice: Giorgio Valentino, 1615.

Scarioni, Francesco. *Centuria di secreti politici, cimichi, e naturali.* Venice: Niccolò Tebaldini, 1626.

Segni, Bernardo. *Il trattato sopra i libri dell' Anima d'Aristotile.* Florence: Giorgio Marescotti, 1553.

Sommario de capitoli della venerabile compagnia di Santa Maria Maddalena sopra le Mal Maritate. Florence: Bartholomeo Sermartelli, 1583.

Sperelli, Allessandro Vescovo di Gubbio. *Ragionamenti pastorali di Monsignor Alessandro Sperelli Vescovo di Gubbio, prelate domestic del sommo pontefice & assistente fatti al clero, alle monache & al popolo, in tre parti distinti.* Vol. 2, *Ragionamenti fatti alle monache.* Rome: Guglielmo Halle Libraro, 1664.

———. *Ragionamenti pastorali di Monsignor Allessandro Sperelli Vescovo di Gubbio, prelate domestic del sommo pontefice & assistente fatti al clero, alle monache & al popolo, in tre parti distinti.* Vol. 3, *Ragionamenti fatti al popolo.* Venice: Paolo Baglioni, 1675.

Tarabotti, Arcangela. *Paternal Tyranny.* Edited and translated by Letizia Panizza. Chicago: University of Chicago Press, 2004.

Thomai, Tomaso. *Discorso del vero modo di preservare gli huomini dalla peste di Tomaso Thomai medico da Ravenna.* Bologna: Clemente Ferroni, 1630.

Traffichetti, Bartolomeo. *Idea dell' arte di conservar la sanità . . . et hora per il medesimo diffeso dalle false oppositioni di M. Matteo Bruni.* Venice: Francesco Gasparo Bindoni e Fratelli, 1572.

——. *L'arte di conservare la sanità.* Pesaro, Italy: Gieronimo Concordia, 1565.

——. *Somma de modo di conservars la sanità in tempo pestilente.* Bologna: Alessandro Benacci, 1576.

Zarrabini, Onofrio. *Delle materie e de soggetti predicabili.* Venice: Battista Somascho, 1587.

Zon, Domenico. *Santuario delle monache.* Venice: Fioravante Prati, 1615.

SECONDARY SOURCES

Agostini, Anna. *Pistoia sul mare: Il cavalieri di Santo Stefano e Pistoia.* Pistoia, Italy: Settegiorni Editore, 2008.

Albala, Ken. *Eating Right in the Renaissance.* Berkeley: University of California Press 2002.

Albini, Giuliana. "Pauperismo e solidarietà femminile nell'Italia settentrionale (secoli XIII–XIV)." *Storia Delle Donne* 13 (2017): 103–126.

Aranci, Gilberto. *Formazione religiosa e santità laicale a Firenze tra cinque e seicento.* Firenze: Giampiero Pagnini, 1997.

Atkinson, Niall. *The Noisy Renaissance: Sound, Architecture, and Florentine Urban Life.* University Park: The Pennsylvania State University Press, 2016.

——. "Sonic Armatures: Constructing an Acoustic Regime in Renaissance Florence." *The Senses and Society* 7, no. 1 (2012): 39–52.

Austern, Linda Phillis. "Musical Treatments for Lovesickness: The Early Modern Heritage." In *Music as Medicine: The History of Music Therapy Since Antiquity,* edited by Peregrine Horden, 213–248. New York: Routledge, 2000.

Bailey, Peter. *Popular Culture and Performance in the Victorian City.* Cambridge: Cambridge University Press, 1998.

Baldasseroni, Eleonora. *Le cavaliere dell'ordine di Santo Stefano: Le monache della santissima concezione di Firenze.* Pisa: Plus, 2008.

Ballester, Luis García. "On the Origins of the 'Six Non-natural Things' in Galen." In Luis García Ballester, Jon Arrizabalaga, Montserrat Cabré, and Lluís Cifuentes, *Galen and Galenism: Theory and Medical Practice from Antiquity to the European Renaissance,* 105–115. New York: Routledge, 2002.

Battistini, Francesco. "La produzione, il commercio e i prezzi della seta grezza nello stato di Firenze 1489–1859." *Rivista di Storia Economica* 21, no. 3 (2005): 233–270.

Behringer, Wolfgang. "The Invention of Sports: Early Modern Ball Games." In *Sports and Physical Exercise in Early Modern Culture: New Perspectives on the History of Sports and Motion,* edited by Rebecca von Mallinckrodt and Angela Schattner, 22–47. New York: Routledge, 2016.

Bigazzi, Francesco. *Iscrizioni e memorie della città di Firenze.* Florence: Per Tipi dell' Arte della Stampa, 1887.

Bijsterveld, Karin. "Introduction." In *Soundscapes of the Urban Past: Staged Sound as Mediated Cultural Heritage,* edited by Karin Bijsterveld, 11–30. Bielfeld, Germany: Transcript Verlag, 2013.

Bijsterveld, Karin, ed. *Soundscapes of the Urban Past: Staged Sound as Mediated Cultural Heritage.* Bielfeld, Germany: Transcript Verlag, 2013.

Black, Christopher F. *Church, Religion and Society in Early Modern Italy.* New York: Palgrave Macmillan, 2004.

Bloch, Amy R. *Lorenzo Ghiberti's Gates of Paradise: Humanism, History, and Artistic Philosophy in the Italian Renaissance.* Cambridge: Cambridge University Press, 2016.

Bonelli, Benedetto. *Notizie istorico-critiche intorno al B. M Adelpreto vescovo e comprotettore della chiesa di Trento.* Trento, Italy: Gianbattista Monauni, 1761.

Botelho, Keith M. *Renaissance Earwitnesses: Rumor and Early Modern Masculinity.* New York: Palgrave Macmillan, 2009.

Brakke, David. *Demons and the Making of the Monk: Spiritual Combat in Early Christianity.* Cambridge: Cambridge University Press, 2006.

Brackett, John K. *Criminal Justice and Crime in Late Renaissance Florence, 1537–1609.* Cambridge: Cambridge University Press, 1992.

———. "The Florentine Onestà and the Control of Prostitution, 1403–1680." *Sixteenth Century Journal* 24, no. 2 (1993): 273–300.

Brizio, Elena. "The Role of Women in Their Kin's Economic and Political Life: The Sienese Case (End XIV–Mid XV Century)." In *Creating Women: Representation, Self-Representation, and Agency in the Renaissance,* edited by Manuela Scarci, 169–181. Toronto: Centre for Reformation and Renaissance Studies, 2013.

Brodman, J. W. *Charity and Welfare: Hospitals and the Poor in Medieval Catalonia.* Philadelphia: University of Pennsylvania Press, 1998.

Brown, Judith, and John Goodman. "Women and Industry in Florence." *Journal of Economic History* 40, no. 1 (1980): 73–80.

Brucker, Gene A. *The Civic Worlds of Early Renaissance Florence.* Princeton, NJ: Princeton University Press, 1997.

Brucker, Gene A., ed. *The Society of Renaissance Florence: A Documentary Study.* Toronto: University of Toronto Press, 2001.

Brundin, Abigail, Deborah Howard, and Mary Laven. *The Sacred Home in Renaissance Italy*. Oxford: Oxford University Press, 2018.

Burnett, Charles. "Perceiving Sound in the Middle Ages." In *Hearing History: A Reader,* edited by Mark Michael Smith, 69-84. Athens: University of Georgia Press, 2004.

Burns, Kathryn. *Colonial Habits: Convents and the Spiritual Economy of Cuzco, Peru.* Durham, NC: Duke University Press, 1999.

Butters, Suzanne. "Natural Magic, Artificial Music and Birds at Francesco de' Medici's Pratolino." In *Sense and the Senses in Early Modern Art and Cultural Practice,* edited by Alice E. Sanger and Siv Tove Kulbrandstad Walker, 31-63. New York: Routledge, 2017.

Bychowski, M. W. "The Transgender Turn: Eleanor Ryekner Speaks Back." In *Trans Historical: Gender Plurality before the Modern,* edited by Greta LaFleur, Masha Raskolnikov, and Anna Klosowska, 95-113. Ithaca, NY: Cornell University Press, 2021.

Bylebyl, Jerome J. "Galen and the Non-natural Causes of Variation in the Pulse." *Bulletin of the History of Medicine* 45, no. 5 (1971): 482-485.

Cabré, Montserrat. "Women or Healers? Household Practices and the Categories of Health Care in Late Medieval Iberia." *Bulletin of the History of Medicine* 82, no. 1 (2008): 18-51.

Camerano, Alessandra. "Assistenza richeste ed assistenza imposta: Il conservatorio di S. Caterina della Rosa di Roma." *Quaderni Storici* 28, no. 82 (1993): 227-260.

Camillo, Elena. "Ancora su Donno Alessio Piemontese: Il libro di segreti tra popolarità ed accademia." *Giornale Storico della Letteratura Italiana* 162, no. 520 (1985): 539-553.

Canosa, Romano. *Il velo e il cappuccio: Monacazioni forzate e sessualità nei conventi femminili in Italia tra Quattrocento e Settecento.* Rome: Sapere, 2000.

——. *La vita quotidiana a Milano in età spagnola.* Milan: Longanesi, 1996.

Canosa, Romano, and Isabella Colonnello. *Storia della prostituzione in Italia dal quattrocento al fine del settecento.* Rome: Sapere, 2000.

Cantini, Lorenzo. *Legislazione toscana: Raccolta e illustrata dal dottore Lorenzo Cantini.* Florence: Albizziniana da S. Maria in Campo, 1804.

Carpanetto, Dino. *Scienza e arte del guarire: Cultura, formazione universitaria e professioni mediche a Torino tra sei e settecento.* Turin: Deputazione Subalpina di Storia Patria, 1998.

Cavallo, Sandra. *Charity and Power in Early Modern Italy: Benefactors and Their Motives in Turin, 1541-1789.* Cambridge: Cambridge University Press, 1995.

——. "Regimes, Authors, and Readers: Italy and England Compared." In *Conserving Health in Early Modern Culture Bodies and Environments in Italy and England,* edited by Sandra Cavallo and Tessa Storey, 23-52. Manchester, UK: Manchester University Press, 2017.

Cavallo, Sandra, and David Gentilcore, eds. *Spaces, Objects and Identities in Early Modern Italian Medicine.* Malden, MA: Blackwell, 2008.

Cavallo, Sandra, and Tessa Storey. *Healthy Living in Renaissance Italy.* Oxford: Oxford University Press, 2013.

Chabot, Isabelle. "La reconnaissance du travail des femmes dans la Florence du bas Moyen Ages: Contexte idéologiques et réalité." In *La donne nell'economia (XIII–XVIII).* Florence: Le Monnier, 1990.

———. "Messer Niccolò degli Alberti, 'pater pauperum': Lettura del testamento." In *L'Ospedale dell' Orbatello: Carità e arte a Firenze,* edited by Cristina De Benedictis and Carla Milloschi, 73–81. Florence: Edizioni Polistampa, 2015.

Chiu, Remi. "Music for the Times of Pestilence, 1420–1600." PhD diss., McGill University, 2012.

———. *Plague and Music in the Renaissance.* Cambridge: Cambridge University Press, 2017.

Chojnacka, Monica. "Women, Charity and Community in Early Modern Venice: The Casa Delle Zitelle." *Renaissance Quarterly* 51, no. 1 (1998): 68–91.

———. *Working Women of Early Modern Venice.* Baltimore: Johns Hopkins University Press, 2000.

Ciabani, Roberto. *Le leggi di pietra: Bandi dei signori Otto di Guardia e Balia della città di Firenze.* Florence: Cantini Edizioni d'Arte, 1984.

Cipolla, Carlo M. "The 'Bills of Mortality' of Florence." *Population Studies* 32, no. 3 (1978): 541–548.

———. *Fighting the Plague in Seventeenth-Century Italy.* Madison: University of Wisconsin Press, 1981.

———. *I pidocchi e il granduca: Crisi economica e problemi sanitari nella Firenze del '600.* Bologna: Il Mulino, 1979.

———. *Miasmas and Disease: Public Health and the Environment in the Pre-industrial Age.* New Haven, CT: Yale University Press, 1992.

———. "The Plague and the Pre-Malthus Malthusians." *Journal of European Economic History* 3, no. 2 (1974): 277–284.

Clark, Stuart. *Vanities of the Eye: Vision in Early Modern European Culture.* Oxford: Oxford University Press, 2007.

Classen, Constance. "Engendering Perception: Gender Ideologies and Sensory Hierarchies in Western History." *Body and Society* 3, no. 2 (1997): 1–19.

———. "The Witch's Senses: Sensory Ideologies and Transgressive Femininities from the Renaissance to Modernity." In *Empire of the Senses: The Sensual Culture Reader,* edited by David Howes, 70–85. Oxford: Bloomsbury, 2005.

Classen, Constance, David Howes, and Anthony Synnott. *Aroma: The Cultural History of Smell.* New York: Routledge, 1994.

Cochrane, Eric. *Florence in the Forgotten Centuries 1527–1800: A History of Florence and the Florentines in the Age of the Grand Duke.* Chicago: University of Chicago Press, 1973.

Cockayne, Emily. *Hubbub: Filth, Noise & Stench in England, 1600–1770*. New Haven, CT: Yale University Press, 2007.

Cohen, Elizabeth S. "Honour and Gender in the Streets of Early Modern Rome." *Journal of Interdisciplinary History* 22, no. 4 (1992): 597–625.

——. "To Pray, to Work, to Hear, to Speak: Women in Roman Streets, c. 1600." *Journal of Early Modern History* 12, no. 3 (2008): 289–311.

Cohen, Elizabeth S., and Thomas V. Cohen. "Camilla the Go-Between: The Politics of Gender in a Roman Household." *Continuity and Change* 4, no. 1 (1989): 53–77.

——. "Open and Shut: The Social Meanings of the Cinquecento Roman House." *Studies in the Decorative Arts* 9, no. 1 (2002): 61–84.

Cohen, Sherill. *The Evolution of Women's Asylums since 1500: From Refuges for Ex-prostitutes to Shelters for Battered Women*. New York: Oxford University Press, 1992.

Cohen, Thomas V., and Elizabeth S. Cohen. *Words and Deeds in Renaissance Rome: Trials before the Papal Magistrates*. Toronto: University of Toronto Press, 1993.

Cohn, Samuel Kline, Jr. "Donne in piazza e donne tribunale a Firenze nel rinascimento." *Studi Storici* 22, no. 3 (1981): 515–533.

——. *The Laboring Classes in Renaissance Florence*. New York: Academic Press, 1980.

Colleran, Kate. "*Scampanata* at the Widows' Windows: A Case-Study of Sound and Ritual Insult in Cinquecento Florence." *Urban History* 36, no. 3 (2009): 359–378.

Colli, Dante, Alfonso Garuti, and Romano Pelloni. *Le mura del silenzio: Monasteri femminili tra Po e Crinale*. Modena: Carpi, Artoli, 2001.

Conway, Melissa. *The Diario of the Printing Press of San Jacopo di Ripoli: 1476–1484; Commentary and Transcription*. Florence: Leo S. Olschki, 1999.

Corbin, Alain. *Village Bells*. London: Papermac, 1999.

Cosmacini, Giorgio. *Ciarlataneria e medicina: Cure, maschere, carle*. Milan: Cortina, 1998.

Crawford, Patricia. *Blood, Bodies, and Families in Early Modern England*. New York: Routledge, 2004.

Creytens, Raimondo. "La riforma dei monasteri femminili dopo i decreti tridentini." In *Il Concilio di Trento e la riforma tridentina: Atti del convengo storico internazionale, Trento 2–6 settembre 1963*, 45–83. Rome: Herder, 1965.

Cusick, Suzanne G. *Francesca Caccini at the Medici Court: Music and the Circulation of Power*. Chicago: University of Chicago Press, 2009.

——. "He Said, She Said?: Men Hearing Women in Medicean Florence." In *Rethinking Difference in Music Scholarship*, edited by Olivia Bloechl, Melanie Lowe, and Jeffrey Kallberg, 53–76. New York: Cambridge University Press, 2015.

Da Calice, Romano. *La grande peste: Genova 1656–1657*. La Spezia, Italy: Cooperativa di Solidarietà Sociale Egidio Bullesi, 1992.

D'Addario, Arnaldo. *La formazione dello stato moderno in Toscana da Cosimo il Vecchio a Cosimo I de' Medici*. Lecce, Italy: Adriatica Editrice Salentina, 1976.

D'Amelia, Marina. "La presenza delle madri nell'Italia medievale e moderna." In *Storia della maternità*, edited by Marina D'Amelia, 3–52. Bari, Italy: Laterza, 1997.

———. "Una lettera a settimana: Geronima Veralli Malatesta al Signor Fratello 1572–1622." *Quaderni Storici*, n.s., 28, no. 83 (1993): 381–413.

D'Amico, Stefano. "Shameful Mother: Poverty and Prostitution in Seventeenth-Century Milan." *Journal of Family History* 30, no. 1 (2005): 109–120.

Davis, Robert. "Stones and Shame in Early Modern Italy." *Acta Histriae* 8, no. 2 (2000): 449–456.

Day, W. R., Jr. "The Population of Florence before the Black Death: Survey and Synthesis." *Journal of Medieval History* 28, no. 2 (2002): 93–129.

Dean, Trevor. "Gender and Insult in an Italian City: Bologna in the Later Middle Ages." *Social History* 29, no. 2 (2004): 217–231.

Dell'Antonio, Andrew. *Listening as Spiritual Practice in Early Modern Italy*. Berkeley: University of California Press, 2011.

Della Robbia, Enrica Viviani. *Nei monasteri fiorentini*. Florence: Sansoni, 1946.

Dennis, Flora. "Sound and Domestic Space in Fifteenth- and Sixteenth-Century Italy." *Studies in the Decorative Arts* 16, no. 1 (2008–2009): 7–19.

Derosas, Renzo. "Moralità e giustizia a Venezia nel '500–'600: Gli esecutori contro la bestemmia." In *Stato, società e giustizia nella repubblica veneta (secolo XV–XVIII)*, vol. 1, edited by Gaetano Cozzi, 431–528. Rome: Jouvence, 1981.

Dijkstra, Jitse, and Mathilde van Dijk, eds. *The Encroaching Desert: Egyptian Hagiography and the Medieval West*. Leiden: Brill, 2006.

Doctor, Jenny. "The Texture of Silence." In *Silence, Music, Silent Music*, edited by Nicky Losseff and Jenny Doctor, 15–35. Aldershot, UK: Ashgate, 2007.

Donadi, Paola. *La regola e lo spirito: Arte, cultura, quotidianità nei monasteri femminili*. Milan: Franco Angeli, 2003.

Doniger, Wendy. "The Symbolism of Black and White Babies in the Myth of Parental Impression." *Social Research* 70, no. 1 (2003): 1–44.

Douglas, Mary. *Purity and Danger: An Analysis of Concepts of Pollution and Taboo*. London: Routledge, 2002.

Dugan, Holly. *The Ephemeral History of Perfume: Scent and Sense in Early Modern England*. Baltimore: Johns Hopkins University Press, 2011.

Eamon, William. *Science and the Secrets of Nature: Books of Secrets in Medieval and Early Modern Culture*. Princeton, NJ: Princeton University Press, 1994.

Eisenbichler, Konrad. *Boys of the Archangel Raphael: A Youth Confraternity in Florence, 1411–1785*. Toronto: University of Toronto Press, 1998.

Elias, Norbert. *The History of Manners*. Translated by Edmund Jephcott. New York: Pantheon Books, 1978.

Evangelisti, Silvia. *Nuns: A History of Convent Life, 1450–1700*. Oxford: Oxford University Press, 2007.

———. "To Find God in Work? Female Social Stratification in Early Modern Italian Convents." *European History Quarterly* 38, no. 3 (2008): 398–416.

——. "'We Do Not Have It, and We Do Not Want It': Women, Power, and Convent Reform in Florence." *Sixteenth Century Journal* 34, no. 3 (2003): 677–700.

Evans, Jennifer. "Female Barrenness, Bodily Access and Aromatic Treatments in Seventeenth-Century England." *Historical Research* 87, no. 237 (2014): 423–443.

Fasano Guarini, Elena. *L'Italia moderna e la Toscana dei principi: Discussioni e ricerche storiche.* Florence: Le Monnier, 2008.

——. *Lo stato di Cosimo I: Le istituzioni della Toscana moderna in un percorso di testi commentati.* Florence: Sansoni, 1973.

——. "Potere centrale e comunità soggette nel granducato di Cosimo I." *Rivista Storica Italiana* 89, nos. 3–4 (1997): 490–538.

——. "Produzione di leggi e disciplinamento nella Toscana granducale tra cinque e seicento: Spunti di ricerca." In *Disciplina dell' anima, disciplina del corpo e disciplina della società tra medioevo ed età moderna,* edited by Paolo Prodi and Carla Penuti, 659–690. Bologna: Il Mulino, 1994.

Finucci, Valeria. "Maternal Imagination and Monstrous Birth: Tasso's *Gerusalemme liberate*." In *Generation and Degeneration: Tropes of Reproduction in Literature and History from Antiquity through Early Modern Europe,* edited by Valeria Finucci and Kevin Brownless, 41–80. Durham, NC: Duke University Press, 2001.

Finzsch, Norbert, and Robert Jutte, eds. *Hospitals, Asylums, and Prisons in Western Europe and North America, 1500–1950.* Cambridge: Cambridge University Press, 1996.

Fisher, Will. "The Renaissance Beard: Masculinity in Early Modern England." *Renaissance Quarterly* 54, no. 1 (2001): 155–187.

Fissell, Mary Elizabeth. *Vernacular Bodies: The Politics of Reproduction in Early Modern England.* Oxford: Oxford University Press, 2004.

Flannery, Michael. "The Rules for Playing Pall-Mall (c. 1655)." In *Sport and Culture in Early Modern Europe,* edited by John McClelland and Brian Merrilees, 183–198. Toronto: Centre for Reformation and Renaissance Studies, 2009.

Franceschini, Giovan Francesco. *Castelfranco di Sotto illustrato.* Castelfranco di Sotto: Biblioteca Communale di Castelfranco di Sotto, 1980.

Frick, Carole Collier. *Dressing Renaissance Florence: Families, Fortunes, and Fine Clothing.* Baltimore: Johns Hopkins University Press, 2002.

Garbellotti, Marina. *Per carità: Poveri e politiche assistenziali nell'Italia moderna.* Rome: Carocci, 2013.

Garrioch, David. "Sounds of the City: The Soundscapes of Early Modern European Towns." *Urban History* 30, no. 1 (2003): 5–25.

Gavitt, Philip. *Gender, Honor, and Charity in Late Renaissance Florence.* Cambridge: Cambridge University Press, 2011.

Geltner, Guy. *The Medieval Prison: A Social History.* Princeton, NJ: Princeton University Press, 2008.

Gentilcore, David. *Food and Health in Early Modern Europe: Diet, Medicine and Society, 1450–1800.* London: Bloomsbury Academic, 2016.

——. *Healers and Healing in Early Modern Italy.* Manchester, UK: Manchester University Press, 1998.

——. *Medical Charlatanism in Early Modern Italy.* Oxford: Oxford University Press, 2006.

Giannetti, Laura. *Food Culture and Literary Imagination in Early Modern Italy: The Renaissance of Taste.* Amsterdam: Amsterdam University Press, 2022.

Giannetti, Vincenzo. *"A vita nuova": Ricordi e vicende della grande operazione urbanistica che distrusse il centro storico di Firenze.* Florence: Cassa di Risparmio di Firenze, 1997.

Giannetto, Raffaella Fabiani. *Medici Gardens: From Making to Design.* Philadelphia: University of Pennsylvania Press, 2008.

Gianturco, Carolyn. "Caterina Assandra, suora compositrice." In *La musica sacra in Lombardia nella prima metà del seicento: Atti del convegno internazionale di studi,* edited by Alberto Colzani, Andrea Luppi, and Maurizio Padoan, 117–127. Como, Italy: Antiquae Musicae Italicae Studiosi, 1987.

Goldthwaite, Richard A. *Private Wealth in Renaissance Florence: A Study of Four Families.* Princeton, NJ: Princeton University Press, 1968.

Gordon, Bonnie. *Monteverdi's Unruly Women: The Power of Song in Early Modern Italy.* Cambridge: Cambridge University Press, 2004.

Goudriaan, Elisa. *Florentine Patricians and Their Networks: Structures behind the Cultural Success and Political Representation of the Medici Court (1600–1660).* Leiden: Brill, 2018.

Gozzi, Marco. "Liturgical Music and Liturgical Experience in Early Modern Italy." In *Listening to Early Modern Catholicism,* edited by Daniele Filippi and Michael J. Noone, 55–78. Boston: Brill, 2017.

Greefs, Hilde, and Anne Winter. "Introduction: Migration Policies and Materialities of Identification in European Cities: Papers and Gates, 1500–1930s." In *Migration Policies and Materialities of Identification in European Cities: Papers and Gates, 1500–1930s,* edited by Hilde Greefs and Anne Winter, 3–23. New York: Routledge, 2019.

Greefs, Hilde, and Anne Winter, eds. *Migration Policies and Materialities of Identification in European Cities: Papers and Gates, 1500–1930s.* New York: Routledge, 2019.

Green, Monica. "Bodies, Health, Gender, Disease: Recent Work of Medieval Women's Medicine." *Studies in Medieval and Renaissance History* 3, no. 2 (2005): 1–4.

——. *Making Women's Medicine Masculine: The Rise of Male Authority in Pre-modern Gynaecology.* Oxford: Oxford University Press, 2008.

Greenfield, Anne, ed. *Interpreting Sexual Violence, 1660–1800.* London: Routledge, 2015.

Grendi, Edoardo. "Ideologia della carità e società indisciplinata: La construzione del sistema assistenziale genovese (1470–1670)." In *Timore e carità: I poveri nell'Italia moderna,* edited by Giorgio Politi, Mario Rosa, and Franco Della Peruta, 59–79. Cremona, Italy: Libreria del Comune, 1982.

Guarnieri, Gino. *L'ordine di S. Stefano nei suoi aspetti organizzativi interni sotto il gran magistero mediceo.* 4 vols. Pisa: Giardini, 1966.

Hahn, Philip. "The Reformation of the Soundscape: Bell Ringing in Early Modern Lutheran Germany." *German History* 33, no. 4 (2015): 525–545.

Hallett, Nicky. *The Senses in Religious Communities, 1600–1800: Early Modern "Convents of Pleasure."* New York: Routledge, 2016.

Hammond, Nicholas. *The Power of Sound and Song in Early Modern Paris.* University Park: Pennsylvania State University Press, 2019.

Harness, Kelley. *Echoes of Women's Voices: Music, Art, and Female Patronage in Early Modern Florence.* Chicago: University of Chicago Press, 2006.

Harpster, Grace. "The Color of Salvation: The Materiality of Blackness in Alonso de Sandoval's *De instauranda Aethiopum salute.*" In *Envisioning Others: Race, Color, and the Visual in Iberia and Latin America,* edited by Pamela A. Patton, 83–110. Leiden: Brill, 2015.

Harter, Karl. "Disciplinamento sociale e ordinanze di polizia nella prima età moderna." In *Disciplina dell'anima, disciplina del corpo e disciplina della società tra medioevo ed età moderna,* edited by Paolo Prodi and Carla Penuti, 635–659. Bologna: Il Mulino, 1994.

Harvey, Elizabeth D., ed. *Sensible Flesh: On Touch in Early Modern Culture.* Philadelphia: University of Pennsylvania Press, 2002.

Henderson, John. "Charity and Welfare in Early Modern Tuscany." In *Health Care and Poor Relief in Counter-Reformation Europe,* edited by Jon Arrizabalaga, Andrew Cunningham, and Ole Peter Grell, 56–87. New York: Routledge, 2005.

——. "Coping with Epidemics in Renaissance Italy: Plague and the Great Pox." In *The Fifteenth Century,* vol. 12, *Society in an Age of Plague,* edited by Linda Clark and Carole Rawcliffe, 179–194. Woodbridge, UK: Boydell, 2013.

——. "Epidemics in Renaissance Florence: Medical Theory and Government Response." In *Maladie et société (XIIe–XVIIIe siècles),* edited by Neithard Bulst and Robert Delort, 165–186. Paris: Éditions de CNRS, 1989.

——. *Florence under Siege: Surviving Plague in an Early Modern City.* New Haven, CT: Yale University Press, 2019.

Herlihy, David, and Christiane Klapisch-Zuber. *Les Toscans et leurs familles: Une étude du Catasto Florentin de 1427.* Paris: Presses de la Fondation Nationale des Sciences Politiques, 1978.

——. *Tuscans and Their Families A Study of the Florentine Catasto of 1427.* New Haven, CT: Yale University Press, 1985.

Herzig, Tamar. "'For the Salvation of This Girl's Soul': Nuns as Convertors of Jews in Early Modern Italy." *Religions* 8, no. 11 (2017). https://doi.org/10.3390/rel8110252.

——. *Savonarola's Women: Vision and Reform in Renaissance Italy.* Chicago: University of Chicago Press, 2008.

Hewlitt, Cecilia. *Rural Communities in Renaissance Tuscany: Religious Identities and Local Loyalties.* Turnhout, Belgium: Brepols, 2008.

Hickey, Daniel. *Local Hospitals in Ancien Régime France: Rationalization, Resistance, Renewal, 1530–1789.* Montreal: McGill-Queens University Press, 1997.

Hills, Helen. "The Housing of Institutional Architecture: Searching for a Domestic Holy in Post-Tridentine Italian Convents." In *Domestic Institutional Interiors in Early Modern Europe,* edited by Sandra Cavallo and Silvia Evangelisti, 119–152. New York: Routledge, 2016.

——. "The Veiled Body: Within the Folds of Early Modern Neapolitan Convent Architecture." *Oxford Art Journal* 27, no. 3 (2004): 271–290.

Hornby, Emma. "Preliminary Thoughts about Silence in Early Western Chant." In *Silence, Music, Silent Music,* edited by Nicky Losseff and Jenny Doctor, 141–154. Aldershot, UK: Ashgate, 2007.

Horodowich, Elizabeth. "Body Politics and the Tongue in Sixteenth-Century Venice." In *The Body in Early Modern Italy,* edited by Julia L. Hairston and Walter Stephens, 195–209. Baltimore: Johns Hopkins University Press, 2010.

——. "The Gossiping Tongue: Oral Networks, Public Life and Political Culture in Early Modern Venice." *Renaissance Studies* 19, no. 1 (2005): 22–45.

Howard, Peter. *Creating Magnificence in Renaissance Florence.* Toronto: Centre for Reformation and Renaissance Studies, 2012.

Howes, David, ed. *Empire of the Senses: The Sensual Culture Reader.* Oxford: Bloomsbury, 2005.

——. "Introduction: Empires of the Senses." In *Empire of the Senses: The Sensual Culture Reader,* edited by David Howes, 1–20. Oxford: Bloomsbury, 2005.

Hunt, John M. "Carriages, Violence, and Masculinity in Early Modern Rome." *I Tatti Studies in the Italian Renaissance* 17, no. 2 (2014): 175–196.

Hyde, Alan. "Offensive Bodies." In *The Smell Culture Reader,* edited by Jim Drobnick, 53–58. New York: Berg, 2006.

Kardong, Terrence G. *Benedict's Rule: A Translation and Commentary.* Collegeville, MN: The Order of St. Benedict, 1996.

Karras Mazo, Ruth. *From Boys to Men: Formations of Masculinity in Late Medieval Europe.* Philadelphia: University of Pennsylvania Press, 2003.

Kendrick, Robert. *Celestial Voices: Nuns and Their Music in Early Modern Milan.* Oxford: Oxford University Press, 1996.

——. "Music among the Disciplines in Early Modern Catholicism." In *Listening to Early Modern Catholicism: Perspectives from Musicology,* edited by Daniele Filippi and Michael J. Noone, 35–54. Leiden: Brill, 2017.

Knox, Dilwyn. "Disciplina: Le origini monastiche e clericali del buon comportamento nell' Europa cattolica del cinquecento e del primo seicento." In *Disciplina dell'anima, disciplina del corpo e disciplina della società tra medioevo ed età moderna,* edited by Paolo Prodi and Carla Penuti, 63–93. Bologna: Il Mulino, 1994.

Korhonen, Anu. "Washing the Ethiopian White: Conceptualising Black Skin in Renaissance England." In *Black Africans in Renaissance Europe,* edited by T. F. Earle and K. J. P. Lowe, 94–122. Cambridge: Cambridge University Press, 2005.

Kvicalova, Anna. *Listening and Knowledge in Reformation Europe: Hearing, Speaking, and Remembering in Calvin's Geneva.* Cham, Switzerland: Palgrave Macmillan, 2019.

Laven, Mary. *Virgins of Venice: Broken Vows and Cloistered Lives in the Renaissance Convent.* New York: Penguin, 2004.

Leong, Elaine, and Alisa Rankin. "Introduction." In *Secrets and Knowledge in Medicine and Science, 1500–1800,* 1–11. New York: Routledge, 2016.

Leong, Elaine, and Alisa Rankin, eds. *Secrets and Knowledge in Medicine and Science, 1500–1800.* New York: Routledge, 2016.

Leuzzi, Maria Fabini. *"Dell'allogare le fanciulle degli Innocenti": Un problema culturale ed economico, 1577–1652.* Bologna: Il Mulino, 1995.

Lillie, Amanda. *Florentine Villas in the Fifteenth Century: An Architectural and Social History.* Cambridge: Cambridge University Press, 2005.

Litchfield, R. Burr. *Emergence of a Bureaucracy: The Florentine Patricians 1530–1790.* Princeton, NJ: Princeton University Press, 1986.

———. *Florence Ducal Capitol, 1530–1630.* New York: ACLS Humanities e-book, 2008.

Loetz, Francisca. *A New Approach to the History of Violence: "Sexual Assault" and "Sexual Abuse" in Europe, 1500–1850.* Leiden: Brill, 2015.

Lombardi, Daniela. "Poveri a Firenze: Programmi e realizzazioni della politica assistenziale dei Medici tra cinque e seicento." In *Timore e carità: I poveri nell' Italia moderna,* edited by Giorgio Politi, Mario Rosa, and Franco Della Peruta, 164–184. Cremona, Italy: Annali della Biblioteca Statale e Libreria Civica di Cremona, 1982.

———. *Povertà maschile, povertà femminile: L'Ospedale dei Mendicanti nella Firenze dei Medici.* Bologna: Il Mulino,1988.

Long, Kathleen. "The Case of Marin le Marcis." In *Trans Historical: Gender Plurality before the Modern,* edited by Greta LaFleur, Masha Raskolnikov, and Anna Klosowska, 68–95. Ithaca, NY: Cornell University Press, 2021.

Logue, Alexandra. "'Saucy Stink': Smells, Sanitation, and Conflict in Early Modern London." *Renaissance and Reformation / Renaissance et Réforme* 44, no. 2 (2021): 61–86.

Lowe, K. J. P. *Nuns' Chronicles and Convent Culture in Renaissance and Counter-Reformation Italy.* Cambridge: Cambridge University Press, 2003.

Ludwig Jansen, Katherine. *The Making of the Magdalen: Preaching and Popular Devotion in the Later Middle Ages.* Princeton, NJ: Princeton University Press, 2000.

Macey, Patrick. *"Infiamma il mio cor:* Savonarolan Laude by and for Dominican Nuns in Tuscany." In *The Crannied Wall: Women, Religion, and the Arts in Early*

Modern Europe, edited by Craig Monson, 161–189. Ann Arbor: University of Michigan Press, 1992.

Makowski, Elizabeth. *Canon Law and Cloistered Women: "Periculoso" and Its Commentators, 1298–1545.* Washington, DC: Catholic University of America Press, 1997.

Mannori, Luca. *Lo stato del granduca 1530–1859: Le istituzioni della Toscana moderna in un percorso di testi commentati.* Florence: Pacini, 2015.

Mantini, Silvia. *Lo spazio sacro della Firenze Medicea: Transformazioni urbane e ceremoniali pubblici tra quattrocento e cinquecento.* Florence: Loggia de' Lanzi, 1995.

Marconcini, Samuela. *Per amor del cielo: Farsi cristiani a Firenze tra seicento e settecento.* Florence: Florence University Press, 2016.

Martines, Lauro. *Fire in the City: Savonarola and the Struggle for the Soul of Renaissance Florence.* Oxford: Oxford University Press, 2006.

Masetti Zannini, Gian Lodovico. "'Sua vità di canto' e 'purità di cuore': Aspetti della musica nei monasteri femminili romani." In *La cappella musicale nell' Italia della Controriforma: Atti del Convegno Internazionale di Studi nel IV centenario di Fondazione della Cappella Musicale di S. Biagio di Cento, Cento, 13–15 ottobre 1989,* edited by Oscar Mischiati and Paolo Russo, 137–139. Florence: Leo S. Olschki, 1993.

Matchette, Ann. "Women, Objects, and Exchange in Early Modern Florence." *Early Modern Women: An Interdisciplinary Journal* 3 (2008): 245–251.

Matthews, Hugh, Melanie Limb, and Mark Taylor. "The 'Street as Thirdspace.'" In *Children's Geographies: Playing, Living, Learning,* edited by Sarah L. Holloway and Gill Valentine, 54–68. New York: Routledge, 2000.

Mazzei, Maria Serena. *Prostitute e lenoni della Firenze del quattrocento.* Milan: Il Saggiatore, 1991.

Mazzei, Rita. "Lucca e Firenze: I lucchesi cavalieri di Santo Stefano in età moderna." *Archivio Storico Italiano* 157, no. 2 (1999): 269–283.

Mazzio, Carla. "Sins of the Tongue in Early Modern England." *Modern Language Studies* 28, no. 3 (1998): 93–124.

McCants, Anne E. C. *Civic Charity in a Golden Age: Orphan Care in Early Modern Amsterdam.* Urbana: University of Illinois Press, 1997.

McClure, George. *The Culture of Profession in Late Renaissance Italy.* Toronto: University of Toronto Press, 2004.

McIver, Katherine A., ed. *Wives, Widows, Mistresses, and Nuns in Early Modern Italy.* Farnham, UK: Ashgate, 2012.

McKee, Sally. "Domestic Slavery in Renaissance Italy." *Slavery and Abolition* 29, no. 3 (2008): 305–326.

Medioli, Francesca. "Lo spazio del chiostro: Clausura, costrizione e protezione nel XVII secolo." In *Tempi e spazi di vita femminile tra medioevo ad età moderna,* edited by Silvana Seidel Menchi, Anne Jacobson Schutte, and Thomas Kuhn, 353–373. Bologna: Il Mulino, 1999.

——. "Monacazioni forzate: Donne ribelle al proprio destino." *Clio: Trimestrale di Studi Storici* 30, no. 3 (1994): 431–454.

——. "To Take or Not to Take the Veil: Selected Italian Case Histories, the Renaissance and After." In *Women in Italian Renaissance Culture and Society,* edited by Letizia Pannizza, 122–137. Oxford: European Humanities Research Centre, 2000.

Mischiati, Oscar. "Il Concilio di Trento e la polifonia: Una diversa proposta di lettera e di prospettiva bibliografica." In *Musica e liturgia nella riforma tridenta,* edited by Danilo Curto and Marco Gozzi, 19–29. Trento, Italy: Provincia Autonoma di Trento, Servizio Beni Librari e Archivistici, 1995.

Mischiati, Oscar, Giancarlo Rostirolla, and Danilo Zardin. *La lauda spirituale tra cinque e seicento: Poesie e canti devozionali nell'Italia della controriforma.* Rome: Ibimus, 2001.

Molho, Anthony. *Marriage Alliance in Late Medieval Florence.* Cambridge, MA: Harvard University Press, 1994.

——. *"Tamquam vere mortua:* Le professioni religiose femminili nella Firenze del tardo medioevo." *Storia e Letteratura* 246 (2006): 1–37.

Monson, Craig. "The Council of Trent Revisited." *Journal of the American Musicological Society* 55, no. 1 (2002): 1–37.

——. *Disembodied Voices: Music and Culture in an Early Modern Italian Convent.* Los Angeles: University of California Press, 1995.

——. *Divas in the Convent: Nuns, Music, and Defiance in 17th-Century Italy.* Chicago: University of Chicago Press, 2012.

——. *Habitual Offenders: A True Tale of Nuns, Prostitutes, and Murderers in 17th-Century Italy.* Chicago: University of Chicago Press, 2016.

——. *Nuns Behaving Badly: Tales of Music, Magic, Art, and Arson in the Convents of Italy.* Chicago: University of Chicago Press, 2010.

Montanari, Massimo. *Gusti del medioevo i prodotti, la cucina, la tavola.* Rome: GLF Editori Laterza, 2014.

Montford, Kimberlyn. "Holy Restraint: Religious Reform and Nuns' Music in Early Modern Rome." *Sixteenth Century Journal* 37, no. 4 (2006): 1007–1026.

More, Alison. *Fictive Orders and Feminine Religious Identities, 1200–1600.* Oxford: Oxford University Press, 2018.

——. "Institutionalization of Disorder: The Franciscan Third Order and Canonical Change in the Sixteenth Century." *Franciscan Studies* 71 (2013): 147–162.

Musacchio, Jacqueline Marie. *The Art and Ritual of Childbirth in Renaissance Italy.* New Haven, CT: Yale University Press, 1999.

Najemy, John M. *A History of Florence 1200–1575.* Malden, MA: Wiley Blackwell, 2004.

Naphy, William. *Sex Crimes from Renaissance to Enlightenment.* Stroud, UK: Tempus, 2002.

Niccoli, Ottavia. "Creanza e disciplina: Buon maniere per i fanciulli nell' Italia della controriforma." In *Disciplina dell'anima, disciplina del corpo e disciplina della società tra medioevo ed età moderna*, edited by Paolo Prodi and Carla Penuti, 929–963. Bologna: Il Mulino, 1994.

——. "Rituals of Youth: Love, Play, and Violence in Tridentine Bologna." In *The Premodern Teenager: Youth in Society 1150–1650*, edited by Konrad Eisenbichler, 75–94. Toronto: Centre for Reformation and Renaissance Studies, 2002.

——. *Storia di ogni giorno in una città del seicento*. Rome: Laterza, 2000.

Novi Chavarria, Elisa. *Monache e gentildonne: Un labile confine; Poteri politici e identità religiose nei monasteri napoletani secoli XVI–XVII*. Milan: Franco Angeli, 2001.

O'Malley, John W. *Trent: What Happened at the Council*. Cambridge, MA: Belknap Press of Harvard University Press, 2013.

——. "Trent, Sacred Images, and Catholics' Senses of the Sensuous." In *The Sensuous in the Counter-Reformation Church*, edited by Marcia B. Hall and Tracy Elizabeth Cooper, 28–49. Cambridge: Cambridge University Press, 2013.

Pagani, Giuseppe. *Memoriale alfabetico ragionato della legislazione toscana dalla prima epoca del principato fino al presente secondo lo stato della medesima*. Florence: Giuseppe Pagani, 1829.

Paolin, Giovanna. *Lo spazio del silenzio: Monacazioni forzate, clausura e proposte di vita religioso femminile nell'età moderna*. Pordenone, Italy: Biblioteca dell'Immagine,1996.

Paster, Gail Kern. *The Body Embarrassed: Drama and the Disciplines of Shame in Early Modern England*. Ithaca, NY: Cornell University Press, 1993.

Patrone, Annamaria Nada. *Il messaggio dell'ingiuria nel Piemonte del tardo medioevo*. Cavallermaggiore, Italy: Gribaudo, 1993.

Payne, Alina. *Vision and Its Instruments: Art, Science, and Technology in Early Modern Europe*. University Park: Pennsylvania State University Press, 2015.

Pedersen, Tara. "Bodies by the Book: Remapping Reputation in the Account of Anne Greene and Shakespeare's *Much Ado about Nothing*." In *Mapping Gendered Routes and Spaces in the Early Modern World*, edited by Merry E. Wiesner-Hanks, 117–131. New York: Routledge, 2015.

Perry, Mary Elizabeth. *Gender and Disorder in Early Modern Seville*. Princeton, NJ: Princeton University Press, 1990.

Piccari, Paolo. *Giovan Battista Della Porta: Il filosofo, il retore, lo scienziato*. Milan: Franco Angeli, 2007.

Polizzotto, Lorenzo. "When Saints Fall Out: Women and the Savonarolan Reform in Early Sixteenth-Century Florence." *Renaissance Quarterly* 46, no. 3 (1993): 486–525.

Pomata, Gianna. *Contracting a Cure: Patients, Healers, and the Law in Early Modern Bologna*. Translated by Gianna Pomata with Rosemarie Foy and Anna Taraboletti-Segre. Baltimore: Johns Hopkins University Press, 1998.

——. "Family and Gender." In *Early Modern Italy: 1550–1796,* edited by John A. Marino, 68–86. Oxford: Oxford University Press, 2002.

——. "Medicina delle monache: Pratiche terapeutiche nei monasteri femminili di Bologna in età moderna." In *I monasteri femminili come centri di cultura fra rinascimento e barocco,* edited by Gianna Pomata and Gabriella Zarri, 331–363. Rome: Edizioni di Storia e Letteratura, 2005.

——. "Menstruating Men: Similarity and Difference of the Sexes in Early Modern Medicine." In *Generation and Degeneration: Tropes of Reproduction in Literature and History from Antiquity to Early Modern Europe,* edited by Valerie Finucci and Kevin Brownlee, 109–152. Durham, NC: Duke University Press, 2001.

Possanzini, Stefano. "Il monastero fiorentino delle Carmelitane in San Barnaba." *Carmelus* 43 (1996): 123–145.

Pullan, Brian. *Tolerance, Regulation and Rescue: Dishonoured Women and Abandoned Children in Italy, 1300–1800.* Manchester, UK: Manchester University Press, 2016.

Quiviger, François. *The Sensory World of Italian Renaissance Art.* London: Reaktion Books, 2010.

Rawcliffe, Carole. "'Delectable Sightes and Fragrant Smelles': Gardens and Health in Late Medieval and Early Modern England." *Garden History* 36, no. 1 (2008): 1–21.

Read, Sara. *Menstruation and the Female Body in Early Modern England.* New York: Palgrave, 2013.

Reardon, Colleen. *Holy Concord within Sacred Walls: Nuns and Music in Siena, 1575–1700.* Oxford: Oxford University Press, 2001.

Rodaway, Paul. *Sensuous Geographies: Body, Sense and Place.* London: Routledge, 1994.

Rodocanachi, E[mmanuel]. *La femme italienne à l'époque de la Renaissance.* Paris: Hachette, 1907.

Rombough, Julia. "Air Quality and the Senses in Early Modern Italy." *Renaissance and Reformation / Renaissance et Réforme,* vol. 44, no. 2 (2021): 39–60.

——. "Noisy Soundscapes and Women's Institutions in Early Modern Florence." *Sixteenth Century Journal,* vol. 50, no. 2 (2019): 449–469.

——. "Regulating Sense and Space in Late Renaissance Florence." *Urban History* 50, no. 1 (2023): 38–57.

Rombough, Julia, and Sharon Strocchia, "City of Women: Mapping Movement, Gender, and Enclosure in Renaissance Florence." In *Public Renaissance: Urban Space, Geolocated Apps and Public History,* edited by Fabrizio Nevola, David Rosenthal, and Nicholas Terpstra, 169–191. Abingdon, UK: Routledge, 2022.

Roodernburg, Herman, ed. *A Cultural History of the Senses in the Renaissance.* London: Bloomsbury, 2014.

Rosa, Gian. *Le leggi penali sui muri di Firenze: Tratti di corda e penna.* Florence: Casa Editrice Nerbini, 1911.

Rosenthal, David. *Kings of the Street: Power, Community, and Ritual in Renaissance Florence.* Turnhout, Belgium: Brepols, 2015.

——. "Owning the Corner: The 'Powers' of Florence and the Question of Agency." *I Tatti Studies in the Italian Renaissance* 16, no.1 (2013): 81–96.

Rothman, Natalie E. "Becoming Venetian: Conversion and Transformation in the Seventeenth-Century Mediterranean." *Mediterranean Historical Review* 21, no. 1 (2006): 39–75.

Ruggiero, Guido. "Mean Streets, Familiar Streets, or the Fat Woodcarver and the Masculine Spaces of Renaissance Florence." In *Renaissance Florence: A Social History*, edited by Roger Crum and John Paoletti, 295–310. Cambridge: Cambridge University Press, 2006.

Safley, Thomas Max. *Charity and Economy in the Orphanages of Early Modern Augsburg.* Atlantic Highlands, NJ: Humanities Press, 1997.

Salzberg, Rosa. "Controlling and Documenting Migration via Urban 'Spaces of Arrival' in Early Modern Venice." In *Migration Policies and Materialities of Identification in European Cities: Papers and Gates, 1500–1930s,* edited by Hilde Greefs and Anne Winter, 27–45. New York: Routledge, 2019.

Sandri, Lucia. "Gli Innocenti e Orbatello nel XVIII e XIX secolo: 'Nocentine' e 'gravide occulte' tra progetti e necessità istituzionali." In *Ospedale di Orbatello: Carità e arte a Firenze,* edited by Christina De Benedictis and Carla Miloschi, 137–145. Florence: Edizioni Polistampa, 2015.

——. "L'attività di banco dell'Ospedale degli Innocenti di Firenze: Don Vincenzo Borghini e la 'bancarotta' del 1579." In *L'uso del denaro: Patrimoni e amministrazione nei luoghi pii e negli enti ecclesiastici in Italia (secoli XV–XVIII),* edited by Marina Garbellotti and Alessandro Pastore, 153–178. Bologna: Il Mulino, 2001.

Schafer, Raymond Murray. *The Tuning of the World: Toward a Theory of Soundscape Design.* New York: Alfred A. Knopf, 1977.

Schutte, Anne Jacobson. *By Force and Fear: Taking and Breaking Monastic Vows in Early Modern Europe.* Ithaca, NY: Cornell University Press, 2011.

Schwartz, Hillel. "On Noise." In *Hearing History: A Reader,* edited by Mark M. Smith, 51–54. Athens: University of Georgia Press, 2004.

Siegel, Rudolph E. *Galen on Sense Perception: His Doctrines, Observations, and Experiments on Vision, Hearing, Smell, Taste, Touch and Pain and Their Historical Sources.* Basel: Karger, 1970.

Smith, Lisa Wynne. "The Body Embarrassed?: Rethinking the Leaky Male Body in Eighteenth-Century England and France." *Gender and History* 23, no. 1 (2010): 26–46.

Smith, Mark Michael. *How Race Is Made: Slavery, Segregation, and the Senses.* Chapel Hill: University of North Carolina Press, 2008.

——. *Sensing the Past: Seeing, Hearing, Smelling, Tasting, and Touching in History.* Berkeley: University of California Press, 2007.

——. *A Sensory History Manifesto.* University Park: Pennsylvania State University Press, 2021.

Speelbery, Femke. *Fashion and Virtue: Textile Patterns and the Print Revolution, 1520–1620.* New York: Metropolitan Museum of Art, 2016.

Sperling, Jutta. *Convents and the Body Politic in Late Renaissance Venice.* Chicago: University of Chicago Press, 1999.

Spierenburg, Peter. *The Prison Experience: Disciplinary Institutions and Their Inmates in Early Modern Europe.* New Brunswick, NJ: Rutgers University Press, 1991.

Stolberg, Michael. "A Woman Down to Her Bones: The Anatomy of Sexual Difference in Early Modern Europe." *Isis* 94, no. 2 (2003): 274–299.

Stoller, Paul. *Sensuous Scholarship.* Philadelphia: University of Pennsylvania Press, 1997.

Stow, Kenneth. *Anna and Tranquillo: Catholic Anxiety and Jewish Protest in the Age of Revolutions.* New Haven, CT: Yale University Press, 2016.

Stras, Laurie. *Women and Music in Sixteenth-Century Ferrara.* Cambridge: Cambridge University Press, 2018.

Strasser, Ulrike. *State of Virginity: Gender, Religion, and Politics in an Early Modern Catholic State.* Ann Arbor: University of Michigan Press, 2004.

Storey, Tessa. *Carnal Commerce in Counter-Reformation Rome.* Cambridge: Cambridge University Press, 2008.

———. "Italian Book of Secrets Database." March 3, 2009. https://hdl.handle.net /2381/4335.

Strocchia, Sharon. "The Nun Apothecaries of Renaissance Florence: Marketing Medicines in the Convent." *Renaissance Studies* 25, no. 5 (2011): 627–247.

———. *Nuns and Nunneries in Renaissance Florence.* Baltimore: Johns Hopkins University Press, 2009.

———. "When the Bishop Married the Abbess: Masculinity and Power in Florentine Episcopal Entry Rites, 1300–1600." *Gender & History* 19, no. 2 (2007): 346–368.

Strocchia, Sharon, and Julia Rombough. "Women behind walls: Tracking Nuns and Socio-spatial Networks in Sixteenth-Century Florence." In *Mapping Space, Sense, and Movement in Florence: Historical GIS and the Early Modern City,* edited by Nicholas Terpstra and Colin Rose, 87–106. New York: Routledge, 2016.

Taddei, Ilaria. *Fanciulli e giovani: Crescere a Firenze nel rinascimento.* Florence: Leo S. Olschki, 2001.

———. "I giovani alla fine del medioevo: Rappresentazione e modelli di comportamento." In *I giovani nel medioevo: Ideali e pratiche di vita,* edited by Isa Lori Sanfilippo and Antonio Rigon, 11–23. Rome: Istituto Storico Italiano per il Medioevo, 2014.

———. "*Puerizia, Adolescenza* and *Giovinezza:* Images and Conceptions of Youth in Florentine Society during the Renaissance." In *The Premodern Teenager: Youth in Society 1150–1650,* edited by Konrad Eisenbichler, 15–26. Toronto: Centre for Reformation and Renaissance Studies, 2002.

Talvacchia, Bette. "The Word Made Flesh: Spiritual Subjects and Carnal Depictions in Renaissance Art." In *The Sensuous in the Counter-Reformation*

Church, edited by Marcia B. Hall and Tracy Elizabeth Cooper, 49–73. Cambridge: Cambridge University Press, 2013.

Terpstra, Nicholas. *Abandoned Children of the Italian Renaissance: Orphan Care in Florence and Bologna.* Baltimore: Johns Hopkins University Press, 2005.

——. "Competing Visions of the State and Social Welfare: The Medici Dukes, the Bigallo Magistrates, and Local Hospitals in Sixteenth-Century Tuscany." *Renaissance Quarterly* 54, no. 4, pt. 2 (2001): 1319–1355.

——. *Cultures of Charity: Women, Politics and the Reform of Poor Relief in Renaissance Italy.* Cambridge, MA: Harvard University Press, 2013.

——. "Locating the Sex Trade in the Early Modern City: Space, Sense and Regulation in Sixteenth-Century Florence." In *Mapping Space, Sense, and Movement in Florence: Historical GIS and the Early Modern City,* edited by Nicholas Terpstra and Colin Rose, 107–124. New York: Routledge, 2016.

——. *Lost Girls: Sex and Death in Renaissance Florence.* Baltimore: Johns Hopkins University Press, 2010.

——. "Mapping Gendered Labour in the Textile Industry of Early Modern Florence." In *Florence in the Early Modern World: New Perspectives,* edited by Nicholas Scott Baker and Brian Jeffrey Maxson, 68–91. Abingdon, UK: Routledge, 2019.

——. "Sex and the Sacred: Negotiating Spatial and Sensory Boundaries in Renaissance Florence." *Radical History Review* 121 (2015): 71–90.

Tognetti, Sergio. "The Trade in Black African Slaves in Fifteenth-Century Florence." In *Black Africans in Renaissance Europe,* edited by T. F. Earle and K. J. P. Lowe, 213–224. Cambridge: Cambridge University Press, 2005.

Tomas, Natalie. "Did Women Have a Space?" In *Renaissance Florence: A Social History,* edited by Rodger J. Crum and John T. Paoletti, 311–328. New York: Cambridge University Press, 2006.

Tomlinson, Gary. *Music in Renaissance Magic: Toward a Historiography of Others.* Chicago: University of Chicago Press, 1993.

Trexler, Richard C. *Dependence in Context in Renaissance Florence.* Binghamton, NY: Medieval & Renaissance Texts & Studies, 1994.

Tullet, William. *Smell in Eighteenth-Century England: A Social Sense.* Oxford: Oxford University Press, 2019.

Van den Heuvel, Danielle. "Gender in the Streets of the Premodern City." *Journal of Urban History* 45, no. 4 (2019): 693–710.

Van der Heijden, Manon. "Women as Victims of Sexual and Domestic Violence in Seventeenth-Century Holland: Criminal Cases of Rape, Incest, and Maltreatment in Rotterdam and Delft." *Journal of Social History* 33, no. 3 (2000): 623–644.

Van Veen, Henk. "Princes and Patriotism: The Self-Representation of Florentine Patricians in the Late Renaissance." In *Princes and Princely Culture 1450–1650,* vol. 2, edited by Martin Gosman, Alasdair Macdonald, and Arjo Vanderjagt, 63–78. Leiden: Brill, 2005.

Vitullo, Juliann. "Taste and Temptation in Early Modern Italy." *Senses and Society* 5, no.1 (2010): 106–118.

Weaver, Elissa B. *Convent Theatre in Early Modern Italy: Spiritual Fun and Learning for Women.* New York: Cambridge University Press, 2002.

Weddle, Saundra. "Mobility and Prostitution in Early Modern Venice." *Early Modern Women: An Interdisciplinary Journal* 14, no. 1 (2019): 95–108.

——. "'Women in Wolves' Mouths': Nuns' Reputations, Enclosure and Architecture at the Convent of Le Murate in Florence." In *Architecture and the Politics of Gender in Early Modern Europe,* edited by Helen Hills, 115–129. Burlington, VT: Ashgate, 2003.

——. "Women's Place in the Family and the Convent: A Reconsideration of Public and Private in Renaissance Florence." *Journal of Architectural Education* 55, no. 2 (2001): 64–72.

Weinstein, Donald. "Fighting or Flyting?: Verbal Duelling in Mid-Sixteenth-Century Italy." In *Crime, Society, and the Law in Renaissance Italy,* edited by Trevor Dean and K. J. P. Lowe, 204–220. Cambridge: Cambridge University Press, 1994.

——. *Savonarola: The Rise and Fall of a Renaissance Prophet.* New Haven, CT: Yale University Press, 2011.

Welch, Evelyn. "Perfumed Buttons and Scented Gloves: Smelling Things in Renaissance Italy." In *Ornamentalism: The Art of Renaissance Accessories,* edited by Bella Mirabella, 13–39. Ann Arbor: University of Michigan Press, 2011.

Williamson, Beth. "Sensory Experience in Medieval Devotion: Sound, Vision, Invisibility and Silence." *Speculum* 88, no. 1 (2013): 1–43.

Woods, Kelli. "Balls on Walls, Feet on Streets: Subversive Play in Grand Ducal Florence." *Renaissance Quarterly* 32, no. 3 (2018): 365–387.

Zardin, Danilo. "Libri e biblioteche negli ambienti monastici dell' Italia del primo seicento." In *Donne, filosofia e cultura nel seicento,* edited by Pina Totaro, 347–383. Rome: Consiglio Nazionale della Ricerca, 1999.

Zarri, Gabriella. "Disciplina regolare e pratica di coscienza: Le virtù e i comportamenti sociali in comunità femminili (sec. XVI–XVIII)." In *Disciplina dell' anima, disciplina del corpo e disciplina della società tra medioevo ed età moderna,* edited by Paolo Prodi and Carla Penuti, 257–279. Bologna: Il Mulino, 1994.

——. "Monasteri femminile e città (secoli XV–XVIII)." In *Storia d'Italia,* annali 9, *La chiesa e il potere politico,* edited by Giorgio Chittolini and Giovanni Miccoli, 359–429. Turin: Einaudi, 1986.

——. *Recinti: Donne, clausura e matrimonio nella prima età moderna.* Bologna: Il Mulino, 2000.

Zarri, Gabriella, Francesca Medioli, and Paolo Vismara Chiappa. "De monialibus (secoli XVI–XVII–XVIII)." *Rivista di storia e letteratura religiosa* 33, no. 3 (1997): 643–715.

———. "Ecclesiastical Institutions and Religious Life in the Observant Century." In *A Companion to Observant Reform in the Late Middle Ages and Beyond,* edited by James Mixson and Bert Roest, 21–59. Leiden: Brill, 2015.

Zolli, Daniel M., and Christopher Brown. "Bell on Trial: The Struggle for Sound after Savonarola." *Renaissance Quarterly* 72, no. 1 (2019): 54–96.

ACKNOWLEDGMENTS

The idea for this project took shape before I had experience working in Florence and when I had much to learn about Italian archives and sensory histories. Delving into the written past in search of ephemeral echoes was, at times, a daunting process, and I have relied on the generous guidance and support of many people.

First, I would like to express my profound thanks to Nicholas Terpstra. Nick, your genuine enthusiasm and support have meant everything; this project is deeply indebted to your mentorship and generous intellect. I'd also like to thank Sharon Strocchia, whose thoughtful insights and encouragement have been a mainstay that I value deeply. Sharon, talking ideas and coauthoring essays with you has been a truly rewarding experience. Nick and Sharon, you are the two greatest mentors a scholar could ask for. Thank you.

Funding from the Social Sciences and Humanities Research Council of Canada, the Ontario Graduate Scholarship, and a variety of internal research grants from the University of Toronto, Cape Breton University, and Acadia University made the research and writing of this project possible. I'm also grateful for the Northrop Frye Centre Graduate Fellowship at the University of Toronto and the Erasmus Plus Fellowship at the University of Tübingen, which offered me the time and space to explore many of the ideas in this book. I have benefited greatly from the generosity of scholars who recommended sources and pointed me in directions I would not have otherwise explored. Particular thanks go to Colin Rose, Sheila Barker, David Rosenthal, Suzanne Cusick, Elizabeth Cohen, and the staff, librarians, and archivists at the Archivio di Stato di Firenze, Biblioteca Natzionale Centrale di Firenze, Archivio Arcivescovile di Firenze, and Archivio dell'Istituto degli Innocenti.

A huge thanks to Emily Silk, Nick Terpstra, and the entire editing and publishing team at Harvard University Press and Villa I Tatti. The reviewers who carefully read this manuscript offered valuable and much-appreciated comments. Chapter 2 builds on ideas first presented in "Noisy Soundscapes and Women's Institutions in Early Modern Florence," *Sixteenth Century Journal* 50, no. 2 (2019): 449–469, while Chapter 3 expands on work I presented in my article "Air Quality and the Senses in Early Modern Italy," *Renaissance and Reformation / Renaissance et Réforme* 44, no. 2 (2021): 39–60. Chapter 4 continues discussions previewed in "Regulating Sense and Space in Late Renaissance Florence," *Urban History* 50, no. 1 (2023): 38–57. I thank these publishers for the opportunity to publish this earlier work.

This project is indebted to many conversations with friends and colleagues who generously discussed ideas with me at various stages. In particular, Sara Matthews-Grieco helped me filter my thoughts while I was knee-deep in the archives; Saundra Weddle, Lucia Dacome, and Natalie Rothman provided thoughtful comments on my writing that played a huge role in improving this book; Natalie Zemon Davis offered steady encouragement over the years and was a model example of academic generosity. I owe a special thank you to Carly Daniel-Hughes, who first created an environment where I could imagine myself in academia. I am immensely grateful for the many friends and colleagues who listened to conference papers, read drafts, asked questions, offered insights, and had post-workshop drinks with me. These include Alexandra Logue, Tyler Yank, Spirit-Rose Waite, John Christopolous, Hana Suckstorff, Ariana Ellis, Vanessa McCarthy, Sara Loose, Daniel Jameson, Lindsay Sidders, Allison Graham, David Robinson, Ariella Minden, Caroline Murphy, and Dani Inkpen; I thank you all. A heartfelt thank-you to my colleagues at Cape Breton University and Acadia University, and to the many students I have been fortunate to work with—your enthusiasm and sharp perspectives continue to inspire me.

The support of my family has meant everything. I'm eternally grateful to my parents, Norah Curtis and Peter Rombough, who remain unwavering in their support and love. My siblings, Adrienne Rombough and Colin Rombough, visited me in Italy, checked in, and sent their support from afar. My greatest gratitude is to my best friend and partner in all things, Daniel Arellano. You have been by my side at every step. Thank you.

INDEX

Note: page numbers in *italics* indicate figures and tables.